Fried & True

TAL

By Fay Jacobs

A&M Books
2007

Fried & True
Tales from Rehoboth Beach
By Fay Jacobs

Printed in the United States of America
First Edition

Cover and book design by Murray Archibald and Steve Elkins
Photo (opposite page) by Steven Billups

Library of Congress Catalog Card Number:
ISBN 978-0-9646648-8-3

Also by the author
As I Lay Frying—a Rehoboth Beach Memoir

*To Anyda & Muriel
and the people on
the porch.*

Winter 2007

ACKNOWLEDGMENTS

Many people helped me with *Fried & True*. Thanks to Steve Elkins and Murray Archibald, who keep letting me have my say in *Letters*. They are my heroes for what they continue to give to the community of Rehoboth Beach and the selflessness with which they give it. Thanks to them as well for the enormous help they have given me in this, and so many other projects. My appreciation also goes to my-son-the-actor, playwright and diversity consultant Eric Peterson, who, in addition to everything else is now my-son-the-editor for his perspective and his lovely words. Much credit to my wonderful draft readers and editors Kathy Galloway, Tom Jones, Pam Kozey, Jennifer Rubenstein, Betsy Schmidt and my partner Bonnie, who were willing, at the risk of personal safety, to give me honest critiques. I love you for that. Extra thanks to Lee Mills, who used his brilliant mind to think about what this book could say and suggested that I say it. Credit too, to Kathy Weir, expert proofreader and reality checker. And of course, thanks once again to my father Mort, who taught me that even the worst event is not so awful if you can eventually tell a story about it. Special gratitude to my *Letters* readers for still being there even after all this time.

A heartfelt hug to you all.▼

Foreword

BY ERIC C. PETERSON

Fay Jacobs is many things to me.

She's a dear friend, a sage giver of advice, a surrogate mother, a confidante, and someone who knows every line of *Funny Girl* backwards and forwards...as do I (it's a curse).

In addition to this, I know Fay Jacobs is a writer.

And by writer, I don't mean that she writes things down; a lot of people do that. Writing isn't something that Fay *does*; it's something that she is. Being a writer the way Fay Jacobs is a writer doesn't just happen when she sits down in front of her computer and begins to type; it follows her everywhere she goes.

She began her enormously popular column in *Letters from CAMP Rehoboth*, a magazine for the gay, lesbian, and straight communities of Rehoboth Beach, Delaware back in 1996. But she was a writer long before that. She's a writer down to her bones. She responds to a well-turned phrase the way a musician might respond to a particularly beautiful tune or an artist might be struck by a particularly stunning canvas.

And all of Fay's friends have said at one point or another, "Um...that's not going to end up in one of your columns, is it?" And the answer, quite frankly, is almost always yes. She can't help it; she's a *writer*. And yet, even when I've cringed at the thought of my antics ending up in print somewhere, I'm the first to laugh loud and long when I see them through Fay's eyes. And even when she knows something won't end up in print, she's been known to write it down anyway, just to get it out of her system.

Fried & True is not only a collection of Fay Jacobs' writings—although her latest columns are all here—it's also about her life as a writer. Among other things, it's about the way her life changed when she and her partner, Bonnie, met Anyda (pronounced like Anita, but with a "d") Marchant and Muriel

Crawford. The two couples were very different. They belonged to different generations and lived through very different times. But Fay and Anyda were both writers, in the true sense of the word. They were both lesbian writers, which made them even more rare, and their resulting friendship even more special. Anyda was, in fact, one of the most important writers in the history of lesbian fiction, and Muriel was her muse. Because of Anyda and Muriel, Fay's first book, *As I Lay Frying*, was published in 2004. Bonnie and Fay's lives changed the day they met these extraordinary women. And Fay's writing changed, too.

Few people who read this anthology will know Fay as I do. For that, I am truly sorry. However, everyone who reads this collection will know Fay's writing—and you know what? That's almost as good as the real thing.

Onward. ▼

Table of Contents

prologue

To be sure, I answered essay questions and scribbled things before that, but they were mostly dreary "What I Did on My Summer Vacation" chronicles.

But in 11th grade English class, taught by a gentleman who looked like a walrus and whose name I have regretfully forgotten, I think I became a writer.

The teacher asked the class to write a thousand words about something that had occurred in the past week.

Lots of things happened that fall of 1964 but none of it included me. The Beatles sang "She Loves You," two teenage girls were arrested for scaling the wall of the hotel next to my building where they thought Ringo was holed up, Robert Kennedy chased mobsters, the Yankees were in the World Series again and *Bewitched* was on the tube.

But for me, it was a dull week. All I did was argue with my best friend over a yellow linen button-down shirt she'd borrowed, took forever to return, and when it did come back it was a mess. Not exactly fodder for *Camille*.

It was so dull that I started messing around, getting pretty silly. ("She took longer to iron that shirt than the Yankees needed to lose to the Cardinals....") and using preposterous metaphors ("The drip dry garment looked like she had scrubbed it raw on a rock in the Amazon.").

Certain that my prior pop quiz successes and mid-term grade would mitigate a D-minus for this particular assignment I handed the paper in with all its obnoxiousness intact.

The walrus loved it. On the top of my paper, circled in red ink, were the words "fetching detail."

Heretofore the only time I had heard the word fetching it involved squeaky toys.

But I looked it up and was surprised to find it synonymous with "eye-catching," "smart," "enticing," and the obtuse "natty."

And so it began. I did very well in English that year, but less well the following as my teacher was humor challenged. She thought me a wise-ass.

But the deal was sealed and I went off to college, became a newspaper editor (keeping a lid on the fetching detail) and then a freelance writer where I could fetch all I wanted.

Then my mate and I started visiting Rehoboth Beach—a gem of a resort town on the Delaware coast, where gays had been vacationing since the early 20th century—albeit very quietly. But by those ACT-UP! 80s, Rehoboth started to attract a more visible gay and lesbian crowd. Out, proud and losing friends by the hundreds to the plague, people came to Rehoboth to eat, drink, soak up the sun and make as merry as possible. As in gay strongholds nationwide, people bonded in newly organized and compassionate communities to fight AIDS and its accompanying homophobia.

By the mid 90s Bonnie and I were loyal Rehoboth weekenders. And I was invited to write a column for a popular local publication *Letters from CAMP Rehoboth*. I wrote about the beach, drag volleyball and boating adventures. Ironically, week after week, the column was pretty much "What I Did on my Gay Summer Vacation." What comes around, comes around again. ▼

"You want to do what?"

I thought I heard my friend Anyda Marchant, lesbian publishing icon and novelist say she wanted to publish my columns in a book.

Clearly this was a mistake. After all, 92 year old Anyda, known to the world as lesbian novelist Sarah Aldridge, was far too literary, too erudite to think my columns worthy. Her own novel, her 14th, *O, Mistress Mine* had just been released. We needed to work on publicizing *it*. What was in the vodka she was serving? Or the scotch she was drinking?

Anyda and Muriel, her partner of 55 years, (yes, 55; somebody please call the American Family Association) just smiled and told me to get to work putting the book together because they wanted it published by spring. And then the conversation turned to politics, squirrels getting into the bird feeder and if anyone wanted another cracker with Double Gloucester cheese.

FLASHBACK

On a Saturday morning back in 1994, I made my way into the cramped quarters of Rehoboth's Lambda Rising bookstore. It wasn't the big place it is now, but its tiny precursor at the rear of the 39 Baltimore Avenue courtyard.

I was there for a reading by Leslie Feinberg, author of *Stone Butch Blues*, one of the first novels ever to address transgender issues. This was a big event for little Rehoboth Beach.

As I squeezed into the minuscule bookshop and listened to the author read, I became aware of somebody setting up two folding chairs just to my left and then two elderly women being seated at my side.

"Do you know who that is?" whispered a woman to my right. "That's Sarah Aldridge."

The name sounded familiar, but rang no particular bell.

"I'll show you her books later."

Following the reading I smiled at the ladies as they rose to leave. One woman was tall, with a long gray pony tail and a somewhat remote, regal look—despite her casual corduroy dyke wear. She nodded to me. The other woman, shorter, stockier and relying on a cane, had twinkling eyes and responded to me with a pixie grin.

Later, I stood before the bookstore's fiction shelves as my friend pointed out a dozen novels by Sarah Aldridge. I saw the imprint of the feminist publishing house Naiad Press on the book spines. Naiad was one of the nation's first and arguably most successful lesbian publishers in this country, and probably the world.

Not much of a fiction reader, I bought the Aldridge book *Misfortune's Friend* for Bonnie to read and wound up getting into it myself. The writer had an old-fashioned romantic style, an impressive grasp of historical detail and a passion for lesbian romance. I enjoyed the book and wanted to get to know the elderly author and her partner, our local celebrities.

After asking around, I realized I had known of the ladies, if not their names. They had actually been founders of Naiad Press. I also learned that Anyda Marchant and Muriel Crawford, both in their 80s had been together almost half a century and that during the past twenty five years Anyda wrote over a dozen novels. Muriel, a former executive secretary, transcribed them and partnered with the author by providing serious scrutiny and feedback for their fine-tuning.

Anyda was a member of the illustrious Virginia Woolf Society, Muriel liked popular mystery writers, and they both liked Dewars Scotch, growing roses, and talking politics.

I asked *Letters* editor Steve Elkins for an introduction and he told me about the Saturday evening "salons" on the ladies' front porch, where everyone is welcome. The following weekend, Steve and his partner Murray took me and Bonnie to meet the ladies. It was one of the most important days of my life.

What can I tell you about Anyda and Muriel? They have been in Rehoboth almost half their long lives.

Not part of Rehoboth's gay community. Not until relatively recently. Anyda and Muriel spent a majority of their lives deeply closeted and silent about their relationship. In fact, Muriel couldn't even say the word lesbian—she coined a new one. When they would see a female couple walking down the street Muriel would say, "Shhhh..." Eventually, they began to call their own kind Shushes.

Over many years, long before I came along to partake, the ladies hosted their front porch cocktail hour with a crowd as diverse as Rehoboth Beach itself—neighbors, clergymen, writers, artists, and politicians. And shushes and gay guys. They loved the boys' attention and the boys loved to come to visit, flowers or homemade goodies in hand.

They were Rehoboth's Gertrude Stein and Alice B. Toklas, serving scotch instead of marijuana brownies. On that expansive front veranda there might be a dozen people, four conversations in progress and visitors coming and going throughout cocktail hour, which started promptly at 5 p.m. and ended pretty much an hour and a half later.

When winter came, the ladies packed up whatever great big sedan they had at the time, Muriel at the wheel, and drove themselves to Florida for the winter months. The writing collaboration continued.

Following our introduction to those wonderful porch gatherings, Bonnie and I became regulars. We heard lots of rich history, including Anyda expounding on the virtues of the suffragettes. I had to remind myself that she was old enough to remember them.

"Oh yes, I saw them taken away in handcuffs from the front of the White House," she'd tell me. Anyda also had plenty to say about the failings of both Herbert Hoover and Tricky Dick Nixon.

Local politics didn't escape scrutiny either, nor did the

deplorable condition of a garden down the street. "They should really be spraying those roses," both ladies agreed, with an unspoken tsk, tsk.

And there's no telling what subject from the past might come up to bring perspective to today's conversations. The female cats, a gray tabby and an all-black beauty, would scamper around the guests' legs and often completely interrupt weighty topics with their trapeze acts atop Muriel's walker.

We'd be on the porch, listening to stories as Anyda and Muriel sat together, facing the street, on a well-worn couch, its sides doubling as scratching posts for the cats. We'd be across from the ladies, in wicker chairs or seated on a weather-beaten yellow vinyl glider, backs to the neighbors and all eyes on the storytellers. Anyda generally sat bolt upright; Muriel sank into the sofa, her feet not touching the floor.

Anyda loved talking about growing up in the Nation's Capitol. "Washington was a one-horse town," Anyda said. "My family lived in the second apartment building ever built in D.C., and I remember going to a tree planting to honor Teddy Roosevelt's son, who had been killed in the war." That would be the first World War.

"My father was a scholar who had been educated by French Jesuits. Books were very, very important. I read my way through the children's section of the D.C. public library and then wanted to start with the adult books. My mother fought with the librarian and won, so I could read the grown-up books."

From what I gathered, young Anyda was a handful. "Oh yes, I was quite pugnacious at the time," she admits, describing how she had to protect her little brother from bullies, and that she herself got into a fistfight or two. "We were odd, we came here from Brazil, you know, speaking a jumble of languages." That jumble—English, French, Spanish, Portuguese —must have served her well, because she eventually graduated first in her college class of 100.

All Bonnie and I wanted to do was soak up this living history. We heard how Anyda received a scholarship from the newborn Women's Bar Association, and it was on to law school in 1930 as one of four women in a class of over 300.

Graduating in the heart of the depression, Anyda took any job she could get—first as a law clerk, then working in the political science department of Johns Hopkins University, and in 1938, a job with the Library of Congress. "I was assigned the magnificent salary of $1,800 a year," she says.

In the meantime, her brother secured a job with the State Department back in Rio. Anyda joined him and their mother in Brazil for two years, just prior to the Japanese surrender in World War II.

"Anyone dry?" Muriel interrupted, holding up her empty glass. That was a cue for Charlie and Betsy, porch regulars and great friends of the hostesses to collect the empties and tend bar.

Anyda looked at me and said "I didn't want to be a lawyer. I wanted to be a writer. I'd been writing since I was a child and finished my first novel at 17. But I got a scholarship for law school, so I went.

"Who had the vodka and cranberry?" Charlie asked, returning from the kitchen. From there, the conversation turned to other things as guests filtered in and out. Dammit, I had a feeling we were just about to get to the juicy part of the story—how Anyda and Muriel found each other and fell in love. Fortunately that afternoon would not be our last salon with the ladies of Laurel Street....▼

September 2003

I don't know how many deviled eggs or Ritz crackers with saga blue cheese I nibbled or how many cocktails I sipped while getting to know Anyda and Muriel. Since Bonnie and I met them in 1994, there's been a lot of scotch and water under the bridge. We cheered the day when we were invited to stop by anytime, not just for Saturday evenings on the front porch.

Whether on the porch with a crowd, or just the two of us visiting in the ladies' back sunroom, it was always a learning experience. We could tell from the living room, with its crammed bookshelves, baby grand piano, twenty year old stereo components and furniture representing several eras, this was a home well-lived and well enjoyed.

As for that juicy part about how A&M met, Anyda insists she just looked out the window of her office one day, spotted Muriel crossing the street, and it was love at first sight. She remembers saying to herself, "That's it." But she couldn't exactly figure out what 'it' was.

At age 38, she had never had any kind of intimate relationship, although she had plenty of unrequited crushes on female teachers and friends. "Besides, there was no way to even picture a life where you would settle down with another woman. It was unheard of. At least to me, in my experience."

"But you knew that lesbians existed, didn't you?" I asked.

"Well, I knew of historical characters, I knew this kind of attraction existed, but absolutely no one talked about it." At the time, over a half century ago, most gay men and lesbians were deeply closeted, feeling shame and furtively making contacts with those like themselves. Forget about books on the subject—the most heralded lesbian tale was *The Well of Loneliness*, and you know how that banned-in-Boston book came out (You don't? Read it, if only to see how great it is to have zillions of lesbian novels and books to choose from these days—ones that don't end in self-recriminations, suicide, murder and despair).

It was Anyda's beloved Virginia Woolf who gave her reason to hope. Woolf's quote, "only women stir my imagination," became her inspiration, and she showed me a book where she had underlined those words. Then she looked at me and said "I read it and I wondered if some kind of life with a woman might be achievable—although it seemed a rather remote possibility. But at some point I realized that it was what I wanted."

At the end of World War II, when Anyda returned to the U.S. from Brazil, she went to work for an attorney in New York City and then received an offer to join the large Washington, D.C. law firm headed by former Secretary Of State Dean Acheson. There, she was one of four female attorneys on a staff of 75 and Muriel was a crackerjack executive secretary. Amid manual typewriters, secretarial stenography, and carbon paper, workplace intrigue came to life.

Muriel had been clandestinely "seeing" another one of the female attorneys. Office romances are always tricky, but I imagine that a same sex liaison in those post-war days was absolutely perilous.

Anyda and Muriel began to enjoy an innocent lunchtime friendship at work as they got to know each other. Soon, Muriel suspected that Anyda's attention was more than just friendly, and Anyda realized that there could be no one for her but Muriel.

But how would she know if Muriel was "that way" also?

"I didn't make it easy," Muriel admits. She had been in the relationship with the other female attorney, on and off, for more than five years. "And I was even dating a man then, because it was the thing to do. Besides, I was told by the woman I was involved with that women could not be together permanently. It was a very confusing time for me. But Anyda was there to lean on."

Sorry to say, I don't know much more information straight from the mares mouths about what happened next. But it's not

7

for lack of prying! But both Anyda and Muriel quickly clam up when discussing their initial attraction and decision to be together.

"But it was the best decision we ever made," says Muriel, smiling.

One clue came from their appropriation of Thanksgiving as their own private holiday; one they always celebrated quietly with each other and later took as an anniversary. Shortly after Thanksgiving 1948, Muriel asked Anyda, who was living in a rooming house at the time, to move into the house she shared with her aunt. Muriel was taking care of her elderly relative and Anyda joined her.

Muriel always says how "very circumspect we had to be. We didn't go to bars. We didn't do anything that would shatter the illusion we were just friends." Actually, it may have been easier to disguise the nature of their relationship at that time—there was a terrible post-war housing shortage and lots of women wound up sharing lodging because of the crunch.

If others suspected, they certainly didn't talk about it. "But if they didn't know, they were stupid," says Anyda, stealing a glance at Muriel, who blushed bright pink.▼

September 2003

SUNNY DAYS, PARTY NIGHTS
AT CARPENTER BEACH

The phrase "Don't Ask, Don't Tell" might have been coined in 1992, but the policy was alive and well in Rehoboth Beach as far back as the 1930s.

Talking to folks who've been in Rehoboth for twenty years or more, you begin to learn just how far back our gay history goes. People who started coming here in the late 1970s learned from their elders of a gay mecca—"although we weren't called gay then. We were still homosexuals," jokes one Rehoboth senior.

Lore has it that the Dupont property, which sat ocean front at Rehoboth's Silver Lake, was where it all began. According to old timers, Louisa Dupont Carpenter, while married to a prominent businessman, was a flamboyant and very independent woman, perhaps even, as Muriel would say, "a shush."

An aviatrix and adventurer, Carpenter was a great friend of the Broadway and Hollywood star Tallulah Bankhead—whose family lived on the Eastern Shore of Maryland off Chesapeake Bay. Louisa, Tallulah, singer Libby Holman and many of their male friends gathered in Rehoboth in the late 1930s and 40s at the family estate.

A large field on the periphery of town doubled as a small airfield to allow celebrities to swoop in and out for private gay weekends. According to reports from those who were there, it was a very cultured, very sophisticated scene and the tradition continued for years. Hundreds of older men would gather at what became known as Carpenter Beach to relax on the sand, set up chess and backgammon boards and play volleyball.

In the 1950s, and well into the 60s and early 70s, since there were no specifically gay bars to frequent, gay life moved exclusively between the beach and private house parties. Even if there was a welcoming bar, liquor laws prevented anyone, gay or straight, from walking around carrying a drink. Under those circumstances, even if gays gathered at a gay-tolerant establishment "it was almost impossible to meet anyone other than the fellow sitting right beside you" says one veteran.

As Rehoboth honed its reputation as the Nation's Summer Capitol, with Washington D.C. legislators and government workers vacationing here with their families, so too were the hundreds of gay government employees seeking anonymity on a beach vacation.

With the hideous threat of exposure that could mean loss of jobs and even prison time, most of the gay people kept strictly to their area of the beach and partied only at their closest friends' homes.

The traditions continued almost unchanged through the early 1970s. Louisa Dupont Carpenter was a fixture here during much of that time, until she flew her plane into a local airport field, with a fatal result, in the early 1970s.

Rehoboth's early gay life was rich and famous.

Muriel, her aunt, and Anyda often came to the beach for weekends. "But if there was gay life here, we certainly didn't know about it," Anyda says.

Anyda handed me a square black and white photo with scalloped white edges. It was a picture of the couple, maybe in their early 40s, standing on the sand at the edge of the water.

"We'd stay at the Dinner Bell Inn and have breakfast at The Robin Hood Restaurant at 3 or 4 in the morning with local fishermen," Anyda remembered.

"It's still there, isn't it, Bouddie?" Muriel asked, addressing Anyda with one of the pet names, origin unknown, she had for her partner.

"Oh, yes, it's still right in the same place."

In those days, the ladies spent mornings on the beach, afternoons fishing off the old bridge over the Indian River inlet and evenings strolling the boardwalk, soaking up the freedom they felt here. I loved to hear their stories.

And as wonderful as it must have been to be in quiet mid-

1950s Rehoboth Beach, it's also sad that the couple had to hide their great love for each other.

But being in the closet didn't mean they kept to themselves. They found full acceptance with their families and neighbors all without saying a word about their relationship. "There was an old style of society, where people just accepted things," says Muriel. "Anyda's mother called me 'Muriel-my-love.' It didn't make a difference. There wasn't the kind of religious bigotry we see today."

On another afternoon with the ladies, while Bonnie was out spraying the backyard roses, I was talking with Anyda about the need to prune the tree on the side of the sprawling single story cottage. I learned that it was under that full-canopied tree that the first of the cocktail salons began.

"Before we had the porch built," Anyda said. "We'd put out some chairs, and the neighbors would spy us and walk up to say hello. We'd offer cocktails and it turned into a lovely tradition. That's how we met Betsy."

They bought their current house in 1965. It was their second Rehoboth cottage, the first being a tiny weekend place on the outskirts of town, surrounded by farmland—where today there are McMansions. When Anyda and Muriel bought that first house in the 1950s, their real estate agent was the mayor's wife and one of Rehoboth's first female agents—which thrilled fervent feminist Anyda.

It was not so thrilling that the local bank refused to grant the two women a loan despite their stellar professional credentials. Muriel, still annoyed, remembers that the bank worried that the women "weren't connected in any way," and it was shocking for two females to purchase a home.

"They thought women were a bad risk even if we had careers. We might have gotten pregnant, you know," Anyda explained, with a wink.

So the couple went to a more progressive bank in town, got their mortgage and headed east to their weekend retreat.

In 1965, still commuting from Washington on weekends,

Anyda and Muriel sold their little home and bought their present in-town cottage. But it took a while to come up with the $32,000 price tag. "It was a leap for us at the time," Anyda says, of a property that's worth millions today.

IF THEY ASKED ME I COULD WRITE A....

Now, more than thirty years later, Anyda, dressed in brown corduroy pants and a blue plaid flannel shirt, with green slippers on her feet, is standing on her porch, a box of crackers in her hand asking me, somewhat impatiently, if I've thought any more about her next publishing project.

With her last novel released a whole six months before, and negotiations with lesbian author Ann Allen Shockley about her new manuscript still in the talking stages, Anyda had to have a new project. Time for some new challenge for the 92 year old. Never mind that she already had me busy writing promotional brochures and press packets, running to the post office and helping with A&M Books distribution. Of course, I loved being part of our local publishing empire. But a book under my byline?

"Tell me again exactly what you had in mind?" I asked.

"A book of your columns. We will publish it. You'll have to get them all together. Just do it." She sounded like a Nike commercial.

"But I have a column due tomorrow, and…well, press releases for your book and…"

"You can do it," she said and turned around to arrange a vase of flowers plucked from her own garden.

Anyda had spoken. There would be a book of my essays. But my deadline for *Letters* was only 18 hours away. First priority would be finishing *that* column. And with our discussion of the threat of imprisonment for the rich, famous and bureaucratic homosexual crowd back in the 1940s Rehoboth, I find it ironic that we haven't come all that far today. In fact, Delaware is going backward. To wit, my next column….▼

September 2003

Frankly, I'm stunned. I hardly believe myself what you are about to read. But it's true, I saw it with my own eyes and I herewith report the following:

I'm a common criminal. Actually, an uncommon criminal, since I'm guilty of a charge that few can claim (so far) and of which no one has ever been convicted. I am guilty of this crime in the State of Delaware and what's more, I am subject to a $100 fine or 30 days in the slammer.

And I'm oh-so-guilty as charged.

My infraction? I married my same-sex partner last month in Canada and then went on a glorious Alaskan honeymoon.

But wait, you say! That was Canada. Delaware does not permit same-sex marriage. For pity's sake they can't even get anti-discrimination legislation onto the Senate floor. So what's your Vancouver marriage got to do with Delaware?

Holy matrimony, Batman, not only is it illegal to conduct and recognize same-sex marriage in Delaware, but anybody who resides in the state and goes some place else (Boston, New Paltz, NY, Canada) to tie the same-sex knot may be subject to jail when they get home. If I'd known this in August I could have been worrying about it for the past six months. I'm astounded that there was something to worry about and I missed it.

Not only is this provision on the Internet in the Delaware Code, but it's sandwiched between all kinds of other punishable offenses. Did you know that two paupers can't marry either? Hell, now there are two counts against me.

I'm so shocked that I qualify for an all expenses paid vacation to the hoosegow I might now be eligible for felon-ness under "unsoundness of mind"—another bridal infraction. Oh, in Delaware it's perfectly alright to marry a lunatic, habitual drunkard, confirmed narcotic user or a diseased person, but lucky for any unsuspecting bride or groom, those marriages are "void from the time its nullity is declared" whatever the heck that means. No jail time, though.

If Bonnie and I are brought in on charges, too bad we're not habitual drunkards or Cuckoo's Nest residents, or we could be annulled and avoid the nasty fine. Don't quote me on this. I'm not a lawyer, I just slept at a Holiday Inn Express on my trip to Florida last week.

Now I don't know if I'm the first person to sound the journalistic alarm about this situation, but I probably won't be the last.

Title 13—Domestic Relations—Chapter 1. Marriage

101. Void and voidable marriages.

(a) A marriage is prohibited and void between a person and his or her ancestor, descendant, brother, sister, uncle, aunt, niece, nephew, first cousin or between persons of the same gender.

(d) A marriage obtained or recognized outside the State between persons prohibited by subsection (a) of this section shall not constitute a legal or valid marriage within the State.

102. Entering into a prohibited marriage; penalty.

The guilty party or parties to a marriage prohibited by § 101 of this title shall be fined $100, and in default of the payment of the fine shall be imprisoned not more than 30 days.

104. Entering into prohibited marriage outside the State; penalty.

If a marriage prohibited by this chapter is contracted or solemnized outside of the State, when the legal residence of either party to the marriage is in this State, and the parties thereto shall afterwards live and cohabit as spouses within the State, they shall be punished in the same manner as though the marriage had been contracted in this State.

Yipes. Now this is pretty scary. While the numbers are not huge, there are several folks I know who have traveled to Canada to get married, both as a symbolic gesture of commitment and, in my case, the logical conclusion to a 21 year engagement. Do we have to pay up or go up the river? If so, do we have to return the wedding gifts? Does Miss Manners even cover these questions?

And if we are jailed, will both marital criminals be in the same cell? If there are more than four of us in a cellblock will it be a tea dance?

I suppose I could work a plea bargain, what with the state trying to save money and all, and get house arrest. I'd be willing to wear a clunky ankle bracelet and be confined to the house for a month. In fact, given my current crazy schedule and obligations, that sounds heavenly. Oh wait, would the Delaware Humane Society step in, call us unfit parents and remove our Schnauzers from the home? This is a question that needs an answer.

So here I sit, shocked and appalled that my goody-two-shoes reputation is shot. I am police-record eligible. How can I plan my calendar if I don't know if I'll be away at the big house? What's a wife to do? Pay the fine? Not me.

In the interim, I must tell you about my annual parental visit to Florida, where, when we weren't sitting in the sun or dining out with the folks, we spent much of our time watching the talking heads on the tube pontificate about gay marriage.

Happily, my family shares my political ideology as well as our personality genes. Which means we were all screaming back at the TV about the prospect of a Constitutional amendment codifying discrimination. My 85 year old father called Rick Santorum an (expletive delete).

Bonnie and I did take a side trip from Sarasota to North Ft. Meyers to check out the community called Care Free. It's a gated community, with well-manicured grounds, a pool, tennis courts and club house that's home to 500 lesbians. Some live there year round and others buy property as weekend or vacation spots. Folks rent out their units too, like our beach resorts, and lots of folks visit Care Free for a week or two each year.

While it was all very pretty and, well, care free, Bonnie and

I couldn't see living in an all-girls-all-the-time environment like that. We love the diversity of Rehoboth and certainly feel as care free here as we can be. Or at least we did until we learned we're scofflaws and could possibly become jailbirds. (I know, it's waaay too late for jail *bait*) We did the crime, will we do the time?

Which brings to mind more questions. Is Queen Latifah still the warden? Will there be women in prison that look like Charlize Theron? If so, I can take 30 days. Will Martha Stewart be there, decorating my cell?

Gee. Will I be sentenced to time in the prison laundry and have to confront my fear of ironing? Will HBO want my story for The Jacobs Redemption? Can you really dig through a cell wall with a spoon? Being taken away in handcuffs should make a nifty front page photo in *Letters*. In the meantime, just call us Bonnie & Snide.▼

Mea Culpa, Mea Culpa. I can no longer keep up the charade. My fear of being found out and thoroughly humiliated is giving me the vapors. So I've got to come out of the closet. The truth is, I don't know your name.

Now it's true that I've never been formally introduced to many readers of this column, so of course, I'm to be excused for not knowing everyone on a first name basis. But quite frankly, when I see some faces around town, day after day, season after season, and I know we've been introduced a couple of quadrillion times, it makes me positively nuts that I can't remember people's names.

And while there's a certain amount of slack to be cut for waiters I see occasionally—before, during and after Cosmopolitans—I'm talking about people I see all the time. People I've had dinner with. Sometimes at my own house. I mean I know who they *are*, I just can't remember what to call them. "Hi, Hon" only works if you're in Baltimore.

I realize that I'm not the only person in my age bracket having this problem. But, by virtue of my mug being in a magazine (okay, I know it's a picture from one of my sporadic thin days, but people on the mailing list from Idaho don't know) a lot of people stop me around town to say hello. I love this, and it's great to meet *Letters* readers, but the problem is that I never know if I've actually met the people before or they're asking about the dogs, Bonnie or some issue I'm in a lather about from reading my column. Half the time even the initial conversation doesn't give me a clue to the person's age, rank or serial number.

Mostly I just sweat and stress out, hoping I can horkle up a name from my hard disk before somebody else arrives and I have to do introductions. Failing an identification, I just stand there like an etiquette moron, while introductions swirl around me. When I do hear a name, it circulates in my ears for about two seconds and then *bang*, it's sucked up into my cerebellum never to be heard from again.

When you think about it, remembering names may be tough everywhere better baby boomers are found, but it's even harder in Rehoboth. I mean out there, in the rest of the world, when you meet couples at an event or party, many of them are heterosexual. Hell, if you can remember that they're Fred and Ginger or Scarlet and Rhett, it's not hard figuring out which is which. Pairs of Toms and Tims, Sues and Debs, and Gertrudes and Alices are a knottier problem altogether. In fact, some couples become proper nouns, like FayandBonnie, SteveandMurray, RobertandLarry. Lots of people remember the couple, but who's who gives them fits. I call it couples dyslexia.

Now all this wouldn't be so totally bothersome if it weren't for the latest research which shows that stress causes memory lapses. I can't remember a name so I get stressed so I can't remember a name so I gets stressed…it's a chicken/egg thing.

But why is it I can remember the complete lyrics to "Jubilation T. Cornpone" from the Broadway bomb *Lil Abner* but I can't remember the name of the maitre d' who gets me the great eight o'clock reservation?

I'd take some of those over-the-counter dietary supplements, but I can't remember which ones to take. It reminds me of the old Carol Burnett gag "Amnesia? I forget what that means."

It's like the friend of mine, who, having MS, gets asked by her doctor if she's having memory lapses. She says "How would I *know*?"

What's a person to do? Short of encouraging people to provide name tags at parties (thank you, thank you, thank you, those who do…) there has to be a way to improve my memory.

So I turned to a computer search.

The dragnet turned up the Cognitive Enhancement

Research Institute, where I found out that a substance called GHB seems to be all the rage for improving memory, but drat it all, its' use is being *criminalized* nationwide. If I landed in jail how would I remember my lawyers phone number?

If carburetor additives aren't the answer, maybe mnemonics is. Whew. If you can remember how to spell that one you're halfway home. Mneumonic systems are mind tools to help remember things. According to lots of people on the internet who want to sell you stuff, linking names to vivid images makes you able to remember all sorts of complex things.

It works by associating one thing with another. You are advised that associations can be made by visualizing yourself being placed on top of the object you want to remember. Whoa. When it comes to remembering people, this gets into a whole different set of techniques, and, frankly, as a permanently partnered woman, I'm not supposed to be going there.

So we move to the next memory tool: the Roman Room Mneumonic. Here, you're supposed to be able to remember whole lists of unstructured things, like a shopping list, by picturing a room that you know very well. Then you assign each item on your shopping list to a thing in, say, your dining room. When you recall the objects in the room, you recall your list.

Sure. Not only couldn't I remember my shopping list, but I forgot whether we had six or eight dining room chairs. All it did was give me a headache and I couldn't remember if we had Excedrin.

At this point I started to explain to Bonnie the memory tricks I'd been describing. She suddenly stands up, taps her head, points to her chest, slaps her behind, smiles and points to her crotch.

"That's it," I said, "You've finally gone round the bend."

"No," she says, "don't you remember the old joke where the woman does these things in the grocery store and when she's asked what in the hell she's doing she says 'Shopping list' and does the routine again saying "A head of lettuce, jug of milk, buns and a little Joy."

Um, not a helpful system.

Let's face it, until scientists come up with some magic solution to memory malfunction, I'm destined to wander throughout Rehoboth bluffing my way through sticky situations. Although I did feel somewhat better this afternoon when I had lunch in the CAMP Rehoboth courtyard and two different people (one I've known for a while) came up and called me Bonnie. It really did make me feel better. I'm sure they know that Fay is the one who writes the column and Bonnie is the one who yells at her for publishing some of her most embarrassing moments, but making an I.D. these days is just not as easy as it used to be.

So at the next party, or beach day or stroll through town, if you say hello and a panicked, quizzical or vacant look crosses my face, help me out here. I promise you, I know who you are. Or I want to know who you are. And you can be sure that I never forget a smile, a kindness or a favor. Now your name may be a different story altogether. Mea Culpa.▼

October 2003

Like detective Kinsey Milhone says, *F is for Fish*. Frozen fish. Oy Gefilte. Over the past several weeks, I've been snarled in the *Search for the Missing Salmon*.

To me, fishing is selecting an entrée. Not surprisingly, to my spouse, it's a sport.

Which is why, on our recent Alaska trip, I spent my morning in Ketchikan on a land tour while Bonnie sought to catch and can salmon. As it turned out, she spent what sounded to me like a disgusting morning playing with chum, and catching a trio of mighty salmon. *The Middle Aged Woman and the Sea*. Hemingway would have been proud.

But you know how the commercial goes by now: Sport fishing excursion: $170; Smoking and flash freezing fish: $120; Hosting a salmon bake at home with fish you caught yourself in Alaska: priceless.

Only it wasn't that easy.

First, we worried that the flash frozen salmon would be shipped home before us, to lounge on our doorstep in the August sun, decomposing. Now that's a *Clear and Present Danger*.

Assured that the catch would not arrive before we did, we moved to wondering how we'd be sure to get the actual fish Bonnie struggled to land—which, I might add, she did to the envy of the four fishermen also on the boat. I mean, how would we know that our FedExed salmon steaks were from the bug-eyed monster my wife caught? DNA?

Patricia Cornwell's coroner Kay Scarpetta not being available, we had to take it on faith. Although, it's mighty tough to take *anything* on faith these days, what with California voters failing to notice that Ahhhnold had no actual platform and holier than everybody Rush Limbaugh turning up as a druggie.

But recent CNN stories notwithstanding, we put aside skepticism, hoped for the best and continued our cruise without worrying. At least about the fish.

White-knuckled, we soared over glaciers in a float plane, survived a tour bus driver shouting "Moose in the road!!!," witnessed fornicating sea otters (you go, girl!), saw clouds part to reveal an awesome Mt. McKinley, and tromped through the woods following a guide who was, literally, loaded for bear.

Taking note of the rifle slung over his shoulder I asked "Ever had to use that thing?"

"No," he said, "you tourists are pretty well behaved." I guess he got the question a lot.

The trip followed immediately on the heels of our August double wedding in Vancouver—Fay & Bonnie, Robert & Larry getting hitched and honeymooned.

The four of us had a great time rafting, despite fretting we'd fall out of our rubber boat into the whitewater, if you'll excuse the expression. Dressed in every article of clothing we'd packed, we resembled South Park cartoons.

In addition, they made us wear rubber suits over all the clothes. We have seen the Abominable Snowman and he is us. The raft trip proved exciting and very, very chilly. The splashing waves gave us a glacial facial, but fortunately nobody fell in. We'd have sunk like the Bismarck.

So, having toured both the great Alaska wilderness and every cocktail lounge on the ship, we headed home with several observations. First, in Alaska there should be a two-pair minimum on socks. Second, if a big chunk of ice falls off a glacier and Leo DeCaprio is not there to hear it, it is still an iceberg. And finally, bears actually do poop in the woods.

I'm still amused by U.S. airport security. To prevent the SARS virus from entering Philadelphia, they asked each incoming traveler, following their eight mile hike through the airport dragging carry-on crap, up two escalators, down one long hallway, over the river and through the woods to baggage claim, to sign a paper attesting to the fact that they did not have shortness of breath. Puleeeze.

Jet lagged, wheezing and recovering from hypothermia, we arrived home to await our souvenir seafood.

Every day, starting September 2, Bonnie or I arranged to check the homefront between noon and 3 p.m. People whispered about a possible affair between one of us and the FedEx girl. Often, we'd post a "Dear FedEx" note on the door, so every burglar in town knew exactly when to strike. Fortunately, we also had the Schnauzer alarm.

Weeks passed, and the mystery of the *Ten Little Filets* deepened. *P is for Pissed*. My God, millions of fish had gone through whole spawning cycles since we last heard from *Moby Salmon*.

Finally, we called Ketchikan (not that easy in itself) to learn that our flash frozen fish was safe in an Alaskan Sub Zero, while parts of the catch went through the smoking process. They said our order would be shipped September 29 to arrive October 1.

Frankly, by this time neither of us gave a damn whose fish it was as long as it arrived postmarked Alaska to prove to increasing numbers of skeptics that Bonnie really caught something and wasn't just blowing smoked salmon.

So now it was the *Hunt for Red (Salmon in) October*. Once again we did the daily FedEx vigil so three hundred bucks of fish sticks didn't thaw on the stoop. Days passed and it was Agatha Christie's *Murder on the Federal Express*. By October 6 we scoped out Food Lion for frozen filets to pass off as the trophy catch.

"Hello, Ketchikan? Where the heck is our fish?"

"Oh, sorry, we've been closed down with heavy fog all week. Nothin goin' in or outta here."

"Our Sockeye Salmon is socked in?"

"Yes, but don't worry, your fish is in a freezer at the airport. It should be able to fly out tomorrow."

Great, my fish is flying stand-by.

I came home today to find Bonnie feverishly stuffing vacuum packed baggies filled with salmon into every crevasse in the freezer.

"So whaddya think? Is it yours?"

"I dunno."

I suggested matching the fish scales on the largest filet with photos of Bonnie holding up her fish for the camera. She chucked a salmon brick at me.

Tonight as an appetizer we had a yummy smoked salmon spread. We followed with fettuccine alfredo and smoked salmon. And tomorrow, it might be Salmon Stroganoff, Salmon Wellington, or Szechuan Salmon. Fish Bake, here we come. We're glad the mystery of *The Runaway Salmon* is solved. As John Grisham might say, now it's *A Time to Grill*....▼

October 2003

I tried to brush the sand off of my shoes, my pants and my dog before getting into the car. I was gritty and sweaty but the deed was done. I had just posed in a beach chair, at the edge of the water, laptop and lapdog on my considerable lap, as I sipped from a Martini glass of faux Cosmopolitan.

All things considered, my friend Murray, CAMP Rehoboth President and photographer par excellence had an easier time with the dog than with me.

Between blinking my eyes at the flash and obsessing about my thighs being an unfortunate focal point, the shoot was a challenge. But at the end of the day, I hoped we'd have a book cover photo.

Of course, we pulled the idea for the picture out of our butts, because there's really no book yet, just a collection of columns, but they do involve the beach, Schnauzers and Cosmopolitans, not necessarily in that order.

I'm alternately freaked out and frenzied. I've re-read eight years of columns, read them aloud and edited out parts that annoyed me the minute they went to press the first time. Then I printed out all the columns, and with the assistance of my "adopted" son Eric, assigned them in yes, no and maybe piles on the floor of my home office. We were in that room flinging paper for days.

Oddly enough, the columns, written every two weeks on whatever topic popped into my brain at deadline time, did tell a story. It's *How I Discovered Rehoboth, Came Here for Gay Weekends, Lived on my Boat, Bought a Condo, Pined to Be Here Full Time and Finally Made My Father Insane Because I Quit My Job and Moved to the Beach.*

Okay, maybe Rehoboth locals would get a kick out of it in book form. Maybe a few weekenders from Philly or D.C. might get a chuckle. Mostly, it will make Anyda happy to have A&M

Books publish another author besides Sarah Aldridge. Muriel seems excited about it too. We'll print a few copies, bribe local stores to stock them and have an adventure.

Actually, I really have to get off my ass and put the thing together because a beach book should probably be published by Memorial Day. Besides, Anyda and Muriel may be the publishers, but writing the check to the printer and cheering me on is the most they are up to doing. So I've got to get busy. But the real urgency is what Anyda matter-of-factly says: "Get to it. I'm old you know."

I know.

Seeing two women in their 90s so incredibly engaged, animated, and energized is fantastic. That it's my pre-natal book they are keyed up about blows me away. After all, they are lesbian publishing royalty.

THE LESBIAN WRITER

Shortly after Bonnie and I met the ladies, we were in their sunroom talking about the Sarah Aldridge novels. Muriel had her checkbook out, writing a check for postage to send a carton of books to a feminist book collective in California. They asked me to walk to the detached garage behind the house and bring back a stack of books they needed. I wended my way past the roses, through some ancient ground cover toward the garage—a structure with a rental apartment above. I slid the heavy door open and it was like walking into a lesbian archeology dig. I found hundreds of cartons, holding thousands of copies of the 13 still-in-print Sarah Aldridge novels.

By that afternoon I'd learned that although Anyda had been penning unpublished lesbian novels since she was a teenager, both she and Muriel spent the 1950s and 60s concentrating on their careers and their clandestine gay life. Anyda was an attorney for the World Bank by this time and Muriel was executive secretary to the president of the Southern Railroad. Both women had enormously high pressure jobs and they loved the work they did.

But by the early 70s, both Anyda and Muriel had health issues. Muriel had lung problems and her blood pressure was off the charts. Anyda was told she had a life-threatening heart condition and the doctor ordered mandatory retirement. So in 1972, Anyda (age 60) and Muriel (age 58) headed to Rehoboth full-time. While they both had wanted to continue their careers, at least the reluctant lawyer would now have the time to write her lesbian novels.

"You know, I had been writing novels all along, and a few of the novels I wrote years ago I did present to publishers," Anyda told me, "but they were turned down flat. I realized I was not reaching my potential because I was not writing about gay subjects. I had a gay mentality, but I was writing non-gay novels, so naturally they had fatal flaws," Anyda acknowledged in her somewhat scholarly voice. "When I came to retire I thought, 'Well, this is the opportunity.'"

Anyda took it and ran. She started writing stories with fiercely feminist themes, strong women protagonists and happy endings. But she and Muriel firmly believed there could be no way to publish such "scandalous" material without disguising the author's identity by using a pen name. Anyda chose *Sarah Aldridge*, a name that sounded vaguely historical and a tad British—by this time Anyda had a bona fide affinity, from both her ancestry and her travels, for Great Britain. She scribbled her novels—rich in both historical detail and romance, in long-hand on yellow legal pads, filling up dozens at a time. Along the way, Muriel, a voracious reader herself, would go over the drafts, making comments or raising questions.

Then, Anyda would dictate them to Muriel for typing. Sometimes Muriel waded through the long-hand drafts herself, muttering and cursing at Anyda's scrawl, as she transcribed. Writing was the easy part; getting published only a dream.

"I wouldn't know where to begin," I said, helping to pack up copies of Aldridge titles *A Flight of Angels* and *The Nesting Place*. "You were so closeted, how did you even know there were readers out there?"

"We had *The Ladder*," said Muriel.

I had heard of the publication, a newsletter of the early lesbian rights organization The Daughters of Bilitis. It was the first American magazine published by lesbians for a lesbian readership. I had read about it and the amazing women, Del Martin and Phyllis Lyon, homosexual rights pioneers, who were behind both the organization and its magazine. *The Ladder* was probably the very first written lifeline thrown to a scattered and mostly isolated population of lesbians all over the country.

Anyda submitted short stories to the publication, marking the first appearance of the Sarah Aldridge byline. And through *The Ladder* Anyda and Muriel met Barbara Grier, the publication's last editor.

By 1972, the magazine had folded, but Grier still had the mailing list—an incredibly valuable commodity of over 3,000 entries. Anyda, encouraged by Muriel, decided she would publish the first Sarah Aldridge novel, *The Latecomer*, herself. "I told Muriel we should start a publishing house," Anyda remembered. "If you had a manuscript of a lesbian novel, you certainly could not find a publisher. But we would do it ourselves and work with Barbara Grier to get the word out with her mailing list."

It was a collaboration that worked—for a long time forward.▼

They would call the publishing house Naiad Press, based on Greek Mythology. Naiads were beautiful water nymphs and Naiad Press would allow lesbian feminist writers' words to flow. Anyda and Muriel put up the $2,000 required, but no printer would touch a lesbian book with the proverbial ten foot pole. After several irritating encounters with insulting printers who refused the job, the women finally found a Florida company, whose only other big client was a Baptist Church. "It was a remarkable combination," Anyda said.

The Naiad Press was officially launched on January 1, 1973, with the publication of *The Latecomer* a year later. The printer shipped the finished books to Anyda and Muriel, who distributed them from their garage. "We were shipping clerks," said Muriel.

Anyda, ever the lawyer, saw to it that by 1974, Naiad was incorporated in Delaware, with Anyda and Muriel, Barbara Grier and her partner Donna McBride as shareholders. Thanks to the large network of independently owned lesbian-feminist bookstores cropping up throughout the 70s, and fledgling gay newspaper outlets, Naiad Press started to make a name for itself.

Through the rest of the 1970s and early 80s, Anyda continued to write novels, with Muriel acting as a sounding board and informal editor. One time, Muriel caught a confusing plot twist in one of the stories requiring Anyda to head back to the legal pads. Although she had to re-write almost half the book to straighten out the plot, she credited Muriel with discovering that "fatal flaw."

In addition to the early Sarah Aldridge novels, Naiad Press began to publish romances, mysteries and novels by other female authors—writers like Katharine V. Forrest, Renee Vivien, Valerie Taylor, and many more.

Anyda was most proud of the business as an incubator for lesbian writers who otherwise might never be published. She and Muriel never expected financial success and never cared if they got any money back on their investments. They used the money made from the sale of *The Latecomer* to pay for publication of the next book, which in turn financed another. And another.

Over the years, Naiad published 12 Sarah Aldridge novels and dozens of other books by lesbians/feminists—surprisingly growing from a small business in the back of a garage to an impressive feminist publishing company with its own warehouse, staff, author list and first-rate nationwide reputation. In the early 80s, Naiad author Jane Rule, who had written the novel *Desert of the Heart*, saw the book turned into the now classic lesbian film *Desert Hearts*. Naiad Press was in the thick of it.

In 1985, Naiad also published the ground-breaking and controversial book *Lesbian Nuns: Breaking Silence*, a collection of true stories.

As Anyda and Muriel continued to tell me the history of Naiad Press, the setting sun indicated the start of cocktail hour, an event not to be ignored. We seemed to be at a stopping point in the Naiad Press story anyway, as Anyda had gotten very quiet. And I knew, from comments Muriel had been dropping, that by the late 1980s the Naiad partnership was on the rocks.

After her second scotch Anyda, who had been very closed mouthed about the whole thing, hinted that the rift involved the direction Naiad Press was taking. Too commercial, not literary.

"We don't really have anything more to say about it," Anyda told me.

Later, I heard from Anyda and Muriel's long-time friend Tom, that Anyda felt Naiad was retreating from its original goal—a publishing opportunity for quality lesbian/feminist writers who might not otherwise be able to publish. As it turned out, the vision Grier and McBride had for the company took Naiad in a much more commercial and controversial direction.

In fact, after researching it, I learned that soon after *Lesbian Nuns: Breaking Silence* was released, Naiad Press sold the rights to one of the interviews to *MS Magazine*, which published it in August 1985.

Apparently, Naiad, with Grier and Johnson at the helm also sold other stories from the book to the men's magazine *Forum*.

Immediately I understood why Anyda has been so reticent to talk. The selling of the chapters to *Forum* must have deeply disturbed Anyda and Muriel on so many different levels.

I found a listing online about a collection of material in the archive at the James C. Hormel Center in San Francisco. The archive contained Naiad Press correspondence from 1971-1994 donated by Barbara Grier. In a description of the material, the archivist notes, "Of particular interest are the files of clippings and correspondence relating to the publication of *Lesbian Nuns: Breaking Silence* edited by Rosemary Curb and Nancy Manahan...Grier's sale of rights to publish excerpts in *Forum* caused a firestorm of controversy within the feminist and lesbian communities. The controversy served to make the book a best seller...."

Well, that answered a lot of questions. Obviously this move by Naiad was the antithesis of everything Anyda and Muriel stood for and saw for the future of Naiad Press.

A&M BOOKS IS BORN

Eventually, Barbara Grier and Donna McBride bought Anyda and Muriel out of Naiad Press and in 1995 Rehoboth's best known publishers started a new company, A&M Books of Rehoboth, once again, out of their home and garage.

As part of the financial settlement with Naiad, A&M Books retained both the existing stock and the rights to all of the Sarah Aldridge titles. And Anyda, at 83, was still writing.

If nothing else, A&M Books would be the avenue for publishing more Sarah Aldridge novels. Although by this time, the

Aldridge novels were joined in gay and mainstream bookstores by an explosion of lesbian-written, lesbian-themed and lesbian-published novels, romances and the new hot genre, mysteries with lesbian detectives, cops and investigators.

Keeping with the style she knew, Anyda kept on writing. With the lesbian publishing industry growing so rapidly—by this time Naiad was joined by several other thriving lesbian publishing outlets—the lesbian community had their own thriving literary culture. And the Sarah Aldridge novels were fast becoming collectible classics.

While continuing to write her romantic novels energized Anyda, she also wanted very much to bring A&M Books to prominence by finding other unpublished authors and letting their words flow as well. It was Anyda's goal.

The publishers have worked on A&M Books projects every single day for over a decade now, at a pace slowed by age, but with more gusto than most people decades younger. A thirteenth Aldridge novel was released and they worked to send out publicity, fill orders and keep the publishing business going. These days, hardly a week goes by without a letter in the A&M post office box from a fan, a former author or a purchase order from a bookseller. Muriel takes care of the checkbook and Anyda does the correspondence. Longhand. Not a computer in the house.

And several of the porch regulars, in addition to stopping by for cocktails and conversation have doubled as shipping clerks, delivering packages to the post office.

Anyda and Muriel humbly accept a little help (like hiring me to do some of the promotional work and mailings), but these fiercely independent women are determined to stay happily and stubbornly self-sufficient.

They both read at least two newspapers a day to stay current. Anyda has a passion for crossword puzzles, *The New Yorker*, and her old muse Virginia Woolf, while Muriel never met a romance novel she didn't love. They cook a bit, entertain guests and keep busy.

Rehoboth residents aren't surprised to see Muriel at the wheel of their shiny maroon late-model Lincoln Town Car, Anyda riding shotgun and navigating, as they go to out to lunch, visit the library or just head east and park by the ocean for a good long look at the seagulls and sand.

Anyda's 14th Sarah Aldridge novel *O, Mistress Mine*, was released by A&M Books last month with a big, celebratory book signing party at the CAMP Rehoboth Community Center. Lots of sales, lots of press. Happy, happy publishers.

And last week the big front porch was closed up for the season. No Florida trip this year. It's just too much stress and difficulty now. So the Florida house has been sold, and the cold months will be spent in Rehoboth. Friends have promised to stop by for cocktails in the back sunroom all winter long and to look in on the ladies every day.

And everyone is pitching in to assist the publishers on their next big project, *As I Lay Frying–a Rehoboth Beach Memoir* by some little-known local columnist.▼

November 2003

According to Oprah, the only wasted day is a day without laughter. It's my motto too. Paying taxes, growing older, or sexual orientation is not a choice, but laughing at yourself is.

I make this point because generally, when absurd stuff happens, I try to keep my sense of humor. That is, until yesterday, when somebody stole my identity.

Why anyone would want my identity, with its maxed-out credit and pathetic portfolio, is beyond me, but steal it they did. Okay, that's not completely true. I pretty much gave them my identity—over the Internet (Fay, call your village, their idiot is missing).

The mess started six weeks ago, when I could still get a good chuckle out of spending two hours on the phone with AOL because somebody in Uzbeckistan had cracked my password. Unable to log on, I'd called AOL. While on hold, I could have read the collected works of Rita Mae Brown.

As it was, wireless phone lodged between my ear and shoulder, I changed my clothes and spent time in the loo. Naturally, the technician finally answered and I had to do the Mexican Hat Dance to get my pants back up without dropping the phone. He pretended not to hear the flush. He explained that I was secure again and issued me a new password. Fine.

Two weeks later, my e-mail went flooey again. This time, the AOL tech had me on my cell phone for forty-five minutes while he coached me on reinstalling my software. I was fixed.

This was a good thing, because I was in the midst of e-mailing columns back and forth to editors and layout designers, trying to make my self-imposed book deadline.

Unfortunately, the fix AOL offered completely screwed up my modem settings, requiring me to have a martini and call Dell Computer. I was getting ticked but still able to find a little humor in this incident.

For instance, Dell keeps you on hold for twenty minutes and then, before you can even say hello, an automated voice asks for your service code. I bent down to find the code on the side of the computer, and saw it was written in 2-point type, impossible for a woman of my age to read, even with peepers on.

"You have 30 seconds to say your service code numbers or press the numbers on your touch tone phone," droned the automated one.

I dove under the desk, plastered my face up against the sadistic code number, and still couldn't read it. Time up! Bang! I was back on hold. Phooey. I wasn't even on the portable phone so I could go get stronger glasses. When the robot came back a second time I punched "O" and prayed.

Finally, a human said, "Your service code, please."

"I can't see it," I said.

"It's on the side of the computer," he said.

"No, I can *find it*, I just can't see it. Can you hold while I get my glasses?"

So I raced off, feeling not at all guilty for making some computer geek wait 30 seconds, when his employer had left me on hold for a long days journey into night.

Returning, I crouched under my desk, peered at the tiny numbers and started reporting them to the farmer in the Dell. Suddenly, I leaned too far with the phone cord, dragging my martini off the desk, followed by the phone, both of which hit me in the head. At this point, I was still laughing. I mean what's a day without laughter, right Oprah???? Even the guy from Dell started to laugh when he heard the splash followed by the crash, followed by a loud word for a bodily function.

Eventually the computer got fixed and my sense of humor lay in wait for the next insult.

So yesterday I got an e-mail from AOL, which looked like all the other e-mails I've been getting from AOL. It announced that since I'd recently had a problem with my password, they needed to verify my billing information. What's more, they needed this verification within 12 hours, or my account would become invalid—as a protection to me, the account holder.

Well, reading this now, it positively screams "dumb schmuck," but at the time I was e-mailing columns to my editor and PR stuff for my job, so I panicked. I followed instructions and went to the recommended web site. It sure looked like AOL—right down to the privacy statement and links.

To make double sure this was legit, I minimized the page and surfed to the AOL home page–which looked identical to the one asking for my financial verification. So I typed in the bank information and all that other secret stuff that makes me Fay Jacobs and hit "submit." The second I did it, I knew I'd been stung. I can't tell you what brought forth the epiphany, but I was positive my screen name should have been ImaMoron@aol.com.

I e-mailed AOL as fast as I could and they confirmed I'd been a victim of fraud—me and thousands of others. Scumbag hackers had cloned AOL graphics and made sport of getting people to spill their financial guts.

I then spent six hours on the phone, alternating between numbing classical music and repetitions of my vital statistics to three credit bureaus, two credit card companies, two banks, the Social Security Administration, Macy's, Nordstrom's, my mortgage company, and the FBI ("Hello, Fraud Department? Can I speak with Clarice?"). By the fiftieth time I dispensed my social security number I started to go paranoid. Was I really talking to my bank or some con artist in Botswana? Would they soon find me locked in the den with newspaper clippings and secret code numbers pasted to the walls like that guy in Opie's *Beautiful Mind* movie?

At one point Bonnie suggested I go ahead and let the con men have my identity. What the hell, I had a perfectly good maiden name to use and I could just start over. I've never been lucky at Roulette or in my investment portfolio. I could give 'em Fay Jacobs and see what *they do* with her. I considered it.

But, having gotten used to me, I went to the bank the next

morning, closed my accounts, cut up my checks, threw away ATM cards and signed up for all new stuff. Hopefully, those hackers who wanted to be Fay J. had nothing left to pilfer. My hope is they'll try to use my accounts, discover them defunct and go victimize some poor schnook who took longer to realize he'd been had than I did.

Of course, all this left me with exactly $6.54 in my wallet and no way of getting my hands on more until payday or my ATM cards arrive, whichever comes first. I thawed the spiral ham left over from last Easter and figured we could wade through the freezer burn and wait it out.

Despite being purple with rage at myself for being so stupid, a couple of good things did come from this debacle. With my new accounts, my checkbook is balanced for the first time in 3 years. And I got the opportunity to warn you to be more careful than I was. Of course, since a day without laughter is a wasted day, I figure those damn con artists owe me 48 hours, some belly laughs and a night's sleep.

Caveat Emptor Computer Dumbbell—let the web surfer beware. ▼

December 2003

Not only am I rewriting draft after draft on my incipient book, but I'm proofing, bribing people to write things on the book's back cover, figuring out Library of Congress applications, ISBN numbers (a convoluted numbering system for the publishing biz), bar codes, cover photo bleeds, nose bleeds and more.

I ran away to the beach to slow down and I've never been so busy in my life. Between my day job promoting downtown, writing for *Letters from CAMP Rehoboth*, promoting and selling Anyda's new book, and this memoir business I don't even have time to whine. Oh? Am I whining? Well that's two more minutes of sleep that has to go.

But progress is good. Last night I caught myself re-writing columns I re-wrote three days ago. I'm past improving them; now I'm just changing them. I've stifled myself. The writing is done. Now it's all about getting it to the printer. And arranging for interviews of Anyda and Muriel, who, all of a sudden, have captured the imagination of feature writers from the *Wilmington News Journal*, *Delaware Beach Life* magazine, and our local newspapers.

I was over at their house the other day, packing books when I heard Anyda ask Muriel if she remembered how a reporter pushed them out of the closet several years before. Muriel frowned and harrumphed, playfully, I hoped.

I recall Anyda showing me the celebratory and flattering feature article, written in the early 1990s, but I hadn't a clue how it all came about. However it happened, I got the feeling Muriel had been none too pleased about it. After all, hiding was an ingrained skill throughout their long lives.

"We weren't ashamed of ourselves," Anyda says, "but other people made you feel that you should be."

"My goodness, you had to defend yourself if someone accused you," says Muriel.

Their words made me think of my own coming out journey and how tough it was to stand up against societal norms, how tough I was on myself and ultimately how difficult it was to feel good about myself again. I eventually did, but I came out in 1980. I cannot imagine the struggle for self-esteem for women raised in the early decades of the twentieth century.

Through the years, Anyda and Muriel remained absolutely discreet while living in Rehoboth, but they began to see changes in town. "I remember, in about 1973, we went to the Boathouse in Dewey," Anyda says. "It was a mom and pop operation and there were men and women there—with juke boxes and a snooker table."

Snooker. That would be English Billiards. I had a feeling the Boathouse had a plain old pool table, but Anyda loved talking about the snooker players. While the ladies ventured there only once or twice, the Boathouse was a huge success. In addition to the hundreds of gay people vacationing in Rehoboth who came to the Boathouse, the club also attracted gay-friendly straight people, including members of the Washington Redskins, FBI and CIA agents and U.S. Senators.

Boathouse regulars remember turning off Route One parallel to the beach and following the stream of mostly boys, some girls, heading from all directions toward the water. In fact, it was so near the water that many nights customers grabbed push brooms to help sweep out bay water that had seeped onto the brick dance floor. Sadly, the bar burned to the ground on April 15, 1982 amid many rumors. Arson by homophobes? Competitors? Or just plain faulty wiring? It was never determined, but the bar is mourned to this day.

"We thought we were very daring to go to the Boathouse," Anyda says, "although we did have some friends in town by that time."

"'Shushes', she means," added Muriel, who says that by the 1990s Rehoboth began to change. "The gay men started coming to town in droves, bringing a lot of money and a lot of renovating!"

In season, visiting gay men rented Anyda and Muriel's backyard apartments, some of them visiting the porch before going out to dinner and becoming dear friends.

"So exactly how did that article about Anyda in the *Journal* happen?" I asked Muriel. She stared at me, then at Anyda and shuddered—still for effect, I think, but I had a suspicion she would have been content to stay underground, in the back of the closet forever.

Through a dozen novels, and with Naiad Press in its heyday, Anyda let penname Sarah Aldridge receive the praise and applause. In 1992 the *Wilmington News Journal* changed the dynamics.

According to Anyda, the newspaper learned of an award Anyda had won for her writing, given at a women's music festival somewhere in the mid-west. The paper put two and two together and asked Anyda for an interview.

"I realized it meant coming out of the closet—everyone in Delaware reads the *Journal*. And I had no objections. It behooved me, since I had a certain position as a novelist. I told Muriel what I wanted to do and asked if it was alright with her."

"I didn't want to, I would have been very happy to stay quiet. I told Anyda to go ahead. But I didn't like it," Muriel said, shaking her head. "Then, on the day after the newspaper article came out, I just slunk into church, very afraid," Muriel remembered.

No need. The novelist and her partner were greeted with wide open arms and congratulations—from the congregation and all of their friends in town.

"Well I never did feel any different," Anyda said.

But Muriel did. "Now I had to go places with Anyda and everybody knew. I couldn't get used to that."

Over 80 years in the closet can do that to a person.

A short time later Anyda and Muriel made their first trip to a gay and lesbian book fair, in Philadelphia. They were setting up a table for A&M Books as Muriel hovered in the background, making herself scarce. "I wanted no part of this at all."

At one point, a young woman, looking a little lost, approached Muriel and asked, "Are you one of the Delaware dykes?"

"I almost fainted," Muriel said.

It turned out that there was a group called Delaware Dykes and members were participating in the day's events. Knowing that did not make Muriel feel at all better.

"But we're used to it now," Anyda said, about feeling comfortable out of the closet and in the spotlight.

"She should speak for herself," Muriel whispered to Bonnie, with a wink.

Shortly thereafter, a few friends arrived bearing flowers and Brie. It was winter, so no official salon was scheduled, but long-time friend Tom was in town, and he, along with friends of his (friends of friends were always welcome) came to visit. It was a typical cocktail hour. Anyda, Tom and friends discussed the headlines while Muriel flirted a little with a young lesbian in the room—that would be 55 year old Bonnie. That Muriel is a scamp. She loves to kiss the girls who visit and once in a while, although I pretend not to notice, she leans forward in her recliner and pats Bonnie on the behind as she passes by. A scamp, I tell you.

When I left that evening, Muriel was busy writing down the names of all of her new friends, so that they, too, could be put on the holiday card list. It was another successful cocktail hour—and they liked nothing better than that.

I try to picture Bonnie and Fay in their 90s, still holding hands, still living independently and still hosting a party. When you have role models like Anyda and Muriel everything seems possible.

Even getting a fledgling manuscript to the printer. ▼

January 2004

Vagina. There, I've said it. I just wanted to get it over with so I could relax. We will, of course, get back to that word presently (don't worry, boys, it's going to be okay).

The past few weeks have taught me a thing or two. No, wait! You're putting this together with that first sentence and imagining that this column is going to include waaay too much information...no need to panic.

The things I learned were about movie stars, local politics, and the power of great theatre.

I'll start with the movie stars. Former investigative reporter-turned biographer Diana McClelland published a book called *The Girls—Sappho goes to Hollywood*. In it, her reporter's quest for historical accuracy brings to light great (and exquisitely documented) lesbian romances of some of our most legendary Hollywood elite. From Garbo to Dietrich to Stanwick to Bankhead, these Hollywood hotties ricocheted through the movie studios and in and out of each other's Hollywood Hills bedrooms. From actresses to screenwriters, costumers to confidential secretaries, Hollywood buzzed with sapphic romance. It's a wonder these girls had any time to make movies.

While most everyone except Garbo had one of those convenient lavender marriages, all this lesbian activity was very well known—only the press respected their privacy. If my generation thinks it's the first to discover "outing" and stepping from the closet, we've got another think coming. Sure, we've heard the rumors before, but this book documents the party like it was Watergate.

While it's great to hear what fun our foresisters were having it's equally disturbing to read of pre-World War II Germany, New York, Paris and Hollywood as openly embracing same sex romance. Exactly what happened to give us the wretched

1950s and 60s…and beyond? Hitler, Fascists, the Hollywood censor machine and America's post-war retreat to conservative values pummeled us.

This tells me that no matter how far we've come in attaining our rights, it could all be swept away in another conservative tide. Like those bright lights long ago in Hollywood and elsewhere, you never know when the dim bulbs are going to take over and try to send us back to the closets. Senator Rick Santorum, call your office.

And that's where empowerment comes in—not just for those of the Sapphic persuasion, but for women everywhere. And there's been a very empowering thing going on for many years now, called *The Vagina Monologues*.

When I first heard of it I was sitting in a New York City cab listening to an ad on a local radio station. It featured two female voices.

"Hello, Box Office, May I help you?"

"Yes, I would like two tickets to the Monologue show."

"What show?'

"You know, The Vagi,um,er,errrrr, Monologues."

"Come on honey, you can say it…"

"Okay, I want two tickets to the (deep breath) *Va-gi-na Monologues*.

"There, I knew you could do it."

Not only was it a clever ad for one of the biggest hit shows New York has seen in years, but it appealed to the inner prude in all of us who find that word, not to mention the subject, difficult to discuss. As it turned out, Bonnie and I had tickets for *The Vagina Monologues* the next day. And to tell the truth, I'm not sure if I ordered my tickets over the Internet for convenience or to avoid having to enunciate the show title.

Which, of course, is the very reason there's an Off-Broadway show called *The Vagina Monologues* in the first place.

As we neared the theatre, I saw the huge marquee sign shouting THE VAGINA MONOLOGUES in letters almost two feet high. Impressive—and a teeny bit scary.

Inside, the crowd was mostly women, but decidedly racially mixed. My gaydar honed in on lots of lesbians, but there were as many straight women—grandmothers, Soccer Moms, a handful of brave men and quite a few youngsters—male and female. I spoke to a woman in the ladies room who had seen the show already and was now back with her husband and adolescent son. "It's important, empowering and hilarious!" she told me. A rave!

And she was right. Eve Ensler's little play (an hour and a half long, with the stories repeated by three actresses sitting on stools on an empty stage) is a knock-out and a sell-out.

The script is a ground-breaking, eye-opening event—very, very funny, but also shocking and poignant. It developed from over 200 interviews where the author asked women of varying ages and backgrounds to tell stories about their intimate experiences. From sex education to sex itself, birthing to violence, the monologues covered it all—including desensitizing the house to formerly verboten language and subjects.

As Gloria Steinem says in the printed play's forward, "I come from the 'down there' generation…where the words, spoken rarely and in a hushed voice…weren't accurate, much less prideful."

And so Eve Ensler went about writing a play that encouraged feminine empowerment by saying the unsayable, celebrating positive attitudes, sharing stories of violence and letting audiences laugh and cry together about a subject most had been forever loathe to mention.

Marlene, Greta and Tallulah would have loved it. ▼

February 2004

Okay. Uncle. I apologize. To readers who took umbrage, and in fact, to those who were purple with rage when I wrote my 2001 column criticizing the then-new Showtime drama about gay men, *Queer as Folk*, I offer a sincere request for forgiveness. I should be flogged.

You know where I'm going.

I'm absolutely, positively head-over-heels addicted to Showtime's new drama about gay women, *The L Word*. I can't take my eyes off it, can't wait for Sunday, and can't imagine television allows us such provocative lesbian voyeurism.

And the truth is, in its own way, *The L Word* flashes the same kind of gratuitous sex and stereotypical mostly white, mostly wealthy gay people, often behaving badly, as *QAF* does.

But frankly, my dear, I don't give a damn. Call me a charlatan, call me a hypocrite, but call me when it's show time. I beg for clemency.

It's amazing, after a lifetime of watching TV characters reflect other people, to finally watch some of our own. It's startling and comforting all at the same time.

Now to be sure, things have changed since 2001. And even as I apologize, I have to defend myself a little.

While I still think the initial season of *Queer as Folk* showed us extraordinarily mean-spirited, sex-obsessed, drug-absorbed characters, it's since gotten better and braver. At the time it was pretty much alone in offering that much sex and salaciousness on television. I was embarrassed that the only purportedly realistic gay characters on TV were those naughty, naughty boys.

But time and trash marched on. Several seasons of racy hetero *Sex in the City* and prime time "reality" slut fests have desensitized us to TV sex and bitchiness. Exactly who's reality do these "reality" shows show? And *Survivor* makes the *QAF* guys seem positively charitable toward one another.

As for scantily clad actresses, we can hardly complain given the recent Janet Jackson bra-ha-ha. Thanks for the mammories, hon. On the radio this morning somebody called it a tempest in a C cup. With all the other nudity in entertainment, why, on the eve of a national primary election, and on a day when countless people were being blown up by terrorists, was Janet's tit front page news? Just asking.

A woman bared a boob at the Superbowl and America acts as if it's the beginning of the Apocalypse. What is wrong with us?

Of course, the fact that Janet wore a nipple shield, on the remote chance that her costume would fall off, pretty much blows Justin's claim of "costume malfunction." Timberlake wins euphemism of the year, though. But I digress.

My point is, that with *Queer Eye*, *Will & Grace*, and politicians weighing in on same-sex marriage, being out is positively in America's face these days. Timing is everything for *The L Word*.

On the cover of *New York* magazine, over a gorgeous photo of all the sexy women in the *The L Word* cast, a banner exclaimed "Not Your Mother's Lesbians."

Gee, I didn't know my mother had lesbians—except for me, of course. But that's a whole other ballgame.

And speaking of ballgames, the magazine story about Showtime's new series made a point. *The L Word* highlights nary a flannel shirt or softball game. Representative of a wide spectrum of gaydom, it's not. The women are all gym-bunny thin with gorgeous clothes, expensive cars and Trump-like careers. It's very, very upscale Los Angeles. One of my friends called it Melrose Place for lesbians. In *The L Word*, Jennifer Beals is to most gay women as *Sex and the City*'s Sarah Jessica Parker is to the majority of straight gals. Hence, it sure is pretty to watch. And not as shocking as it would have been only a few years ago.

But if we think the three years since the debut of *Queer As*

Folk have made a difference in the way we perceive television or movies, what about 18 years?

I remember attending the 1985 premier of the movie *Desert Hearts* in Washington, DC. Most AARP-eligible lesbians remember the film as the very first movie featuring a lesbian love story where two women actually rode off into the sunset together—rather than some tragic ending where calamity befell one or both of them. *Personal Best* premiered in 1882, but predictably Mariel Hemingway went back to boys by the end.

But I remember the *Desert Hearts* premier like yesterday (probably better than yesterday, alas), seeing hundreds of women converging on the theater and loitering outside. I'd never seen so many lesbians in public before. Seedy bars in bad neighborhoods, yes, but here we were along Pennsylvania Avenue in the nation's capital. The motorists driving by had never seen such a thing either, leading to, I swear, a number of screeching tires and at least two crunched fenders in the half hour before the theater doors opened.

But it was inside the theater where history happened. The audience watched, transfixed, as prim Helen Shaver and cute Patricia Charboneau, a "hottie" in today's vernacular, met, intrigued each other and had an affair—including a beautifully filmed love scene.

As the women kissed, you could feel tension in the theater. At a literally climactic moment, somebody got carried away and screamed, "Oh my!" The rest of the crowd burst out laughing.

Heterosexuals had been watching themselves clasp and gasp on film since *Birth of a Nation*, but this was our very first chance to experience a filmed love story about people like us. It was magic.

So, too, is *The L Word*.

Of course, by comparison, *Desert Hearts* was G-rated for clasping and gasping. *The L Word* has abundant sex, lingerie, strong language, strong women, nudity and more abundant sex.

It's great and terrible all at the same time. Sure, I wish there was more diversity in the characters, less sex for sex sake, and a cast that looks more like lesbian America.

But why quibble. The show is about people I know, have known, or might know in the future. And despite its flaws, that makes it very, very special.

Time wounds all heels. I'm sorry I was so hard on your show, fellas.

The L Word is for learned my lesson.▼

March 2004

I took a walk up memory lane and into the Twilight Zone last weekend.

The place was the Chelsea Pines B&B in New York City, where I climbed toward heaven in a five-story walk-up and came face to face with memories of my high school prom. Yes, me in a dress. If staring at my old prom pictures didn't make me feel ancient, schlepping up those guesthouse stairs surely did.

About a year ago, in a search of lodging in New York, I discovered that my former high school prom date Jay (Fay and Jay, it was cute) was now the proprietor of an internationally known gay B&B in the Big Apple. If we'd only realized then, what we both know now, we'd have saved ourselves a lot of angst.

But each of us, having found our way out of the closet in our own sweet time, reconnected last weekend and laughed our heads off about it.

When Bonnie and I arrived at the guesthouse, my high school honey's front desk staff greeted us warmly, with devilish grins. "Where's your corsage?" said the cute staffer. Uh, oh. Infamous. He smirked as he offered us a tour.

Jay's father had owned a movie theatre, and Jay was the proud owner of thousands of fantastic old movie posters, hundreds of which adorned the B&B walls. Each room in the 25-room building was named for an old-time movie star, and the place was high homosexual and positively wonderful.

The general manager pointed us (up) to our fourth floor Donna Reed Suite to await our host. Like luggage-laden Von Trapp Family Singers, we commenced the climb from base camp to summit.

Oh boy, (pant, pant) to borrow a line from playwright Neil Simon, if I had known the people on the second floor I would have gone to stay with them.

Winded but no worse for wear, we arrived at Donna Reed, flung open the door and (cue the eerie *Twilight Zone* music) discovered why the front desk clerk smirked. Enlarged, grainy, frightening Xerox copies of my 1965 prom pictures, yearbook photo, and other assorted artifacts adorned the walls over the movie posters. Bonnie and I used up what little breath we had left laughing.

I especially appreciated the Thelma & Louise-ish picture of me, behind the wheel of my parents' sports car, wearing a ridiculous grin and humongous, dramatically pointy white sunglasses.

Actually, when I got finished laughing and gasping for oxygen, I was touched that Jay had saved all that stuff for, omigod, 39 (!) years. It doesn't seem possible.

But almost four decades later it is. And while I haven't changed much (Ha!) movie posters sure have.

"He knew her lips, but not her name..." "Backlash! Suspense that cuts like a whip!" and my favorite—certainly prior to political incorrectness—Donna Reed starring as Sacagawea.

The film was *The Far Horizon*, IN TECHNICOLOR no less, and it was a far horizon indeed to see my high school photo plastered in the middle of the poster. Bonnie, staring at the yearbook graduation picture laughed that she had Jimmy Carter type lust in her heart at the sight of that innocent young thing. Weird!!!!

When our host arrived, he came bearing flowers and a huge smile. We stared at each other, searching for our former young selves in the middle-aged gay people we'd become. I recognized him right away, even if he was letting his natural blonde grow in (!!). I noted that perhaps he'd forgotten I was always a red head.

We only had the afternoon to reminisce, because Jay lives the life we used to: he works at the Chelsea Pines during the week and then he and his partner flee the city Friday nights for their weekend home in the Berkshire Mountains. We told him of our five years commuting to Rehoboth.

Jay learned that Bonnie and I were celebrating what would have been our 22nd anniversary, if we hadn't eloped to Canada last August, creating a muddled anniversary date. I learned the fascinating tale of his buying a run-down rooming house filled with "bums" and slowly converting it to the now-thriving gay guesthouse. It was a lovely reunion and we talked of doing it again, maybe here at the beach.

As for the rest of the weekend, it had lots of blast from the past qualities. On Saturday afternoon we went to the Television and Radio museum on 52nd Street to see part of a documentary series on gay images on TV. The Saturday showing was The Early Years and included a 1964 episode of *Espionage*. Filmed in black and white, one year before my high school graduation, the program looked as prehistoric as my prom pictures.

Jim Backus played a diplomat investigating a rumor that one of his staff was (big wide-eyed intake of breath) "a homosexual." Lines like "You realize he is an expert in...antique furniture!!!" (gasp!), and "Isn't he a little...light on his feet?" made the audience wince, then giggle. Frankly, as dreadful as the televised homophobia was, the treatment of women in the episode was even more disturbing, so lots of us have come a long way baby.

And we went a long way, baby, all weekend. For the record, we'd get dressed for the whole day in the morning, and not return to Mt. Donna Reed until bedtime. One Stairmaster session a day was plenty.

We spent time downtown in Chelsea and the Village, then uptown to Bloomingdale's and Broadway. By Sunday, we toasted to our anniversary at a girl bar called The Cubby Hole on West 4th Street in the Village.

In a very back-to-the-future moment, we played the state-of-the-art satellite jukebox, which can summon every recording ever made, and chose "our" song from 1982—Anne Murray's "Can I Have This Dance."

As we sipped a drink and, to quote Anne Murray, "swayed to the music," Bonnie slipped a bar matchbook over my way. She'd written our phone number on it, with the words "call me."

Cue the *Twilight Zone* music.

Okay, we're back, if not to the future, at least to the present. We've got six months to argue about whether to celebrate our anniversary again in August.

In the meantime, if you happen to be heading to NYC, we heartily recommend the Chelsea Pines Inn. I'm sure my photos have been stripped from the walls by now. And I understand that the James Garner suite is fabulous. It's on the ground floor. ▼

Much to Bonnie's relief, I've kept the following story to myself for three long years. But the time has come to, well, come out of the closet about the riding mower.

I've decided to do this, since I finally heard a more dramatic lawnmower story than our own. And the new story falls under the mantle of "no event is totally horrible if you can tell a good story about it."

So just let me say that when my friends up the street told me their lawnmower tale, I had to tell you ours.

I'll start by saying the obvious. Almost nothing is private in this town. I say "almost," because the truth about our lawnmower has somehow eluded the community hotline. It's about the only thing that has.

If I show up at a CAMP event or some happy hour with a friend in tow but no Bonnie, she'll get a call within minutes wanting to know who I'm running around with. Don't try to pull anything off in this town. The whole population works for *Magnum P.I.*

We were practically on the news when one of our cars went to the shop. Coming home we stopped by our local fancy car lot to ogle. Bonnie stared adoringly at a Mercedes convertible and the proprietor, to stem her drooling on it, offered to let Bonnie drive it for the day. With our car in the shop, it was an offer we couldn't refuse.

Not fifteen minutes after I got back to my office, I got not one but two phone calls congratulating us on the new convertible. In the seven minutes my spouse had been home, two busy buddies cruised by the driveway and zeroed in on the trophy car.

"Get that thing back to its home NOW!" I hollered to Bonnie, not wanting to spend the rest of the day denying the purchase or the rest of the year convincing people we hadn't bought a sexy speedster in lieu of paying the mortgage.

Which brings me back to the riding mower. One day, shortly after Bonnie's dreams came true and we purchased a tractor to trim the crabgrass, Bonnie came home with an extraordinarily sheepish look on her face.

After serving me an anticipatory Grey Goose martini, offering me some un-requested canapés and sitting down next to me in an uncharacteristically humble pose, Bonnie said she just HAD to confess.

"What????"

"The only reason I'm telling you this is that I'm sure you'll hear about it any second. I'm surprised the phone isn't ringing now."

"What, What?????" I stammered, looking to see if the two dogs at my feet were healthy or if the sky was falling.

She then described her trip to have the blades sharpened on her pet lawnmower. Apparently this took a day or two and involved leaving the lawnmower at the kennel overnight—I have no idea about this stuff.

However, upon picking the beast back up and loading it into the truck, as politicians are fond of saying, "Mistakes were made."

Suffice it to say, when Bonnie and her mower stopped at a traffic light, Bonnie glanced in her rear view mirror to see her prized mower lurch backward, then fall out of the truck onto the pavement. Good God! If a car had been back there it would have been vehicular mower slaughter. As it was, it was just plain mower slaughter.

"I thought the mower sharpener man tied it down and he thought I tied it down," Bonnie said, staring at the floor.

Apparently, the behemoth yard vehicle landed on the pavement on all fours, bounced and returned to earth somewhat splayed, its wheels going east and west, it's hood cracked and several of its vital organs hemorrhaging fluids.

A car screeched to a halt behind the mess, and a quartet

of young men ran to aid the mortified dyke in distress. They scooped up the machine with most of its parts and hoisted it back into the truck. Bonnie, completely humiliated, having caused a huge traffic back-up, and sure that she was already on candid camera, transported the patient right back to the stunned mower repairman.

Ultimately, he fixed the thing so it would mow, but cosmetically it's been a candidate for *Extreme Makeover* ever since.

So, what could be a worse, therefore a better, story? Well, my friend the boat captain also owns a riding mower and she lives adjacent to a canal off Arnell Creek. Uh huh. She was going for that last, errant blade of grass, at the very edge of the lawn, by the bulkhead at the water, and…Geronimo!!!!!!!!!

Fortunately it was low tide.

Fortunately she wasn't hurt going in.

Unfortunately this tractor driver is also the owner of a very expensive computerized prosthetic leg.

Now I have to stop here and tell you how much I admire the captain. She's made an amazing and audacious recovery from the accident that caused her to own this high-tech kneecap and all that goes with it. She's able to captain boats, play golf, and do far more athletic things than I can on my own two feet. It's amazing and wonderful.

However, the leg is not waterproof.

That's right, not only did she drown her $1000 lawn mower, but she shorted out her amazing, golf-enabling, trick knee that costs forty-five times what the lawnmower cost. Euwwwww.

Thank goodness her mate came running when she heard the scream and the splash, and all was well that ended well. For the driver. The mower was given a decent burial and last I heard, the snazzy prosthetic leg was beeping and blinking like an extra-terrestrial and will probably have to be Fed-Exed overseas for an overhaul.

Shortly the story will become funny at that house on Arnell Creek, just as Bonnie dumping her mower out of the truck has become humorous in our house (although when she sees this in print, my luck may run out).

But you know, as I write, Bonnie is outside, riding our poor banged up tractor. It mows a lopsided swath, is missing its hood and one headlight, but like the Energizer Bunny, it keeps going and going.

As Bonnie and the bummed up mower wobble by the window there's an analogy in all this. Even as I type, words that would have been on the tip of my tongue a decade ago, are now retrieved a whole lot slower. And lots of us are becoming chronologically, aesthetically challenged. But while we may not be spanking brand new anymore, and some of us may not have all our parts, we're all still going strong. And that's a good thing.

Of course, now Bonnie is lusting after one of those new John Deere mowers at Home Depot. She hasn't had the nerve to start lobbying for one. Yet. ▼

April 2004

I've been thinking about wine a lot lately. Well, not first thing in the morning with Boone's Farm apple in a paper bag. Although I actually did think about it first thing in the morning, when I helped promote the April wine and food festival in town. While I was consumed by wine the minute I walked into the office each day, luckily I wasn't also consuming.

One thing I learned by being involved in the wine fest is that all bets are off. Everything I thought I knew about wine is up for grabs.

No vinophile, my first taste was sipping Manischewitz at the Jewish holidays. I'd rather drink Robitussin. Actually, I suspect that the infamous Kosher Concord grape is from France's illustrious Nyquil region.

Although even Kosher wine is improving. In fact, there's a web site called Kosher Wine Connoisseur, which, only a few years ago would have been a major oxymoron. Apparently, some of the stuff is really good now. But that news does little for the fact that my introduction to wine gave me a sugar high and cured bronchitis.

By high school, we'd sneak across state lines to small towns where you could drink legally at 18 and get away with it at 16. At that point we thought we were real cool to get the boy with the most upper lip fuzz (as opposed to the women with the most upper lip fuzz now that we're in the AARP) to buy us bottles of Lancers in those darling red crockery bottles. I don't remember what it tasted like, but we thought we were really cool for drinking it.

In college I moved on to Mateus, a vaguely foreign-sounding imbibement which, concurrently made us feel sophisticated and nauseous. It's a wonder we ever sipped wine again.

Welcome to the 1970s. It was all Chianti in cute straw-covered bottles, with or without spaghetti. And a little Blue Nun. Public relations programs all over the country are still citing those Anne Meara/Jerry Stiller radio ads as an example of the greatest brand identification ad campaign of all time. All of America was drinking that sweetly anemic German Leibfraumilch wine. Ptooey.

I think it was replaced in the 80s by Riunite on Ice, remember that one? After that, Chardonnay became the rage and it's still hanging on.

Around about 1985 though, George DeBeouf importers played the brand ID game again and gave us Beaujolais Nouveau. They got everybody excited about a grape that had gone from the vine to the liquor store in about fifteen minutes. Okay, it was longer than that. But it was very, very new wine.

On the third Thursday in November, regardless of when the wine from the Beaujolais region of France was actually harvested, DeBeof released that year's Nouveau. Sometimes it was really good, and sometimes it was swill. But it always came with big fanfare, pretty labels and parties starting at one minute past midnight on release day. In New York one year, an entire motorcycle gang of wealthy wine drinkers from the Hamptons drove their Harleys to the docks and welcomed the freighters with the first batch. Now that was a PR man's dream.

In our house we always gamble on the Nouveau for Thanksgiving, but our favorite wine is actually Chateauneuf du Pape. I was introduced to it in the late 70s through friends with an educated palette (and wallet). I loved the hearty Burgundy wine, loved its romantic sounding name, and loved remembering all the celebrations it invoked.

All that love was reinforced on a 1998 France trip when we literally stumbled upon the region and the ruins of the actual Chateau of the Ninth Pope. After drinking and dining al fresco with the sun, the vineyards, the divine food, live chickens strolling around, and the imposing, crumbling chateau neuf itself in the background, I was in love to stay. It happens to be a great wine, but with the romance of that afternoon, it could have been Welch's grape juice and it would still be my favorite.

So by this time, while I'm no connoisseur, I figure if wine costs a lot, has a real cork, and comes in a bottle instead of a cardboard box, it's the good stuff.

But no! Now I learn that real cork, in addition to being expensive, can develop a smelly, nasty fungus called cork taint to contaminate even the most lovingly cellared wine. All of Europe seems to be talking about, "When good corks go bad!"

That being the case, synthetic corks are popping up. However, they take the Incredible Hulk to pop them up. I tried to smell one once and had a dozen dinner guests laughing at me.

"Good thing I didn't try to smell a screw cap!" I joked. But now it's no joke.

The formerly déclassé screwcap is entering the upscale wine market. Who knew. The new screwcaps are in. Come on baby, let's do the twist. I'm sure some of it is expert marketing (shades of Blue Nun) but the truth is, I just tasted some really good wine in a screw cap bottle. Although the first few times it's hard to be serious telling someone to unscrew the wine so it can breathe.

What's next, a good vintage in a box with a spigot? The answer appears to be yes. Some West Coast wineries are actually experimenting with good wines in the old bag-in-the-box. They call them cask wines, but it's really just a sack of wine. I hear they're pretty good. Are we being manipulated? Maybe a little. But wineries are finding ways to make good wines more accessible at smaller prices.

And I find that admirable. In fact, I was really impressed by the various wine reps and winery owners who visited Rehoboth for the wine tasting weekend recently. Bonnie and I sampled some wonderful selections, and enjoyed as many events as we could.

Apart from the wine itself, my favorite moment of the weekend happened at the Bedazzled B&B's Friday afternoon wine tasting. More than a dozen folks stood around the living room, some talking amongst themselves, some listening to a description of the wines by the visiting vintner and some taking a look at the dazzling movie memorabilia in the room.

Suddenly, the flat-screen HDTV, that had been playing old TV shows flashed with the most stunning scene. There it was, in black and white, Judy Garland and Barbara Streisand doing a duet. If, for some reason, it had been important to know who was straight and who was gay in that room, you would have had no trouble with the head count. All the gay people immediately stopped talking and stared at the two icons on the screen. Gawwwd, we can be so predicable at times!

But it was a magic moment of wine, women and song. I'll drink to that. ▼

May 2004

I want to simplify my life but I don't have time.

It's the latest self-help craze. You can go on the web and find hundreds of sites touting the pleasures of veering into the slow lane. From simplifylifedotcom to simplelivingdotnet, people are rushing to tell you how to slow down.

I originally thought I was simplifying my life by moving to the beach. Ha! I'm busier than ever. So the thought of slowing down intrigued me.

I was stymied from the first. "Write down all the things that are complicating your life...."

If I had time to write down all my complicating factors I'd never have gotten my book to the printer.

Skipping to a list of small steps you can take to simplify things, I sought to identify a magazine that I subscribe to, but don't have time to read (add "and feel guilty about not reading" for those of us of the Jewish persuasion).

Okay, I've subscribed to *People* magazine since the day it was first published in 1974, but now not only don't I have time to read it, but ninety percent of the stories are about celebrities I've never heard of. That they are celebrities without passing through my radar, or even my gaydar in the case of Peter Paige and the whole *Queer As* crew, scares me. I have left the popular culture zone and I'm in a purgatory between cool adult and doddering biddy. Will somebody please tell me why I should know the name (never mind how to pronounce) Avril Lavigne?

Zapping *People* was the easy part. Unfortunately, as I tossed the invoice into the trash, I unearthed a *New Yorker* solicitation.

Now a few years ago, in an effort to keep navigable paths in my home, Bonnie and I adopted the "nothing comes into the house unless something goes out" rule.

With a slot now open on my periodical list, I ordered the venerable *New Yorker*. I won't have time to read that either, but it will look much more erudite than *People* stacked on my coffee table.

Seeking more ideas I checked out realsimple.com, and found that it's just another magazine wanting me to subscribe. False advertising!

Flunking magazine deletion I moved on to "identify responsibilities you've taken on that you are better off without." Whoa. That's the whole adulthood thing. I could get rid of it all if I could just go back to fifth grade (of course then I'd have to learn to be a computer whiz).

Let's see, I would be vastly better off without the responsibility for paying my mortgage or pharmacy co-pays, but I'd be homeless and anxious. No good. There must be some responsibilities I can delete. Maybe plant watering...I have a 15-year old Jade plant with baby Jade plants sprouting in pots all over the house. I could recover about 15 minutes a week if I just stopped watering. Of course, I'd have to spend weeks watching the plants shrivel and croak, so it's not a wise trade.

I love the hallmark advice of the simplification movement about "finding a quiet time for yourself, when you can turn off the TV, CD player, computer and cell phone." I already have a time like that. It's called bedtime. Next!

Anti-clutter activists define simplification as getting rid of what's bogging you down. Okay, that would be my thighs, and I've been trying to get rid of them for years.

Apparently, clutter is the enemy of simplicity. To get rid of unnecessary possessions, simplifiers want you to ask yourself "If a natural disaster approached and you had to get out of your house suddenly, what would you take?"

Purportedly this answers clutter problems. But I don't think I'd be happy living with just 27 photo albums, an 8x10 glossy signed by Sharon Gless, and extra underpants.

I'm a closet case. Once I managed to come out of the closet it's been impossible getting me back in there to organize the thing. It's overstuffed with wardrobes in three different body sizes—current, the elusive one-size-down, and pup tent in case I revert.

I understand we're supposed to mark time on our calendars specifically for clutter clearing, scheduling it like any other important activity. Would that be the twenty minutes after the full day's work and right before the next political fundraiser? I could unclutter instead of showering and dressing, certain that showing up nekked, with poor hygiene would limit future invitations and give me more time for clutter removal.

One book on simplicity asks why we hang onto so many possessions. Keep reading and they suggest...get this, converting to Buddhism. Folks, I want to throw away tchotchkes not convert to a new religion.

"Why do we get so buried and overwhelmed by our stuff?" asks a clutter guru. I was tempted to scoff until I opened a kitchen cabinet last night and got caught in a Tupperware avalanche. Here's the real question. How many plastic won-ton soup containers do I need? And frankly, where do the lids go? Are they in the crawl space with solo socks from the dryer?

Buried in burpware, I managed to kick some of the containers toward the trash can, but they immediately became dog toys and are now cluttering up a dozen different places in the house.

Who started this simplification craze anyway? I checked the credentials of one clutter management expert and want to know what it says when the author's first book is *Simplify Your Life*, with her second, *Panic and Anxiety Disorder*. Coincidence?

Let's face it, simplifying takes a lot of time. One suggestion had me subscribing to *Simple Living* magazine, getting a pack of index cards, and jotting down favorite tips. They suggest listing one idea per card, subject on the back, details on the front and then, after incorporating the tip into my life, checking it off in red pen. If I took time for that I'd have to give up the quiet bedtime thing.

"Do it now!" is another simplifying mantra, so you don't

have to take time to write the chore on a list. Hell, I'm a "do it now" kind of girl. Especially when it comes to ordering a second Cosmo. Actually, in the do-it-now spirit, I'll wrap it up here and e-mail this column to *Letters* immediately.

As the Simple Simon's say, simplify your life and you can do what you love and love the life you live! Hey, overscheduled, and cluttered though I may be, I already do. Right now, for instance, I'm heading out to acquire another soup container, then going to another political fundraiser. But the day after this edition comes out, I'm having a great big yard sale, selling off baby Jade plants, books I can part with, a sofa (no points here, another one is entering the house the same day) and all the tchotchkes I can schlep to the driveway. Of course, it's to make room for upcoming book cartons!

Stop by and simplify my life. Or at least say hello. ▼

May 2004

I didn't believe this adventure was real until I actually felt the book, my book, in my hands. Although a lot of things had happened prior to the cartons of books showing up on my driveway. Some things relative to *As I Lay Frying*, even involved money—amazingly, coming in, not going out. Last month I sat at a table at the CAMP Rehoboth Women's Conference, and blindly, 63 people plunked down $15 for a book that hadn't even been released yet. These brave souls will pick up their signed copies at an upcoming book party at CAMP. If nothing else, they'll make decorative doorstops.

Okay, this is where the fraud theory comes in. Fraud, not Freud, although he probably thought this up. Psychologists say that actors, singers, and writers—although I bet it happens with everybody at some point—get carried along in their careers, taking it on face value that their good reviews, compliments and reputation for whatever it is they have done are, if not deserved, then at least a lucky accident.

I've had a good run. People seem to like my columns. Folks come up to me in restaurants saying "Aren't you Fay Jacobs?" and when I admit it they give me compliments to be polite. Of course, some people just say "I thought so" and leave, which is always a little worrisome.

But according to shrinks, one day, when we least expect it, creative types wake up with the petrifying certainty that today is the day the public will realize they've been duped and all the movies, songs or novels are absolute and utter crap, the creators a fraud.

I was sitting at the computer when I saw the printer's truck backing into my driveway. Fraud washed over me. I immediately knew that my life's work should be in a landfill. The manuscript would be best encased in lead and buried with nuclear waste. My writing career was a freak accident. I was a deceitful hoaxer. If I went outside I'd be pelted with rotting produce.

Can I tell the truck driver that Fay Jacobs entered the witness protection program? Shall I send the shipment back? I won't answer the door. Let the dogs go insane.

I got up from the computer and looked out the door.

"What the hell are you just standing there for?" Bonnie hollered as she pushed past me to open the door and help the truck back in. "Snap out of it!"

There's nothing like your spouse looking at you as if you are Mr. Potato Head to get you moving.

So we got the books unloaded. My garage looked like a QVC warehouse. And I was certain that every single book, minus the 63 copies for the fools who pre-ordered, and one for my father, would be in my garage until the end of time or Joan Rivers' retirement, whichever comes first.

I have to admit. This well of fraudiness lasted, waxing and waning in severity, becoming especially virulent the day that I opened our local paper to find the following:

BOOK PUBLICATION PARTY AND BOOK SIGNING MAY 22

A&M Books of Rehoboth Beach announces the publication of As I Lay Frying—a Rehoboth Beach Memoir *by* Letters *columnist Fay Jacobs. The book is a collection of Jacobs' CAMPout columns published over the last several years.*

CAMP Rehoboth will host a book party and signing on Saturday, May 22 from 4-6 p.m. at the CAMP office and courtyard.

"We're thrilled to be able to publish this collection of lighthearted and witty essays, based on Jacobs' understanding of our unique gay culture," says publisher Anyda Marchant.

As book jacket announces, "the columns of Fay Jacobs cast a witty eye toward contemporary culture and life in a gay-friendly resort town. The essays tell a story that is sometimes provocative, sometimes political, occasionally heartwarming and always hilarious."

Stop by the CAMP Rehoboth office on May 22 to hear the

author read from her new book and host a book signing as well. Refreshments will be provided.

READING AND SIGNING: MAY 22, 2004

On the day of the book signing, I knocked back a couple of drinks at the Blue Moon Bloody Mary bar, said "here goes" and headed next door to the CAMP office.

While fear of fraud may have abated somewhat relative to book content, I realized that people would now learn my other dirty little secret—that thing about not remembering anybody's name.

I can get by with the generic "Hi there!" only so many times, deceitfully appearing to know everyone. I cover my disability in various ways—eavesdropping until a name comes up; enlisting trusted friends to whisper names in my ear; or proclaiming, "Well, if it isn't Bonnie & Clyde," when confronted with a couple whose names have gone missing.

Help me. I knew that if anyone did buy my book, they would approach my signing table, thrust the book at me and say, "Just inscribe it to me."

Ba-da-bing. Screwed.

"Pssst, Pam," I whispered to my dear friend who understood my appalling affliction. "Help me out here."

We agreed she'd sit to the left of me, whisper names as people approached or intercept people she didn't know and say "Hi, I'm Pam," to prompt a revealing answer.

It was a plan.

Oddly, there were a lot of people gathering. Happily there was wine. Steve introduced me to the crowd, a sea of familiar faces, a puddle of whom I could name. There were friends and strangers.

I got up to read, having chosen a column about taking a station wagon full of fugitive felines across state lines, out of the clutches of the ASPCA and off to a no-kill shelter. It was an adventure that included shrieking and cat fights and that was just me and Bonnie. Bodily functions were involved, which I hasten to add did not originate with me and Bonnie.

I read the story. People laughed.

The reading went well, the signing went well thanks to Pam's name game, Anyda and Muriel watched it all with glee and we sold a heck of a lot of books.

Whooo Hooo.

Afterwards, Anyda and Muriel and dozens of our friends, young, old and in-between gathered on Laurel Street, in the house and on the porch, to raise a glass to A&M Books. The publishers glowed.

Sweet.

Well that was fun. How long will the other several thousand books stay in my garage before they get hauled off to Mt. Trashmore?▼

June 2004

Now I'm being spied on. And not by Attorney General John Ashcroft, who I would expect to do so. No, I'm being spied on by my own household computer. Although Ashcroft may have my file on his desk as well.

Is this what being published brings? Is it the result of my name and the word lesbian being inexorably linked in some Google algorithm? Or maybe it's random. Or maybe it's not.

Now before you call me completely paranoid, I have to tell you that this was NOT to be my topic for this column.

In fact, I was surfing the net for confirmation about a factoid I wrote about Cicadas—those beady-eyed disgusting shrimp-sized bugs that have descended on the D.C. metro area in recent weeks.

I was set to tell you that there are about a million reasons why I love that I moved to the beach, but right up there, especially this month, is that I missed the attack of the 17-year locusts. I'm delighted that the vermin don't cross the Chesapeake Bay and invade Delmarva.

Truth is, I was going to relate my run-ins with the swarm of Brood X Cicadas (not to be confused with Generation X, which swarms in our local watering holes) that came out in both 1987 and way back in 1970. Point of fact, I came out in 1980, having nothing to do with locusts. But those tales will have to wait.

A funny thing happened on my way to the Cicada story. My computer was invaded by spyware. I went to Google to search for Cicadas and I got an eyeful of pop-up ads, followed by strange grinding noises from my hard drive and then my computer went on a slow-down strike. I could eat my dinner, and in fact, did, while waiting for Google to do a search. I came back and tried to get my e-mail but the machine worked like it had swallowed a fistful of Quaaludes.

When the thing worked at all it was with pop-up ads for casinos, prescriptions by mail, liposuction clinics, and methods of enlarging an organ I do not have.

"You have just won!!!!" "Get the drugs you need!" "Sweepstakes Winner!!!" and my favorite, "Be Bigger and she'll love you!" Boy, are they barking up the wrong tree house.

I tried to close the ads and the computer froze up like a lesbian in a room full of Promise Keepers. Did this have something to do with the wireless cable doodad under my desk that's been blinking at me ever since I threw over dial-up for broadband?

"Hello, Comcast? My computer pops up then poops out."

"Hmmmm. It sounds like spyware has invaded your system."

Do I call Bond. James Bond? Do I go to the C.I.A.? Ghostbusters?

The tech support guru explained that my computer had a bad case of this spyware phenomenon. It's not a virus or a worm, mind you, but software that watches what you are doing and zaps you with ads against your will. I'd rather have a virus.This feels more like a rapist.

How the hell did this happen?

"I have no idea," said techguy, "but it happens a lot."

"But my machine was fine yesterday."

"Yeah, it can happen in a minute. One click, one piece of spam, you never know."

Then he told me to go to Download.com and find a free software called Spybot, download it and run the program on my machine. If the instructions hadn't come directly from Comcast, I would have been very wary, indeed. But I checked out the site, downloaded the program and ran the "Search and Destroy" feature. I would have laughed at the video game nomenclature if I hadn't been so pissed off.

But here's the shocker. The Spybot program located 66 different spyware programs that had invaded my computer between noon yesterday and today and were lurking there just waiting to help me enhance my breasts. Or my bank account. Or my sex drive.

In the ten minutes it took to seek all the spies and destroy them, I learned spyware names like Scratch and Win (at least it wasn't scratch and sniff), Gratisware (thanks for nothin'), FunWeb (who says?), I-SPY (does it come with Bill Cosby?), ICU2 (not if I see you first), and my favorite, Usucker (exactly).

We're all suckers, sucked in by this marvelous technology and then at the complete mercy of tech support crews who are now more valuable to us than doctors or plumbers.

When I ran my first search and destroy mission and found all those intruders I realized that the proverbial once was not enough. Five minutes after cleaning my computer off, the damn things were back again, popping up in my face with their sleazy, sneaky messages.

Aha! Following search and destroy, I had to immunize. That's right, I had to run part two of the program and inject my computer with anti-spyware serum. The program had to immunize my computer against all known bugs, viruses, Trojans, and everything but Whooping Cough.

Of course, part of my weekly routine will now include updating my spy software for new bugs and running my weekly search and destroy missions. Ugh, and I had vague hopes that my life was getting simpler.

The good news is that there seem to be dozens of programs available to combat this twenty first century problem (some solutions for free, some, of course, for hefty fees).

Just so you know, spyware can also be called adware or malware. This malicious programming consists of files that allow the people who think them up to snoop on your browsing activity, see what you purchase and send you "pop-up" ads they think you will love. They are sadly mistaken if they think that everybody who surfs the CAMP Rehoboth site (or Matt Drudge, or CNN.com) wants their member enhanced. Or needs Cialis. Or wants a new mortgage. Okay, here's the thing. I just realized that I hate pop-up ads worse than I hate Cicadas.

I'd rather be bombarded by flying beady-eyed shrimp-bugs (which I was, on Charles Street in Baltimore, in my Mustang Convertible, in 1987, but I didn't get to tell you all about it because of malware!!!) than bombarded by virulent and disgusting pop-up ads on my own home computer.

And the government wants us to use completely computerized voting for the November election? I'm even more opposed to that idea than I was yesterday, before a brood of spyware infested my computer. I'd rather walk ankle deep in dead Cicadas (which I did in 1970 in Bethesda, Maryland...) than have to worry that malware and spyware will invade and hijack our critically important upcoming national election.

I say bring back paper ballots and number two pencils. I say we should all demand paper back-up and whatever other measures are necessary to make sure that computer hackers, netspys, software terrorists or virtual Cicada swarms don't make technological idiots out of us all.

Spyware. It's a brand new fear factor. Trust computers? I'd rather eat a Cicada. ▼

June 2004

"Is that a henna?" I was asked last night at a party.

"Um. No."

"It's real? You got a tattoo? No you didn't, it's a henna."

"No, it's a real tattoo."

"You didn't. It's henna."

"I did. It's not."

"I can't believe it. You're having a mid-life crisis. Tell me the truth, did it hurt?"

"You betcha!!!!"

I must have been in some kind of altered state as a result of the hoopla surrounding this book business, otherwise this never would have happened.

On Memorial Day Weekend, under threatening skies (although I wasn't personally being threatened, which makes this whole thing extra weird), I went to the Ancient Art Tattoo Studio on Route One and got tattooed. I've got a rainbow-colored seahorse etched into my ankle. Bonnie got one too. Now we don't have to invite people home to see our etchings, they travel with us.

So, in 21st century vernacular, I've had my body modified. I would have thought that the first modification I'd ever try would be liposuction, but instead of shedding something I've actually had something applied.

And I love it. Now. The morning after the modification fest my spouse and I looked at each other, looked at our ankles, and said, "Holy _____. Do you believe this?"

But of course, buyer's remorse is moot. No three-day rescission clause on this baby. It's a keeper.

And I'm still trying to piece together the events that led to my foray into body art. Me, who pales at dental anesthetic and freaks when the pups get kennel cough boosters. How did this happen?

It started with our son the actor Eric, whose corporate career in diversity work once took him to a classroom discussion of Native American dream interpretation. One of his recent dreams had featured a giant turtle and he and the instructor decided that his good luck totem would, forever more, be a turtle.

What followed was pretty natural. Eric installed turtle lawn art at his Capital Hill townhouse, decorated the coffee table with gift turtles from friends and relatives, and pretty much had a cool little collection going.

Until Memorial Day weekend when he started to, as Emeril Lagasse says, notch it up a little. Bam! He wanted a big old turtle tattoo.

"Okay, lesbian moms, are you going to get tattoos, too?"

Oddly enough, this was not a question out of the blue. Over the past few years, we've flirted with the idea. Much like we've flirted with Cadillac Escalade ownership or the cutie cashier at the hardware store. But it didn't mean we planned on actually taking either of them home with us.

We'd often thought about getting a little seahorse stenciled on a shoulder blade or other circumspect site. Why this design? According to Bonnie, all of Baltimore's old-time lesbian bars (and there were surprisingly many) had a seahorse symbol by the door. The seahorse represented a species where boy seahorses birth and nurture babies, while mommy seahorses play softball or something. The symbol has completely fallen off contemporary gaydar, but it's still a cute tattoo image.

Fast forward to Route One, May 29, Ancient Art Tattoo. Now, if any son of mine is going under the needle, the operatory better be sparkling clean and sanitized. Peggi Hurley, an award-winning tattoo artist and a woman who knows a thing or two about body art runs a clean as a whistle shop and takes her craft seriously. In fact, she worked with the state government and the health department on tattoo parlor regulations. So it was Peggi we went to see.

The place was packed. While Eric searched through patterns for his turtle of choice, Bonnie and I flipped through pages and pages of massively inappropriate and ugly, if not frightening, selections. Vipers, Harleys, naked ladies, barbed wire. I think not.

One young girl eyed a sweet little puppy template for her rump. I didn't want to be the one to tell her that it was destined to become a Shar-Pei. Likewise, the chippy who wanted Snoopy on her ultra flat stomach—when this young woman is nine months pregnant Snoopy could quite possibly explode. At any rate, he'd have jowls by 2034.

And these gals were giving us advice. I'll admit, it was disconcerting hearing body art counsel from sweet young tattoo candidates with pierced eyebrows, tongues and goodness knows what else. One Valley Girl could have strained linguini through her ears. When I couldn't quite understand what one girl was saying I realized she was trying to orate with a brand new tongue stud. I think she told uth getting a tattoo doethn't hurt. Hell, it already hurt feeling like Grandma Moseses.

Finally, we located a viable seahorse design. Incredibly, we didn't go screaming out the door.

Okay, we'd had the advice, next came the consent. Naturally, Eric knew he had to go first if there was any chance we'd follow. For forty-five minutes he sat in that chair, smiling and chatting as Peggi engraved a Native American turtle totem on his upper arm.

When it was my turn, I showed Peggi the seahorse I wanted and told her I was wavering between shoulder blade, lower back or the flight or fight response. She was so nice and reassuring, and so quick to suggest that I'd really rather have a tattoo where I could show it off, I immediately agreed to the ankle site.

Well. Only after she started buzzing me with the black ink outline did I realize just how good an actor our boy Eric really is. Getting tattooed hurt like hell. Although, I was somewhat distracted by Bonnie, who had turned ghostly pale and seemed to be panicking. At that moment I realized she had banked on my chickening out and she'd be spared. "Fooled her!" I thought, although that was little consolation. Fortunately my seahorse tattoo was just a 15-minute job, and pretty soon I was out of the chair and pain-free, watching Bonnie cave to peer pressure and get her very own seahorse appliqué.

Truthfully, the whole thing was pretty shocking. I hadn't felt like this much of an outlaw since 1970 when I accidentally wandered into a campus Vietnam War protest and got tear gassed. Even then, all I had to do was be hosed down. Jeesh. Now I'm seahorsed for life.

"Okay," said Peggy, as our trio stood stupefied, staring at our body art, "go home and wash with mild soap and water, keep it clean and have fun."

Our seahorses hurt like mild sunburn for a week and then they were fine. We are both delighted with our pathetic little middle-aged rebellion. If this is a mid-life crisis, we can only hope that the nursing home folks will be admiring Peggi's handiwork when I'm 112.

Of course, as we drove to New York to visit my parents last week, I wondered if I was the only AARP member in history worried about telling an octogenarian dad about a tattoo.

Got ink?▼

July 2004

My partner Bonnie did a brave, tough, loving thing last week. She played the slots with her mother. Okay, you have to know the history to understand the depth of this gesture. My mother-in-law is an unrepentant gambling addict.

For the better part of Bonnie's 50-something years and the entirety of our 22 year relationship, we've been yanking Mom out of various casinos and bingo parlors—often just a step ahead of the mortgage man.

Now it's tough enough for gay people to deal with family baggage related to our sexual orientation, but add addiction to the mix and you have bona fide American Tourister.

For my part, I couldn't understand what was so bad about bingo. It's a game we played in school. What????

Then Bonnie took me to the bingo hall. No church basement this. Lights flashed, bells went off and a herd of Winston-puffing gamblers sat glued to their cards, some playing 48 games simultaneously. I was so inept I couldn't even manage one game card efficiently. Mom, and the 85-year old woman to my left could dab their total of 96 cards with the permanent marker digit dabber and then swoop in to mark mine before I realized my number had been called. I couldn't even get out of their way in time to avoid having my forearms dabbed like a Jackson Pollack canvas.

Permanently marked in bright colors, I watched the bingo-mania give way to the next phase of the evening: the unfortunately named ripoffs. These are instant games where you rip off five tabs to see if you've won. The bingo mavens rushed the ripoff counter, pitched large bills at the clerk and commenced ripping numbers like crazed pigeons pecking seed. Winners traded winning tickets for more ripoffs, losers shed the debris on the floor. By night's end, nobody had any money as we waded knee deep in cardboard toward the exits. I was beginning to understand the problem.

Next we heard that Mom went on a Bingo Bus—a five-day tour from Maryland to South Carolina and back, stopping for a chance at big jackpots at all the hot bingo mills en route. All I can say is that by the time bingo Mom and the other gaming nuts got back, they'd gambled non-stop for days, sitting on the bus or in bingo parlors with their ankles swelling like soccer balls. For five days, nobody wanted to miss a G-18 to go potty. Yuck.

But it was the time we opened our credit card bill to find it speckled with charges from Glen Burnie Bingo World that the poop hit the propeller. After a text-book intervention, the requisite crying and teeth gnashing, followed by the eventual acceptance of consequences, we all wound up at Gamblers Anonymous.

Bonnie and I joined the GamAnon family sessions. Personally, I think the gamblers were all in a room trading tip sheets while we entertained ourselves with sob stories of the pissed and penniless.

Actually, I think Bonnie and I were the entertainment, since the group couldn't figure out how we were all related. "Oh, you are so lucky to have a best friend accompany you here…" I'm pretty sure we were the only lesbians they'd ever encountered, and I'm positive I was their first Jew.

Be that as it may, life continued with Mom on the wagon occasionally and back on the bingo bus more often than not. But, as they say, life is what happens when you have other plans. Five years ago Mom was diagnosed with ALS or Lou Gehrig's disease.

The disease is as cruel and as powerful as addiction. Combine the two and you have a woman who has trouble walking, talking and swallowing but who can con her equally elderly neighbor into taking her to play bingo three nights a week.

Necessity forced Mom to move to an assisted living facility and when she could no longer gamble, things got really ugly.

One night Mom mounted her mobility scooter, crashed through the nursing home doors and headed for that neighborly getaway car waiting to take the fugitive to the bingo hall. She was apprehended in the parking lot. You gotta laugh. I think.

Now I know many gay people who have had to take care of aging parents who had often made their children's lives hell because of sexual orientation issues. But in the end, whether the parents came to terms with their gay children, or were merely senile enough not to remember the family schisms, lots of relationships were pasted back together before, or just as, it was too late.

In Bonnie's case, her Mom was failing fast, refusing to be fed through her tube, resisting anything to help herself, and generally giving up.

Bonnie showed up at the nursing home and said to Mom, "If you don't eat, how will you have strength to go to the Slots at Charlestown?" The patient lit up, furiously punched the bell for the nurse to get her dressed and off they went.

While Mom could hardly move or sit up in her wheelchair, she knew which slot machines she wanted and which were unacceptable. Finally, at the very perfect machine, twenty bucks in quarters got swallowed before Mom started to tire. Then, the old lady strained to push the button on the one armed bandit one last time and bang! She hit for a sizeable jackpot.

"I never thought I'd do this again," Mom scribbled on her note pad, her only means of communication. "Love U."

Acceptance, forgiveness, amnesty. It works both ways. We should all be so lucky. ▼

June 2004

Just in case *Letters from CAMP Rehoboth* was thinking of conducting a readership survey, I'm here to say they shouldn't bother. Letters has a huge readership. I know this because following my column about my getting my ankle tattooed, I had hundreds of people, many of them complete strangers, come up to me, asking me to prove that I actually got the tattoo.

This resulted in my having to stand on one foot while lifting the tattooed ankle high enough for people to see my seahorse body art. I fell over a lot. If we happened to have the conversation by a fire hydrant I looked like a urinating Schnauzer. It was not my most graceful week, but I can certify to a vast readership.

And speaking of vast readership, the good news is that I was recently asked to pen a column for the national GLBT magazine *The Advocate*.

Time out here: readers, do you know the meaning of the acronym GLBT? A straight friend of mine thought it was a sandwich, "I'll have a GLBT on pumpernickel toast, please." Actually, GLBT stands for Gay, Lesbian, Bisexual and Transgender, the diversity of our "gay" community.

So the good GLBT news was that I was asked to write a national column. This was also the bad news, since I was asked to come up with ideas for a suitable topic in three days. No pressure.

The magazine was trying out new writers for a possible rotating spot writing the back page essay. Think Andrew Sullivan, Michaelangelo Signorelli. Urvashi Vaid. Serious writers. Very humbling.

While the editors had read excerpts from my book and decided they liked "my voice," they gave me the impression that my usual skewed look at life, liberty and the pursuit of column fodder was a little too cavalier for their gay news publication. They wanted something more weighty and erudite. Kinda like that play *I Love You, You're Perfect, Now Change*.

I toyed with writing about scientist Steven Hawking's shocking admission that he miscalculated black holes and they don't swallow matter into the great abyss after all, but I had no idea what the hell he was talking about.

I tinkered with the latest findings of the food police, who just announced that certain vegetables, like broccoli and spinach may help older women keep their brains sharper. I began expounding on the theory but couldn't concentrate. Somebody find me an asparagus spear.

Taking a cue from all the writing coaches I ever had, I decided to pitch them stories about two things I am comfortable covering: the gay marriage debate and the upcoming elections. Before I could get the first sentence down on paper I got an e-mail from the editor requesting story ideas on anything but gay marriage and Kerry-Edwards. Kill me now.

Stymied, I knew my traditional methods of vetting column ideas wouldn't work. Stories arising from everyday disasters at home ("Lawnmower falls from pick-up truck") were too mundane, ideas from weird internet stories ("Nude man covered with nacho cheese arrested.") were too silly, and great, big, ponderous social issues were really out of my league.

After two hours of staring at my computer screen and coming up with not so much as a paragraph I gave up. Hell, it was only a chance to write for a national publication. No big deal. Auuugggghhhh!!!!!!

I turned on the TV. There, before my eyes was a commentator discussing gay rights legislation, along with film of two menopausal middle-aged lesbians feeding each other wedding cake. "Gee," I said to Bonnie, "remember when the only pictures of gay people on TV were parading drag queens and dour dykes on bikes? Things have really changed."

Bing.

So I proceeded to write a column pointing out the incredible change in the televised image of gay people over the past decade. I had a grand time, noting that once there were only disco bunnies and bull dykes on the screen no matter what the topic.

Part of the column questioned why mainstream media didn't go out of their way to show the diversity within the gay community. "After all, the far right has a huge investment in demonizing us and it wouldn't have served their nefarious purpose to make movies about middle aged women purchasing antacids at K Mart or handsome young men delivering Meals on Wheels."

Hey, CBS, CNN and the rest. Earth to networks: Homosexuals are not homogenized. All heterosexuals are not members of Hell's Angels or the Mormon Tabernacle Choir. All gay men don't wear thongs or Vera Wang. All lesbians can't dive under your hood and rebuild your carburetor. There are eight million stories in the naked city and not all of them are naked."

I went on to talk about the improving image of gays on television, saying it was about time, and being very glad for the adjustment. My entire theory was that the change was good. As a zinger at the end of the column I added a line about hoping the news outlets would still humor me once in a while with a shot of a bare-breasted parade marcher. Made my point, end of column. Finito.

I e-mailed the column to the editor, nervously awaiting a reply, my nationwide writing career hanging in the balance.

The next day I got a note back. The editor chopped my essay to bits, and told me it was a good start. He loved the last line and said I should expand on that theory. What does it mean for our community to have normalized images of gays on TV? Is this good or bad for our identities and should we be worried?

Worried? What worried me was that the editor pretty much eviscerated my story and wanted me to fill in with a theory I'd never really considered.

Okay, what does this new image of GLBT people in the news mean? Hmmmm. Is it a totally good thing? The editor got me thinking. So I gave his premise a whirl, argued both sides of the question and added back a couple of my favorite axed lines.

By the next day I heard from the editor again, with word that the column was just what they were looking for and that it will be published August 17. Go figure.

In the meantime, for the record, despite what I say in *The Advocate*, I think it's pretty swell that images of gay people on TV have improved a heck of a lot. And while there may be lots of gay people who still prefer to be seen as social renegades, I'm quite happy to see our community viewed for all its diversity, thank you.

So I guess my writing style has been broadened by this experience. I learned I can be more flexible. Although I don't think you'll find me being more argumentative or weighty (unless it's a column on the *South Beach Diet*) in these pages. But I hope I get another swipe at that kind of thing on a national level.

But take it from me. I really love our new TV images. It's about time.▼

July 2004

Apparently, my choice of a new car means I'm actually a gay man.

And the strange thing is this is not the first time my lesbian credentials have been questioned. In several episodes from my past, people have gingerly asked, and in one incident actually shouted "are you sure you're not a gay man????"

Now don't go queasy on me. It's not like the plot of *The Crying Game* (Surprise!!!) or anything. It's just that sociologically I seem to exhibit some fairly stereotypical gay male behavior.

For one thing, I'm a musical comedy queen. I know the lyrics to every obscure song in the whole Broadway cannon. I can actually sing all the words to "Shipoopi" from *The Music Man* and everything from Liza Minelli's *Flora the Red Menace*. The Liza thing is a ten-pointer on the poofter scale.

I may have been the only lesbian at Follies to recognize a song from 1947's *Finian's Rainbow*.

And a few years ago, when my sister and I were nostalgically recalling those controlled-substance-filled 1960s, she admitted that while she was in a haze with Jefferson Airplane and *White Rabbit*, I was the only person she knew to puff on weed and go over the rainbow listening to Judy Garland records—how gay is that?????

More recently than Haight Ashbury, when I was looking to purchase my Rehoboth home, my adored realtor ferried us around extolling the virtues of square footage and environmentally friendly heating systems. All I focused on was curb appeal.

"I love those columns!!!!" I squealed.

"Are you sure you're not a gay man???" he shouted.

Okay, so I have tendencies.

But apparently the new car sealed it. According to a web

site listing official auto choices for gay men and lesbians (yes, really), my old car was the official lesbian car, the Subaru Outback. But my new car, a diesel powered VW Jetta was listed as the number one choice of gay men. My garage has had a sex change.

How could that be? I thought my choice of a diesel car made me (all together now) a Diesel Dyke.

Not only was I stung by the accusation that I had purchased the wrong car for my sexual orientation, but I was still smarting over the unfortunate premature demise of the Subaru. It only had 120,000 miles on it, which, ask any lesbian, is mere puppyhood.

Only last week, Bonnie and I discussed getting a new car. Hell, we could get $3000 in trade for the Lesbaru. While the thought of a new car was appealing, the words "paid-off" were far more attractive. Uncharacteristically we decided to do the prudent and practical thing and hang onto the car for another year or so.

Woman plans; God laughs and then blows your car up.

Last Saturday on Route One, right in the middle of rental rush hour, the Subaru's engine ignited like a Weber kettle grill. I pulled off onto the service road by Coastal Gallery and asked the proprietors if I could leave a large smoldering metal sculpture in their parking lot. Bonnie came to collect me.

Later, we learned that the Subaru had blown a head gasket—which sounds really awful unless you saw the gasket I blew learning that my $3000 Subaru was now worth bupkus. Nada. Nothing. Toast.

And while this was a terrible blow, I stood there and laughed like the village idiot. It reminded me of the last time I had an automotive asset one minute and a steaming pile of liability the next.

It was back in 1978, with my woozy Judy Garland days behind me, but my non-lesbo musical comedy obsession still flowering. I was on my way to a rehearsal for *Gypsy* (how gay is that!) in Annapolis, Maryland when my elderly 1964 Corvette suddenly lurched and left me with some kind of car part dragging the pavement beneath my wheels.

With the metal scraping the street, I produced hideous noise and sparks.

"If I can only get two more blocks to the theater," I thought.

Unbeknownst to me, just ahead, on a narrow one-way street was a freshly poured speed bump. By this time, the dragging metal on my undercarriage was red hot from being scraped along the road.

My car went over the speed bump with its front wheels, but when the sizzling car part hit the brand new asphalt it sunk into the speed bump like a sack of anvils into a loaf of Wonder Bread, welding me to the street.

Jeesh. No matter how I tried, the car would not move forward one more inch. Traffic backed up behind me, with people finally getting out of their cars to look and laugh. Grown men knelt down on their hands and knees, peeked under the car and howled.

Suffice it to say that when a flat bed truck backed up the street in front of me and tried to dislodge my vintage sports car from the road, the rear axle fell off, turning my pride and joy into a pile of antique rubble.

Meanwhile, it turned out that the culprit in this tale was a dangling leaf spring, which, more like a stereotypical gay man and unlike most lesbians I know, was an item I had never even heard of.

But now, finally, I may have found a way to dispel this long-held notion of my unnatural kinship with the G rather than the L in GLBT.

Since the diesel car gets great fuel mileage, Bonnie has chosen to use it for her business, leaving me with the other family vehicle. Of course, like most of my men friends, I long to drive a Lexus, Cadillac CTS, or the Guppie-approved Jetta. Give me a luxury car with On Star any day.

But no. I got my lesbian cred back. You'll now find me riding around in a four wheel drive mini SUV Chevy Tracker, complete with surf fishing license tag. A personal butchmobile.

Although, if I pull up beside you, windows open, CD player cranked up, it won't be hip-hop. It will be *Hello, Dolly.*▼

August 2004

Not only is Big Brother watching, but he knows where you are going and how fast you get there.

Yes, folks, two decades past the infamous 1984 that Orwell warned us about, the truth is far worse than we feared. And the culprit is E-ZPass.

Don't get me wrong. I love zipping through toll booths, without wrestling with quarters and dimes. I adore shooting right through the express lanes while hapless motorists fiddle with electric windows and lollygagging toll payers. I'm positively giddy about getting tolls deducted from my debit account and never worrying about a fist full of silver sliding into my gearshift to screw up my transmission.

But holy moly, don't ever run afoul of the bureaucrats who monitor the whole East Coast E-ZPass Grid. It's an army of public servants like you've never encountered before.

I fear I am forever doomed to be an E-ZPass scofflaw, evermore labeled an E-ZPass reprobate, possibly with my name and tag number emblazoned on a web site akin to the ubiquitous sex offender warnings.

And it's all over 35 cents.

Imagine my surprise one day, when I opened the mail to find a "Notice of Enforcement Action for delinquent toll payment" from my friends at New Jersey E-ZPass. There it was, a crisp, clear photo of my late lamented Subaru's rear end, with its clearly visible RB sticker, luggage, license plate and yapping Schnauzers.

Holy Batman! They got us on Candid Camera. And I owed thirty-five cents and a twenty-five dollar payoff, er...administrative fee.

I did kind of recall one instance on a recent return trip from New York when I zipped through the E-ZPass lane on the Jersey

Turnpike and thought I heard bells go off. It couldn't have been for me, I was an E-ZPass member in good standing.

Or so I thought.

I immediately called New Jersey E-ZPass, which, after a mind-numbing selection of numerical menu choices, finally allowed me to speak with a cousin of Lily Tomlin's Ernestine the phone operator. I explained my receipt of the violation notice and got bounced around to several disinterested parties before I was finally told to call Delaware where I belonged.

Ladies and gentlemen, our own E-ZPass squad was not significantly better. They officiously explained that my account balance had ebbed to zero and they were unable to retrieve more moola from my bank.

Oh really? Why? What went wrong to turn me into a moving violation? I confirmed my debit card number with the customer disservice operator and oops, Delaware E-ZPass had that silly little expiration date written down wrong.

"Our fault," said the clerk. "I'll correct it."

"Okay, but can you call New Jersey and keep them from putting out an all points bulletin for me? Can you get me off the wanted list? Take my photo out of the Cranbury New Jersey Post Office?"

No, their supervisors did not permit them to call New Jersey. While I could see why they didn't want to, I couldn't understand why I had to be the one to expunge my record and clear my own name. After all, Delaware goofed.

Needless to say, it took about eleven phone calls to the Garden State to clear up the matter and ended with me sending E-ZPass a check—a check!—for thirty-five cents.

Days later, that Subaru went to the great turnpike in the sky, but not before I unnapped the Velcro and snapped the E-ZPass transponder ("Beam me up, Scotty") off the windshield.

As we had occasion to travel back and forth to Wilmington several times over the past two weeks in our new car, I could be found approaching all toll booths by holding the transponder aloft like the Statue of Liberty's torch and hoping Big Brother could validate me.

At one point, Bonnie failed to wave the transponder at the right moment. She did not have to ask for whom the toll belled, it belled for thee.

Envisioning her spouse spending long days journeys into nights bouncing around the SleazyPass phone system while being entertained by Muzak, she knew she was in trouble. She pulled over and went directly to the toll booth staff and turned herself in.

They let her pay the toll in cash (imagine that!), seconds, I'm sure, before that GreedyPass administrative fee would have kicked in.

When the officer saw our temporary tags, he went pale, realizing we were in real jeopardy and immediately entered our new car into the system. I can't imagine what the E-ZPass forensic team would have done with a photo of a violating VW using the transponder from a deceased Subaru. I think the officer saved us from death by hanging. Or at least hanging onto the phone until we wanted to die.

So that, I thought, was the saga of E-ZPass. Until today, when I retrieved my mail and found a Second Notice of Enforcement Action from the State of New Jersey. Apparently, they'd processed my thirty-five cent check, but forgot they forgave the wretched administrative fee.

With phrases like "Delinquent Toll payment," and "Civil Penalty and $200 fine," staring up at me from my violation notice, I am sending New Jersey the damned $25.

I obviously do not have the required inter-state negotiating skills to get this thing cleared up any other way. I doubt that the entire Delaware River and Bay Authority could straighten this thing out. I'm sure the Boss, Bruce Springsteen himself, couldn't use his Jersey influence here. Frankly, I'd call the Governor of New Jersey for help, but McGreevy has his own problems....

E-Z? My ass.▼

August 2004

You probably haven't seen the film *Connie and Carla*. The critics savaged it so badly that its writer/star Nia Vardalos probably thinks of it as her big fat Greek tragedy.

Well, I'm here to tell you to rent it immediately. It's too late to catch it on the big screen since it disappeared faster than a Madonna movie at Cannes. But the drubbing it got from the critics was not only unfair, it was endemic of the diarrhea of the mouth that critics seem to get when faced with a movie that might appeal to people over a certain age—like anybody who has already been through orthodontia.

If I sound mad, I am. While *Connie and Carla* is spectacularly silly, it also has a sweet little message attached about not so sweet discrimination.

So what happens? The critics, in an effort to show off their incredible knowledge of the whole cross-dressing genre, pick the living daylights out of it as they make unfavorable comparisons to every gender bent costume movie in history.

"as in *Some Like it Hot* blah, blah, blah..."

"Not as clever as *Victor/Victoria* blah, blah, blah..."

"A cross between *Priscilla Queen of the Desert* and *Tootsie*, blah, blah, blah..."

The dolts completely missed the point. *Connie and Carla* is not a knock-off of any of those films. It's a love letter to them.

I'm not giving anything away by telling you that this movie is a laugh-out-loud story of two female musical comedy wanna-bees, on the run from gangsters, who hide out as Los Angeles drag queens.

Toni Collette partners with Vardalos and she really does look like the quintessential drag queen. Plus, Stephen Spinella (the original Broadway star of *Angels in America*) is terrific as a man cautiously trying to reconnect with his straight sibling (played by an adorable David Duchovny).

Now I'm not just writing a film review here. It's more like a critics review. If those movie critics had stopped showing off their fancy turn of a phrase for a minute they would have noticed that the script made you think about weighty issues, the Botox craze, discrimination and self respect, even as the gals warbled hilarious (and hilariously costumed) snippets from *Oklahoma*, *Yentl*, and, forgive them, *Jesus Christ Superstar*.

Watching two straight chicks get a taste of anti-gay discrimination is illuminating for the audience, just as it is for the film's characters. And you get a real good look at a straight man fighting to understand the world experienced by some people who have learned, finally, to like themselves.

I will NOT tell you the name of the musical comedy icon with a wonderful cameo in the film, but you will howl. Critics be damned, rent the movie and have a good laugh with a side of pride.

The same can be said for the Ashley Judd-Kevin Kline film *De-Lovely*. I de-loved it. Although I have to admit that in this case the critics, well, had a case.

They took the film to task for its clunky "is this a hallucination or is there really a Broadway producer talking to an aging Cole Porter about his life story" structure. Yeah, it was pretty stupid, but the fact remains that once they got on with it we had two hours of stunning 1930s and 40s fashions adorning Judd and Kline as they sang Porter's magnificent, sophisticated songs.

As if that wasn't plenty, the love story was real, and the film's depiction of it rang very true. Linda and Cole Porter were devoted to each other despite the fact that throughout their marriage he had same-sex relationships on the side, and, according to rumors, she might have done the same.

In the film, they pulled no punches and presented the complicated relationship with taste and tenderness.

Again, it was a tidy little grown-up movie whisked out of theatres by a gust of film criticism that didn't give audiences the chance to discover this gem for themselves.

At this point, give me a flawed (although not seriously) *Connie and Carla* or a slightly weird *De-Lovely* instead of a violent, gory, special effect clogged mega-budget adventure flick any day.

The good news is that the Rehoboth Beach Independent Film Festival is coming up shortly, with no end of grown-up movies on the roster. As Cole Porter wrote, Rehoboth, "You're the Top!" ▼

September 2004

A Borscht Belt comedian once said, "Anyone who owns their own home deserves it." He was being snide. He was referring to me. Like everyone else, we've been spending recent sunny days taking care of all the exterior maintenance that must get done between the last beach day and that sudden cold snap that makes it unpleasant to run around in shorts mowing, mulching and, excuse the expression, spreading your seed.

Over the past few weeks home maintenance drama has reared its ugly head at Schnauzerhaven, and I, for one, am glad I can still laugh. Actually, I'm glad I can still stand up, given the amount of Kudzu and other propagating weeds I've bent over to yank from my shrubbery. Naturally, I bent over only when people I knew drove by. That's not curb appeal.

Embarrassing as it was, that was nothing compared to the garage door incident. On my way to work one morning I backed out of the garage and ran over a plastic flower pot. No big deal. I'd sweep it up later. It was just debris from the dead geraniums from our front stoop, now replaced by the soon to be dead Mums.

But as I backed down the driveway, pushing the remote control to close the garage, the door stopped a foot from the garage floor. That would be a Schnauzer escape route for sure. Damn. The broken pot had rolled directly in front of the little electronic eye on the garage door.

I brought the door back up and got out of the car in my tidy little morning meeting suit, and swept up the pile of dirt and plastic pot shards.

The same kind of luck that had me crouching in the shrubs only when friends drove by now had me returning to the car at the exact moment our sprinkler system activated and shot me and the interior of my car with the kind of spray normally used to separate fornicating dogs. I own my own home. I deserved it.

Actually, when we first had that sprinkler system installed, its timer-regulated debut performance coincided with my letting the dogs out. One of the sprinkler heads came up directly under a squatting Schnauzer who clearly got a surprise and a complimentary enema. But I digress.

Here's a thought: Why do we spend more time shopping for supplies for home maintenance than actually doing the projects? Come on, you know you do it. Gotta get those outdoor furniture covers. And the Styrofoam spigot covers to prevent frost in the water lines. And don't forget the waterproofing for the deck. This past Sunday we lollygagged up and down the aisles at Lowe's, pondering the merits of a long pole with a nozzle on it and then spending considerable time selecting the perfect lawn fertilizer—so much time in fact that we ran out of time to clean the gutters or treat the crabgrass. Is this something that's a choice or are we born this way?

But by far my favorite home maintenance moment recently was the discovery that I could be a contestant on that terrifying, chilling, hit TV show. Not *Fear Factor*, not *Lost*, not even *Live with Regis and Kelly*—but the HGTV show *House Detective*, where the home inspector tells you all the hideous things festering in your basement. It started when I went to our spare closet to liberate my winter clothes. What were these strange white stains on the black pants? The splotches of grey powder on the brown sweater? Mildew! And I don't even live on a boat anymore.

Not only did this situation necessitate my having to buy back my clothes in bulk from the dry cleaner, but the interior of the closet and walls in the room had to be washed down with a bleach solution. Now there's a lovely way to spend a pretty fall day. I really have to thank my spouse for taking on that chore, although I'm reasonably sure she just didn't want to see me wearing Playtex Living Gloves and cursing like a washer woman.

Of course, once the surface mildew was banished we had

to deal with the real problem: (cue the scary music) The Crawl Space. How I ever came to own a home with something called a crawl space is beyond me. I am not a member of the Addams Family. Just the thought of the space and the things that could crawl in it make me nuts. I picture a certain scene from *Raiders of the Lost Ark*.

In this case, curious George, I mean Bonnie, gleefully volunteered to crawl on her belly under the house to see exactly what was growing, oozing, fulminating, or otherwise turning to penicillin in the muddy petrie dish under our spare room. Is there a fungus among us? Is my life partner under the house with some nascent life form? As Bonnie shimmied away from view, I stood by, reading aloud from the newspaper: "three bedroom, two bath CONDO...."

"The moisture barrier seems okay," Bonnie yells.

What the hell is that? To me, a moisture barrier is a Totes umbrella.

"I don't see any black mold," comes a faraway voice. Is that good? Is green mold better? Does it have anything to do with the stuff that's in plastic containers at the back of my fridge?

Eventually my mate emerged, smudged and mud-caked, saying we needed a professional opinion. Which, we got, thanks to a recommendation from a trustworthy realtor.

Here's the upshot. We've got a moisture problem under the house thanks to a badly graded property and not enough vents. No black mold, though. So we don't have to bulldoze. "It's not bad. I've seen lots worse around here," said the contractor.

So we're going to disinfect under the house, install a mess of vents with undulating fans, hook 'em up to electric and blow out the crawlspace on regular intervals. My guess is we'll be dry as a bone in no time but the house will periodically sound like a 747 taking off. Oh, and installing the vents will cost slightly more than an Olivia Cruise. But then I own my own home. I deserve it. ▼

October 2004

As a distraction from the presidential race, Bonnie, who feared I was headed for the funny farm from those moronic talking heads on TV, took me to an actual farm instead.

As a distraction from the results of said election, which I am not going to mention, as I just ate, I will share my rural adventures with you.

Our destination was Hillsville, Virginia, in the southwest section of the state—in hillbilly vernacular, Bonnie's father's "home place" and home to some of Bonnie's most treasured relatives.

Feeling like that traveling gnome in the TV ads, I tried to unwind as we headed down Route 81 into some beautiful fall foliage and weird sights.

First there was Foamhenge—a life size Styrofoam replica of England's Stonehenge, propped in an open field off the highway. Somebody had waaaay too much time on their hands.

Next, on an even more rural route I saw my first wild turkey outside a shot glass.

Zipping past signs for Taters, Maters & Pumpkins, we arrived in tiny Hillsville.

The relatives were great, welcoming us with bounteous hospitality and politely overlooking our Kerry-Edwards bumper sticker.

In between a local pumpkin festival, biscuits and gravy, and a visit to a historic mill along the Blue Ridge Parkway, I glimpsed a newspaper headline about John Kerry "outing" Mary Cheney.

Oh, for pity's sake. She's been a professional lesbian for years. Wanting the scoop, I grabbed my cell phone but found no signal anywhere throughout the state park. Desperate, I eyed two female park rangers who looked, very, um, strong and handsome in their uniforms. Should I sidle up and say, "How 'bout that big old lesbo Mary Cheney???" Not only was my cell phone out of range, but my gaydar didn't seem to be working either. Couldn't tell. Chickened out.

As we drove past the New Hope Primitive Baptist Church, where Bonnie vaguely recalled attending church services with her grandparents, my cell phone warbled. Despite the static I thought I recognized Kathy from the CAMP office wanting to know if I wished to comment on the Mary Cheney story to the *News Journal*.

If I knew something about it I would have. Before I lost the signal entirely I explained that I was in a rural news blackout and couldn't possibly comment intelligently.

My god, I was missing the biggest lesbian flap of all time. No cell service, no internet, and, when we got back home, nothing on TV but Nascar, god help me. I was so frustrated I wanted to go out into the woods and poop with the bears.

Resigned to complete ignorance about what was undoubtedly hot news, I told Bonnie I was going out to visit Uncle Seldon's cows. A gaggle of relatives watched, amused, since nobody before me had ever announced a cow visit. Tromping through the field, careful not to step on what I was told were cow pies, I came to an area of taller grass.

"I wouldn't cross there," Bonnie said, chasing after me.

"Why not? There are footprints here, somebody's been through."

Whereupon I plunged ankle deep in water, realizing too late, that the footprints belonged to Flossy and her friends. One look at my bovine buddies and I knew where the cheese brand Laughing Cow came from. Bonnie couldn't resist either.

"Hey, cows, what do you know about this Mary Cheney thing?" They turned their backs and lumbered off. I tried not to take it personally.

Chagrined, and with soggy socks, I returned to the farmhouse to provide more guffaws for the kin.

"What are the hay bales for?" I asked.

"Well, we'll bring some into the barn and then we'll..."

"Why have them delivered to the field if you are going to move them to the barn?" I asked earnestly.

"Delivered ????" an aunt stuttered.

Call me pathologically urban, but I thought giant farm vehicles delivered the bales directly to the field from some kind of hay bale dispensary. Who knew that the field itself manufactured the hay and a farm vehicle came along, scooped it up and spit it out as a bale. Duh. For the rest of the weekend the clan retold my hay bale faux pas to whoever arrived at the house. They enjoyed toying with the damned Yankee more than watching Dale Earnhardt, Jr.

But alas, eventually it was time to go North. We'd had such a genuinely wonderful visit I almost forgot about the presidential race, not to mention my ignorance of the biggest dyke drama since the unfortunate Anne Heche.

We bade a fond farewell to Hillsville and headed home. Despite my best attempts, I was still incommunicado, with only the farm report and bluegrass music on the radio. Not a word about the Veep's Uber-lesbian daughter.

On Skyline Drive, frustrated by the news vacuum, I suggested we sight-see. "There's a waterfall at the next rest area described as the closest waterfall to any parking lot in the Shenandoah Valley—only a 1.5 mile round trip from the parking lot."

So we got out and walked. Straight down a long and winding trail. The descent was tricky, but not too awful.

We finally made it the three quarters of a mile down to the waterfall, and it was indeed a lovely sight.

Not so lovely was the sight of me, wheezing and bitching on the way back up. Geez, it didn't seem that steep on the way down. I tried to keep a game face for those dumb folks still passing us on their way to the stupid waterfall, but the climb up was an ordeal. I needed a Sherpa, pitons and oxygen.

Amid my struggle to ascend, a man passed us, carrying a three-year-old on his shoulders.

"Things could be worse," Bonnie said, "you could be carrying that weight."

"I am," I said, "but it's on my thighs."

With aching calves and burning lungs, I rested on a boulder mid-way up and wondered if it would be fatally embarrassing to call a park ranger to haul me out on a gurney?

Eventually we made it back to the parking lot base camp, where I leaned on the hood of the car, gasping for air.

"Gotta stop smoking," I said.

"You don't smoke," said Bonnie.

"Right," I said. "Then why was this such a bitch?"

"We're old," she said. "Those endorphins will kick in soon and you'll feel great."

Well, my endorphins did kick in, but it wasn't until I finally got my hands on a newspaper and read, with disgust, that Lynn Cheney called Kerry's mention of her daughter a "cheap and tawdry political trick."

That just goes to show how ashamed she must be of her own lesbian daughter. You'd think Kerry had outed her six year old child. No, Kerry merely referred to her 35-year old political operative daughter who was running the campaign that supported a constitutional amendment against her own lifestyle.

Forget the trek up from the waterfall. After this election, gay pride is the uphill climb. I'm rested and ready.▼

December 2004

Apparently it does come from toilet seats.

Bad luck, that is. One night during this holiday season, a friend ran shrieking from bathroom to bathroom in my house. At first I thought it was the bean dip, but no, he was just noisily slamming the lids down on the commodes.

"Whew!" he said, returning from the relay, according to the Feng Shui guru, if a toilet seat lid is up, money flies out of the house. Lid down, the cash stays. I think it works with luck, too."

Like we had any cash or good luck to go flying out in the first place. But I humored him and promised to keep the lids shut. Then I promptly forgot about it, Kohlers resuming their flaps up position.

Now I'm rethinking this Feng Shui-bad luck connection. Within days of the lavatory warning I was struck down by some kind of kidney infection. "Maybe you got a stone," the ER doctor said. If there was a stone in there, it was Mick Jagger.

Consequently, I spent from the Sunday before Christmas to New Year's Eve running a bizarre fever, moaning and watching TV. Although it's tough to know what came first, the moaning or the TV.

Have you watched in the daytime? It's enough to make you sick, so imagine somebody feverish dealing with it. You get reruns of *Magnum P.I.* (Selleck acting butch), and *Murder She Wrote* (they should investigate Jessica Fletcher as the world's most prolific serial killer; wherever she goes, somebody turns up dead). Then there's *Montel* (lowlifes screw up and blame their parents), *Judge Judy* (lowlifes get punished); *Life in the ER* (lowlife gets shot) or *Dr. Phil* (lowlifes on parade).

Ordinarily I like Diane Sawyer and *Good Morning America*, but even she started to rile me. If I see one more wedding dress segment, interview with mothers-to-be or honeymoon getaway promotion I'm going to scream. Would it kill them to have gay people on once in a while? We lead very interesting lives. Would it hurt to include gay couples in cooking segments, health and relationship features or, heaven forfend, those damn wedding stories? If they're going for human interest, it would be human and actually interesting.

But as bad as the programming is, it's the commercials that defy logic. Daytime watchers must be fools for "only on TV" product sales. You know, the "For just $19.95, we'll send you the (insert superfluous invention here)...."

Wanna paint? There's the Edgemaster—with the built in self-guiding beveled edge. "Guides itself without getting so much as a drop of paint places it doesn't belong—no need for tape, no hassle or we'll buy it back! Paint ANY room with ANY paint in just one hour!!!" Hell, I can paint any room in an hour but nobody in their right mind would let me.

Then there's Gator Grip—"a tool that replaces a whole tool kit! Fits over a thousand nuts, bolts and fasteners for just $19.99. But wait! It gets better!" screams the announcer. Call now and we'll throw in this Ratchet Handle absolutely FREE, you get both for just $19.99.

If you didn't get the FREE ratchet handle, what would you do? Excuse me, I'll stick this on my finger and screw a 24x18 deck together. "Reach any loose screw!" Hmmm, that's you, folks, reaching for a VISA card.

I loved the Original Pillow Back Rest (just two payments of $19.99!). The announcer shrieks of comfort at its best and a pioneering shape, perfect to lean against to watch TV, use flat out as a pillow, or save nuts and berries in its little hidden side pockets. I'd stash Ambien there so I wouldn't have to watch this stuff.

"But Wait! If you order RIGHT NOW, you get a special pillow case, to fit your Original Pillow Back Rest!" Hell, if you didn't get it FREE you'd need three seamstresses and an architect to design a pillow case for this lumpy sack of foam. If I wanted to prop up on something that lumpy I'd lean on a Schnauzer.

BUT THERE'S MORE!!! My favorite ad is for Moving Men. "Not those moving men," hawks the announcer, to video of moving trucks, "these Moving Men!" (video of hand holding plastic cocktail coasters). "These Moving Men make moving furniture fun! Even a loaded bookcase (video of bookcase doing a triple salcow across floor) practically floats along! If these aren't the best helpers ever, send them back for a full refund!" Including, presumably, compensation for lumbar surgery. BUT THERE'S MORE!!! Call now and we'll double your order! 8 Moving Men for just $19.99!

I'd seen the ad three times before I realized they never showed how to put these Tiddly Winks under the hefty furniture in the first place. But wait! Maybe if you call right now they'll throw in Ahnold Shwartzenegger.

I got it! To get Moving Men under a piece of furniture, dismantle it with Gator Grip, then use Edgemaster to patch the paint where you effortlessly slid the armoire into the wall. Rest up from hernia surgery on your amazing Pillow Back Rest. Find Percocet stashed in its little pockets.

The best thing about recovering from my bad luck mystery illness was the cessation of enforced daytime TV. But, the fact is that good luck wasn't exactly breaking down our door. I've never won Powerball, Publisher's Clearing House, or so much as a dime at the Slots.

So what can it hurt to shut a toilet seat? I realize that buckets of cash and good luck may have already escaped (the porcelain horse is out of the corral????) but I'm looking for a sea change of luck right about now.

I hope the coming year brings good health and good fortune to my household and yours. And that Diane Sawyer hears my plea and gives us a little homosexual parity on *Good Morning America*. And that while my back is turned, Bonnie isn't seduced (But there's MORE!!!) into purchasing the Edgemaster.

But heck, the Gator Grip might come in handy if the toilet lid falls off from all the slamming. Keep yer lids on, kids.▼

January 2005

That's my Amazon number. Today. At 3:26 p.m. It fluctuates
wildly. Of all the books Amazon sells, my book is ranked at
130,706. All things considered, I think that's pretty damn good.
I guess it's all that holiday buying. Of course, tomorrow *Frying*
may rank in the 300,000s or worse.

With the exception of my family and friends whose stories,
if not names, are in the book, and a few loyal Rehoboth locals,
I had no idea who in the world would buy or read my book.

I still have no idea, but somebody is. While 130,705 books
are selling better than mine (*DaVinci Code*, 398; that
oldie/goodie *To Kill a Mockingbird*, 705; and Augusten
Burroughs' hilarious memoir at 171), more than a million books
are selling worse than mine—including one by Al Gore at
number 541,456. Al Gore for pity's sake! Okay, okay, it's one of
his older books.

But who's buying *As I Lay Frying*? I swear, it's not my family. They stopped shilling for me in 1961 when they purchased
27 boxes of Girl Scout Thin Mints so I could win a cookie
badge.

A lot has happened since that girl scout started scouting
girls and writing about it. And a lot more has happened since
last May when my book came off the press and into the garage.

As a result of press releases sent by the A&M Books publicity department (one part Anyda, two parts me, stir) gay and lesbian book stores began ordering the book.

Here in town, Lambda Rising bookstore ordered 20 copies
as well as extras for their D.C. and Baltimore shops. The two
Rehoboth Avenue bookstores ordered a dozen as did a shop in
Dewey Beach and another in our sister city of Lewes, DE. Then
they all ordered more. And more. By the case, like Cabernet
Sauvignon.

This was getting weird. Wonderful, but freaky.

Then I got a phone call from the Insightout Book Club, a GLBT (not a sandwich) version of Book of the Month Club. Their executive editor received a copy of my book and a gushing review from a Delaware reader. The editor told me that much to his surprise, he finished the book in one sitting, laughed his head off and wanted the book for the club—in hardcover no less.

With visions of Certificates of Deposit and press junkets in my head, I received the contract from Insightout. Here's how it works: They pay you an advance, in my case, the equivalent of one mortgage payment. And I have a cheap mortgage. It's a far cry from those $2 million advances you hear about, but then again I'm not Hillary Clinton (and I'm glad...).

So the book club manufactures the book itself, promotes it in their member magazine and tries to sell their version to club readers who don't know who the hell I am. In reality, they have to sell a gazillion books for me to make any more money than the advance. But that's okay, since the club has a gigantic membership list and being a club offering is publicity you cannot buy at any price.

This was getting to be fun. I admit it.

I almost passed out a week ago when the book club's January edition arrived in my mailbox with a full color image of *my* book cover taking up the entire front cover of *their* magazine. I'm no Kate Moss but I'm a cover girl. Revenge of the nerds.

Selling on Amazon.com on the other hand requires fortitude and the hide of an elephant. It's great when Amazon sells my book at full price with A&M Books getting the wholesale price. The problem is, folks sell used copies on the page where Amazon has the book listed. There's a link to a herd of entrepreneurs re-selling the book. Some offer *Frying* at a slightly lower price, with the book described as "used, acceptable condition, some markings." Perhaps they did use it as a doorstop. Or "perfect condition, never read." It begs the question why?

There are also copies for $27.99, listed as signed collectibles. Just put me on a shelf with the Hummels and Lladros.

By far the most irritating used book advertisement had the thing going for $2.40 with the comment "well used. There is a rip in the cover and a large ding on the back cover but it does not effect (sic) the pages." I bet it doesn't affect the pages either. What did they do, use the book to shore up a table leg?

The online reviews are fun, too. The publisher gets to post reviews for the book and we submitted reviews from the *Washington Blade*, *OutTraveler* and *Lambda Book Report*.

Readers get to publish reviews, too, and I'm happy to report that the ones from readers I don't know are just as good as the ones I paid my friends to write.

So that's the scoop. By today, the Insightout Book Club web site had my book listed as a best seller (!) in the lesbian memoir category. I surmise there aren't a whole lot of contenders, but seeing myself as Best Seller #7 was a kick.

Reports from independent bookstores out in the hinterlands are good, too. I've shipped stock to stores from Minnesota to Maine, Arizona to (get this) Alabama.

A distributor has picked up the book (along with the Sarah Aldridge titles) for West Coast distribution and we have just signed a contract with a distributor in jolly old England.

It's all happening so fast, I'm dizzy. In fact, Bonnie clicked the garage door opener yesterday, letting us into the book depository and we started counting the remaining cartons. It seems like a second printing is on the horizon.

Needless to say, Anyda and Muriel are assembling all the press clippings and reviews, and are tickled by the success of A&M Books' latest opus. They are delighted that another author is now published under the A&M imprint.

Meanwhile, I added all of the Sarah Aldridge titles to my Amazon.com account last week, and already we've had a few sales. Neither Anyda nor Muriel have a clue about dot.coms so I'm printing pages out for them so they can see that the Sarah Aldridge books are being advertised and sold the new millennium way.

Of course, I haven't the heart to tell Anyda that one of her thirty year old titles is on the Amazon sales scale at number one million, six hundred thousand and something. I think Amazon has sold one copy of that novel in three months. But give it time. If we sell a few more a month she will be right up there with Al Gore.▼

January 2005

Somebody help me here. I'm confused. It's Super Bowl eve, and CNN is crazed over how the NFL will protect the children of America from another accidental breast at half-time.

Baby-faced, uber-trustworthy Paul McCartney has been imported to make sure that a Janet Jackson redux is not even a remote possibility. We recall that one year ago Janet's bitty titty had the Federal Communications Commission and the Concerned Women for America in a sizzle over that naughty wardrobe malfunction. Just this morning, a commentator, tongue firmly in cheek, hoped that this year, McCartney wouldn't accidentally sing Oobla Dee Oobla Bra....

I'm confused, because right in the middle of TV's talking heads expounding on the Super Bowl horror of a nipple making a forward pass, I was treated to a commercial for Levitra.

Now it used to be that advertising for ED drugs, as the common medical malfunction used to be called, was discreet, with spokesperson Bob Dole talking about the little blue pill that would help men with the long-closeted condition.

These days, though, we have romantic television images of very young, exceptionally virile men, and their grinning female partners touting the drug as providing a longer-lasting, better experience. They imply that the drug is not so much for dysfunction as for dissatisfaction.

All well and good, if in between commercials all those concerned mothers aren't getting hysterical about a breast on the 50-yard line. Evidently they have no problem with women broadcasting their thoughts on the quality of erections, but the sight of a female breast makes them queasy. What the hell is that?

Never mind that warning on the Cialis commercial (or is it Levitra again?) telling men that if their erections last longer than four hours they should seek immediate medical help. Go explain that to the kids. (Hell, explain it to me.)

Conservatives, emboldened by what they thought was an election mandate, but what was, if a victory at all (paranoid lefties unite!) just a razor thin win, have gone bonkers. Recently they flogged the entertainment industry over that frighteningly salacious character SpongeBob Square Pants. To hear Dr. James Dobson of the Family Research Council tell it, the problem is not so much SpongeBob himself—although I'm sure he's a little light in the swim fins for Dobson's taste—but that the We Are Family Foundation produced a video for the schools starring SpongeBob, Barney and a variety of other subversive cartoons. Dobson says that the Foundation is, gasp, "pro-homosexual with a sinister agenda."

That sinister agenda teaches youngsters about tolerance by suggesting they take the following pledge: "To help...make America a better place for all, I pledge to have respect for people whose abilities, beliefs, culture, race, sexual identity or other characteristics are different from my own."

Disgusting, don't you think?

Dobson heard the pledge and urged parents "to keep a close eye on your sons and daughters. Watch carefully everything that goes into their little minds."

Little minds, indeed.

All this wouldn't be so frightening if the media didn't find it contagious, spending the entire pre-Super Bowl week tittering, if you'll excuse the expression, about Janet Jackson's 2004 one-point conversion.

Since then, the FCC cracked down on Howard Stern, Dr. Dobson squeezed SpongeBob and right here in Rehoboth, the Film Society got the evil eye for showing a movie that was no more graphic than many others at the multi-plex.

Then came *The Vagina Monologues*. Last weekend, CAMP Rehoboth presented a production of the show at the Rehoboth Convention Center and I was lucky enough to be the director. We drew two sell-out audiences—mostly women, but a nice contingent of men as well. And the diversity astounded us all. Gay, straight, young old, Goth girls, Red Hat ladies, women in Ralph Lauren, flannel shirts, the works.

I had imported three actresses from my old Maryland theatre days and we had a blast putting the show together. Believe me, after working with the script for days on end, hearing the word vagina repeated or discussed a hundred times, we got pretty comfortable with it.

Which is why it was hilarious that at first mention of the play's title in area newspapers (not using the word vagina in any of the headlines, I might add), there was an outcry from some Sussex County folks, hollering that the play promotes lesbianism.

Frankly, the play is 90% heterosexual. But let's face it, 10 percent homo in a sea of hetero is red meat to those conservatives.

Never mind that the play had been on Broadway since 1997 (with the word Vagina in 6-ft letters on the marquee) or that it has been done in 76 countries, translated into 35 languages and produced in thousands of communities.

I was most amused by one newspaper, which printed *The Vagina Monologues* press release, but changed the headline to read "Tickets going fast for play."

But the capper was the ride into town two days before the show to read the Convention Center marquee: CAMP Rehoboth Monologues 8 p.m.

I guess the City staff comes from a more repressed generation.

But there's a big difference between keeping "Vagina" off the marquee (now there's a mental picture) and renaming the play "CAMP Rehoboth Monologues." I don't exactly know how that happened but it gave us a laugh.

In fact, at the show's dress rehearsal, the actresses started substituting the words "CAMP Rehoboth" every time they were supposed to say the V-word. We all had a good howl.

So what do we do about this selectively outraged society

and the free press that gives them more air time and credence every day?

I say we make good and sure the world is still safe for the mention of biologically correct body parts and small spongy cartoon characters. I say we fight to make sure the FCC allows us to watch programming that's at least as explicit as commercials hawking "a quality sexual experience."

It's going to be a fight, but there are signs we will eventually win. My optimism comes from a four year old. As her mother prepared to leave for the Convention Center to perform in the "CAMP Rehoboth Monologues," this child sat on my living room carpet amid a pile of well-dressed Barbie Dolls. But one was buck naked.

"We need to put her clothes on," the child calmly said, "so you don't see her vagina and her bum." Good girl.

But while we wait for the toddler generation to grow up, we can pray that the vituperative conservatives don't try to put words like vagina back in the closet. Hell, we hope they don't try to put gay people back in the closet.

And I so hope that nobody at the Super Bowl drops their drawers, alludes to a penis, or puts one small breast forward for mankind.

People will laugh so hard they'll miss the Levitra commercials. ▼

February 2005

Hallelujah! After years of offering up my unsolicited opinions, this week I actually got a formal request for my preferences. I'm a Neilsen Family!!!!

Yes, after my more than half a century of watching the boob tube the ratings folks finally found me and want to know what I watch.

For fifty years the Neilsens have gotten their information from couch spuds watching *Car 54 Where Are You*, *The Gong Show*, *Mr. Ed*, and, my choice for situation comedy sludge *The Beverly Hillbillies*. Meanwhile, my favorites, *Route 66*, *Cagney & Lacey*, and *Designing Women* suffered premature rejectulation.

It's about time they queried (queeried?) somebody who dotes on PBS, devours the news and lies in wait for high-toned TV dramas. Actually, there hasn't been a really high-toned TV drama since *Playhouse 90* went off the air in 1961. But I'll take *West Wing*.

So can this be my opportunity to bring a more cultured, erudite and discriminating queer eye to the ratings pie? No, the truth is that I'm going to have to admit to shilling for *The L Word*, and never missing that new Monday night disaster *The Medium*. The acting is painful and the dialogue embarrassing, but like a traffic crack-up on Route One, I have to stare. Just as those *Brady Bunch* fanatics and *Dynasty* suckers ponied up the truth about their viewing habits, I too, am determined to reward the Neilsen people for their faith in me by simply returning their diary with my actual television choices for sweeps week 2005.

Oh, but if it had been that easy.

They give you a damn diary for every working TV in your house. Hell, the one in front of the treadmill has been off since my 2003 flirtation with the Adkins Diet.

But there's the Sony in Bonnie's home office droning on all day long as white noise while she works. At any given time she has no idea whether she's watching an old Victor Mature movie or an Abmaster infomercial. Is this even watching? Do we dare give people the impression that each morning, somewhere in Delaware, somebody's actually paying attention to an old *Who's the Boss?*

Here's a question: does proper diary entry require intent or actual consciousness? What about those 10 p.m. episodes of *Law & Order* where, despite our best efforts we watch the gruesome murder but doze off, mouth agape, on the sofa before the jury comes back?

If they'd asked us to be a Neilsen Family 20 years ago this wouldn't even be a question. Our diary would show *St. Elsewhere* and *Hill Street Blues* followed by Johnny Carson, followed by Dave Letterman. Back then, I never even understood why they broadcast 10 o'clock news. "I can't believe people don't stay up for Carson," I'd sneer.

Somewhere in the early 90s, following that wicked lesbian kiss on *L.A. Law*, the question morphed into, "Do you believe people don't stay up for the news?"

Now, without Delmarva 10 p.m. news I'd have to wait until morning for word of the number of chickens with influenza.

But here's the real question. If we-are-fa-mi-ly Neilsen, who's included? The dogs watch Animal Planet when we go out. Should this be in the diary? I really need to know.

On our bedroom TV, our late-night choice is the Travel Channel. We routinely fall asleep somewhere between the Grand Canyon, Monster RVs and an Albuquerque Chile Cook-off. Is everything after toothpaste and before REM sleep legit?

So this week I've been busier running back and forth, pen and diary in hand, between TV sets than I ever was on that treadmill. Frankly, it's a wonder I've had time to watch anything. But I did make certain I reported taping *The L Word* in its 10 p.m. time slot, while watching *The Academy Awards*, a.k.a. The Gay Superbowl on another channel.

I also let the Neilsens know that while I was watching Hilary Swank's va-va-voom backless gown, I was taping that cutie on *Cold Case*. Then, I propped my eyeballs open and watched, and duly recorded that I watched, the repeat of *The L Word* at midnight. The things you do for love.

One day, as I loped between the living room (CNN *People in the News*) and Bonnie's office (the fifth *Murder She Wrote* of the day) it occurred to me that perhaps these opinions were not as crucial as some I could offer about the actual content on television. Especially on news shows.

Like what's with the U.S. Armed Forces spending 200 million dollars to train new translators and logistics experts because they kicked out a whole lotta smart gay people because of "Don't Ask, Don't Tell?" Hey, Neilsens, I got those stats this week on CNN. Somebody do the math and give me the ratings for that stupid Pentagon policy.

And then on *Larry King, 60 Minutes* and the rest I heard about "reporter" Jeff Gannon, in reality a schmo named James Guckert, who's had a daily press pass to the White House for over a year so he could lob softball questions to the President. His questions also included overt criticism of liberals and inaccurate information about pretty much everything I hold dear.

Never mind that Guckert (Delaware's own, by the way), purporting to be a family-values Conservative, is linked to various X-rated gay escort service web sites and other risky business. What a family values hypocrite.

And legendary reporter Helen Thomas lost her front seat in the pressroom. I give this shameful situation terrible ratings.

But no, during this Sweeps Week ("Woman has 160 lb. tumor!" "Stars Without Make-Up!") people will probably just fill out their diaries with nights spent watching contestants wade through worms on *Fear Factor*, shove miniaturized cameras into open wounds on *CSI*, and argue with each other as they bungee-jump canyons in *The Amazing Race*.

I'm off to watch all the political shows I taped on Sunday morning so the Neilsen's know I support network news divisions. These are the real reality shows.

But then like the dyke drama whore I am, I'll be watching—and notating—my third re-run of *The L Word*. Dear Diary, long live lesbian visibility on TV!

And thanks for asking.▼

April 2005

In our gay community, in addition to our biological families, we often build families of affinity. I'd never had a biological brother but in my nuclear family of affinity I had four. And now there are three. Bonnie and I loved Robert from the minute we met him in 1991. We laughed together at Halloween parties where we were Robert Goldilocks and the Three Bears. We got serious in D.C. for the 1993 March for Equality, and we luxuriated on three awesome European vacations. Robert and Larry gave us the inspiration and push we needed to move to Rehoboth full-time; and finally, we had the most wonderful adventure of all, our 2003 double wedding in Vancouver, British Columbia.

Robert was loving, funny, and incredibly brave. But certainly, Robert could be a quirky brother.

He had a fanatical obsession with vehicular cleanliness. He had to sell his own black BMW because he couldn't keep it clean enough for his own standards. He told me he'd never speak to me again if I bought that black Subaru. I did and he forgave me, but continually rolled his eyes when studying, really studying, the dirt splatter on its hood.

Robert was the only man I've every known to insist on routinely taking vacation rental cars through the car wash. In France, we had to purchase a special sponge so he could properly wipe down the rented car in Provence. We toured castles and car washes. And we learned the translation for Hot Wax in many different languages.

In 1997, the four of us went on a 10-day trip in our 27 ft. boat from Rehoboth to New York Harbor to Fire Island. With every squeal of glee from Bonnie crashing the boat through the waves, we got an expletive from Robert as he grabbed for towels to wipe salt from the bow.

Robert was known for his refreshing, if occasionally astounding honesty. I'm sure he was always a candid person, but somehow in the late 1990s one of those fantastic brain surgeons who kept him with us for so long must have removed that little filter from his head—the one that keeps most of us from saying, out loud, every single thing we think.

Not so our Robert. If he thought the house you were thinking of buying was ugly, he'd tell you. If he hated a paint color you chose, he'd tell you. And he was usually absolutely right.

The day I showed up in my first pair of cropped pants—the things we old people used to call pedal pushers, I asked Robert if I looked okay in them. He studied me for an uncomfortably long moment and said, "Yes. Much better than you looked in the shorts yesterday."

I'll think of Robert every time I buy a car, pick paint colors, and especially when shopping.

I'm also going to celebrate Robert's life by remembering his love for Larry and the strength of their 30-year—THIRTY YEAR—relationship and a great marriage by any standard, and one to tell our foolish government about. I'm going to celebrate his great eye for design, his heavy foot on the car's accelerator, his love for his Schnauzer Mitzi and his incredible courage. Where, following a troubling diagnosis, and surgery after surgery, many of us might have given in to depression and given up, Robert kept up his gym regimen, stayed with the Atkins diet, went rambling in England, rafted in Alaska and glowed when Larry bought him a wedding ring. And, with Larry's steadfast and loving help, Robert kept his sarcastic sense of humor until the very, very end.

But there really isn't an end. If you have been riding around Rehoboth in a dirty car, get thee to the carwash as soon as you can. Robert's watching. And I've promised him that Bonnie and I will try to do better. We really will. I missed him so much this morning I bought a 10 wash coupon book at the Rehoboth Car Wash. Robert will be impossible to forget.

Especially during the hot wax cycle. ▼

May 2005

I'm on a quest to find my inner dyke.

In contrast to my long-standing and well-deserved reputation as a non-athletic, non-mechanical, non-outdoorsy brand of lesbian, I'm surprised to find myself tackling some of my demons.

It would be a midlife crisis if I was going to live until 114. Suffice it to say that after a winter of losses and stress, I'm following my insightful counselor's advice to "take some time for yourself" and dabbling in new experiences. Herewith is the first.

Golf.

In the cupboard of dykedom, golf is a staple. And with CAMP's Women's League starting for the season, if I wanted to see my friends it would have to be on the fairway. If only I could get that far.

Day One: I rendezvoused with Bonnie and my brave friend Barb at the driving range. Immediately, I broke a strict golf tenet. I parked in the nearest spot I found. "Nooo!" Bonnie hollered, noting that my car was dangerously close to the 9th hole and therefore a candidate for boinking with golf balls the size of hail. I moved the car.

Next, I purchased the storied bucket 'o balls and strode up to the driving range tee for a lesson in swinging the club ("Practice like an elephant swinging its trunk."). So I stood there in full view of traffic swinging my arms like Babar and fighting the urge to make circus sounds. Then I moved on to aiming for the ball on the tee. Whack. Nice for bocce ball.

From what was, for me, the dribbling range, we proceeded to the Par 3 course. As explained to me, Par 3 meant that I had three chances to humiliate myself before I was technically worse than the median average.

I teed off, but was teed off. I had lost my concentration.

As a wordsmith I was struck by the apparent contradiction in the term par. Why, I wondered, was below par on the course a good thing and feeling below par after a night of Grey Goose on the rocks a bad thing? Conversely, being above par has always meant better than average to me, so why, when I hit the ball 8 times before it reached the green was that not, as Martha Stewart would say, a good thing. You see my point?

Day Two: On my way to the driving range, I stopped at our local golf store, because much like the White House Press Corps and Congressional Democrats, I needed balls.

Ah, so many choices! What's more, here was a whole shopping experience I'd never discovered. Golf shirts, golf shoes, wind pants, gadgets, fuzzy animal golf club covers—I was overwhelmed. Bonnie managed to get me out of the store with a dozen pink golf balls and a rubber suction cup for the end of my putter so she wouldn't have to hear me groan when I reached down to the cup to retrieve my ball. If it should ever land in the cup.

Back at the driving range, I managed to try out most of the borrowed clubs in my bag and actually fire a ball or two briefly into the air. Incoming!

Day Three: Dressed like Nanook of the North and trying to remain upright against a 30mph bluster in the parking lot of the golf course, I wished I'd bought those wind pants. Barb and her partner Evie, organizers of the aforementioned CAMP league showed up with snazzy wind wear and a special clear plastic golf cart cover with zip up windows. I felt like I was riding in *Oklahoma*'s Surry with the Fringe on Top—"with isenglas curtains you can roll right down, in case there's a change in the weather."

A change in the weather I get. But when it starts *out* this bad, I questioned the point of going. But off we went, dressed like Arctic Circle explorers, blowin' in the wind.

Despite the gale force gusts, or perhaps because of them, I overcame my convoluted swing ("You look like you're chopping wood!" "Wimpy, Wimpy, Wimpy!" "This isn't softball!") and marched steadily forward on the course, 20 yards or so at a time. Then, occasionally 30-40 yards. One time the wind caught my ball and accidentally tossed it onto the green, where, to my delight, I soon sank a putt, meaning one over par and a bogey. I asked what Humphrey Bogart had to do with it. Nothing.

My self-congratulatory phase ended when I realized that the next hole was three football fields away, around a corner and past the 7-11.

And it was getting colder out. Say, do those little knitted golf club covers double as hats?

Day Four: Barb drops off a copy of *Golf for Dummies* at my office. Should I take this personally?

Facing those demons: League day approached. I was afraid of embarrassing myself. My insecurities reared their little golf club covered heads with flashbacks of my being the last one picked for sixth grade softball and the first double fault in the sleepaway camp tennis match. My athletic prowess can best be summarized by my status on Bonnie's former softball team. I always wore my sneakers to sit on the bench so in case somebody didn't show up, they could send me to right field to avoid forfeiture.

So I was worried. It's not like softball, basketball or volleyball where a klutz like me is never invited on the team. In our Women's League, all levels of players need apply—in fact, it's encouraged. So while that provided some comfort, I still had the pre-tee-off heebie jeebies. I may have had a dozen pink Nike orbs, but did I have the balls to do this?

League Day: I arrived at the course to find a gaggle of golfers ready to set out and golf carts lined up nose to bumper like a Disney World tram.

Off we went in foursomes, with my quartet consisting of Barb, who wanted to keep an eye on me, and two other players. It was sunny and windy, the course looked beautiful, and I hesitantly stepped up to the tee for my first shot. Amazingly, the ball went up in the air for a short distance.

Since we were playing "best ball" I didn't have to struggle to keep up. Everybody just used the site of the ball that traveled the farthest for the next shot. It was actually fun. And once or twice, the quartet was reduced to using my ball. Of course, theirs went farther than mine, but they had landed in water or sand.

One time, I whacked a shot towards the rough and when it landed, three cute bunnies flew out of the woods, hopping for their lives. They were adorable and I was out in nature. Imagine that.

Our foursome laughed, talked, and scooted along the fairway, leaning out of the carts to retrieve balls like polo players leaning from their horses. I received lots of good advice.

Overall, I made a bunch of crappy shots, dug up an unfortunate amount of sod, whiffed the air instead of the ball a few times and occasionally got a "nice shot!" from my companions.

It goes without saying that I enjoyed the beer and postgame analysis at the 19th hole. At that part of the sport I am above par, meaning good. Or would that be below par, meaning good? I really need an answer on this.

And, prior to next week's League night I intend to do two things: practice a little at the driving range and find some fuzzy golf club hats that look like Schnauzers.

When the going gets tough, the tough go shopping.▼

May 2005

It happens to me every few years.

No, not getting a Social Security statement lengthening the time until I can retire with full benefits. But that is a bitch. This is an entirely different kind of getting the shaft.

Eye glass prescription change? Yes, but not as regularly, if you'll excuse the expression.

Guessed yet? It's the every half-decade trip to the doctor for what we shall euphemistically call study hall.

That's right, in the organ recital of life, the colonoscopy is your sonata's fifth movement. Or, as the prep for this procedure goes, probably your fifteenth movement in as many hours.

Ah yes, roto-rooter time.

The reason I'm writing about this scatological subject is that three times in the last month I've heard of people who have been diagnosed with a preventable cancer, all because they were afraid of, or couldn't be bothered, with this test.

And here we are, facing Memorial Day weekend, thinking about fun in the sun and I'm writing about this shitty topic. But let me assure you, it's even crappier to be Queen of Denial about your colon. The damn test is an inconvenience, yes, but not painful at all, and one little rear ender can cure unbelievable future heartache.

I also have it on good authority from the editor of this publication that it's even less of a bother for gay men than for us gals. You figure it out.

So what's the test like? No big deal. But here's some practical advice:

Follow the pre-test directions exactly. If the test is Monday, you are supposed to have only a liquid diet on Sunday. Do it. But on Saturday night you might want to eat enough for the Israeli Army because it will be at least 36 hours before you can have another morsel. This is the only hard part of the test.

As for the liquid diet, choose Jello and bouillon, not Cosmos and Margaritas. But it's survivable.

Then, around 5 p.m. on Sunday you have to drink a small bottle of liquid that tastes like salt water. Prior to my first exam of this type, my doctor made a terrific suggestion. He told me to get 8 ounces of the strongest (non-alcoholic) liquid I could think of and use it as a chaser for the prep cocktail.

I chose Blue Gatorade, which, if you've never tasted it, can make your ears fold up.

I understand that there are now tablets you can swallow to avoid this liquid loading, but you have to take more pills in an hour than Liza Minelli takes for a whole week, so it may be a bad trade-off.

Still the rear admirals try to make this process as easy as possible. The prep is manageable.

But here's the important part: whatever stuff you swallow, there are immediate consequences. Stay close to home. In fact, stay home. Between 5 p.m. Sunday and Monday morning you will be very, very busy. The company making the prep potion isn't called Fleet for nothing. They should include Reeboks.

Thank god I got that new Comcast digital video service where I could pause *The L Word* every five minutes while I raced to the bathroom. In this case the L in *L Word* stood for Ladies Room. But the truth is, if you stay up until about mid-night, you might be finished spring cleaning entirely by that time and can sleep through the night.

And now, one of the most disgusting and shameless pro-mos you've ever heard: since one critic actually said that my book, *As I Lay Frying—a Rehoboth Beach Memoir* made great bathroom reading because it contained short, fun chapters, it might be just the thing to get you through your Colonoscopy prep. Now there's a ringing endorsement if I ever heard one.

Sales pitch aside, my favorite part of this whole medical process happens on the morning of the test, when the doctor's sadistic receptionist says "Good morning!" with a cheery smile to everybody who walks in. This, to haggard people who she knows have been up all night sprinting to the chamber pot. We're all there for the same tailgate party, and not the kind with beer and pretzels. It's galling.

Meanwhile, a nurse sticks her head out a door and into the waiting room. "Fay Jacobs?" she inquires.

"That's me, I say, "I'm ready for my close-up Mr. DeMille."

I changed into a paper dress, layed down on my side and waited for them to put the scope where the sun don't shine. The doctor asked if I wanted sedation.

"Do bears poop in the woods?" I answered, realizing my unfortunate choice of clichés.

Ask for a little sedation, but not too much—a 60s era haze, not a falling down drunk. You want to be relaxed but conscious to watch the incredible journey through your intestines on the 25 inch plasma TV in front of you.

Frankly, a few years ago, I would have found this disturbing, but after the oozing, glowing, pumping stuff we see on *CSI*, a clean colon is positively charming.

"Well, you should have no discomfort at all, says the doc, you have a pretty straight colon."

"Well, if I do, it's the only thing straight about me."

We laughed and I could see my colon jiggling on TV.

As we viewed the scope rafting its way down the Rio Grande, I'd had enough sedation to start seeing Hans and the Wookie wending their way through space, or Katharine Hepburn and John Wayne rafting towards the waterfall in *Rooster Cogburn*. Or was this *Rear Window*?

Within minutes, the rear guard retreated, the Disneyland ride was over and I got a clean bill of health and a Polaroid photo of my guts as a souvenir.

That was it, nothing to it, over and done for five years.

Starving, I went immediately for a Mumbo Jumbo burger.

So please have it done if you've been stalling. I can't stand to hear any more horror stories that didn't have to happen. With just an ounce of intestinal fortitude, many things are preventable.

Put that Colonoscopy on your to-do list, in your Blackberry, on a note on the refrigerator door or wherever you write things down now that none of us can remember a damn thing.

And here's to one of the very best things we can do for ourselves, our families and our future. A toast to your next colonoscopy! Cheers, L'Chiam, a Votre Santé, or, as Broadway's Sweet Charity used to toast, "Up yours." ▼

May 2005

We're forever sitting around with our friends, postulating about old age. As Bette Davis famously said, "Old age is not for sissies."

Spending time with Muriel and Anyda, who are lucky enough to be able to stay in their own home and care for each other at their age, is an inspiration. But I fear they are the exception rather than the rule.

Proud and extraordinary women, the ladies make concessions to age, but carry on with only a small bit of extra help. Charlie takes care of the garden and makes the salon night appetizers the ladies used to make; Lois Ann, the friend they call daughter, handles outside maintenance and backyard cottage details. Their friend Carolyn cleans the house for them once a week. Carolyn started out as a hired house cleaner and thirty years later, 'though she has her own professional career, she still comes once a week to straighten up. By this time, she is a dear friend. Bonnie chauffeurs Muriel to the library. Actually, Muriel often drives her beloved Lincoln on the way to the library, but if she tires from book browsing, she will give up the wheel to Bonnie for the return trip.

At home, Muriel scoots around in her wheelchair, propelled by foot power, to cook breakfasts, including microwavable grits or eggs, while Anyda does the carrying of dishes, food and utensils to the table. It's a slow process, but it gets done.

Until very recently, almost all of the household chores got done by the ladies themselves, albeit at a crawl. Now, a little more help is accepted, but not much more. Neighbors do the grocery shopping and newspaper recycling. Other folks make sure that the liquor doesn't run out.

Several years ago, when the octogenarians were still making an annual trek south to Florida in the winter, we went to visit them at Lighthouse Point just outside Ft. Lauderdale.

They had a small ranch home, surrounded by grapefruit and orange trees, in a quiet community. Anyda and I chatted about books and politics. "That Newt Gingrich is properly named," Anyda said, looking at a newspaper headline. "He is a little lizard." Bonnie and Muriel concurred as they concentrated on their hands of cards.

"Gin." Muriel quietly announced with a coy smile as she beat Bonnie at the game again and again.

During that long-ago Florida visit Anyda asked me to read the latest book she was working on and make editing suggestions. I was flattered and nervous. Editing for an icon can be daunting indeed, but Anyda relished talking about her characters, their motivations and their feminist triumphs. Those discussions were the very beginning of my working affiliation with A&M Books.

As for their yearly drive south, they always traveled in a big sedan, with boxes full of the yellow legal pads for whatever novel Anyda was currently writing and with whatever cat happened to be making its home with them at the time.

"At motels on the way, the cats would always wind up under the bed," Muriel told us, "and we would have to call the front desk and ask for a clerk to come and retrieve the cat for us before we could leave." According to Anyda, several of the clerks came away with battle scars. One time, they had to have motel staff disassemble an entire bed frame to recover a recalcitrant feline.

Those winters away from Rehoboth were good for their health, and gave them some exercise as well. Before Muriel's hip started giving her trouble she had been an avid tennis player. Rehoboth old timers remember watching Anyda going into the A&P to shop, while Muriel remained outside practicing her tennis game on the side of the building. Along with tennis, both Anyda and Muriel loved golf, and were two of the founding members of the Rehoboth Yacht and Country Club. Of course, in those days (and maybe today, for all I know) there was no family membership for their kind of family.

During their Florida winters, Muriel continued to play tennis. Anyda, acknowledging that Muriel was the only athlete in the family, would agree to step onto the court to lob tennis balls over the net so Muriel could practice. Into their seventies they played tennis, or their version of it, several mornings a week and spent part of each day tending the garden.

In the afternoons, Muriel devoured books by Sidney Sheldon or Danielle Steele, while Anyda wrote her own stories, or gave *The New York Times* and *Washington Post* crossword puzzles their due.

During our Florida visit, as they did with many friends passing through the area, the ladies graciously opened their home for overnight guests and happily accompanied us out for crab cakes and white wine at places famous for fresh Florida-caught seafood and views of the Intercoastal Waterway. We had to fight for the check. Sometimes we would win.

As recently as two years ago, the ladies made their last trip South. That time, they reluctantly accepted the generous assistance of their close friend Curt as chauffeur.

Bonnie and I adored their industriousness in the face of advancing age. Prior to leaving for the journey, "We'd go out in the morning and open up the big trunk on the car," Muriel told me, "Then we'd go back inside and get the suitcases."

"We would take the empty suitcases and place them in the trunk, wide open. Then we would go back inside and start to bring out the clothes."

'You packed the suitcases in the trunk?" I asked, trying to picture the ladies walking out their front door with arm loads of golf shirts and khaki pants, not to mention unmentionables.

"We could never have gotten them out of the house filled, so we came up with this plan," Muriel said, looking at Anyda for concurrence.

"Oh, yes, this was the easy way." Anyda said, describing the reverse tactic once they arrived at their winter home.

On our now long ago Florida visit we shared cocktails and

conversation much as we had been doing in Rehoboth. But having three days of quality time was very special.

Knowing the ladies these last eight years or so has been a gift. All the same, I would have loved to meet them when they were younger. We could only imagine their youth and enthusiasm for everything they did. We loved digging through their slides of Rehoboth summers and trans-Atlantic travels on the original QE2 for the World Bank. "Oh, yes, Muriel got to go with me several times, on ocean liners and trains through Europe. The World Bank was a very progressive organization, you know."

I guess so.

As much as we tried to dig for more details about the closeted life of lesbians in post-war Washington, D.C., the ladies preferred talking about the present.

And presently, they were managing just fine, in their Rehoboth home, doing their publishing tasks, enjoying the antics of their cats and basking in the friendship of the whole neighborhood and then some.

Anyda's eyesight has been deteriorating and she often uses a big magnifying glass to read. Muriel cannot hear much without her hearing aids, but she's finicky about wearing them. And when she does have them in her ears, we can be deep in conversation and I'll see her go to adjust them. I wonder if she's turning them on or turning me off.

As another nod to passing time, Anyda agreed to let Bonnie put her sunroom love seat up on a six-inch platform so it would be less of a struggle to get up and down. When Bonnie worried that the legs of the loveseat might slip off the platform, Anyda came up with a plan. She asked her neighbor Hayden to rinse out four cat food cans, nail them to the platform and lodge the sofa legs in them. It was a look. But it worked.

And while the ladies are doing well on their own, they are quick to let us know that they are fully prepared for the future. Anyda Marchant the attorney made sure of that. Anyda's correspondence, book drafts and other papers will go to the Lesbian

Herstory Archives in Brooklyn, NY...some day.

"I've promised all of this to the archives after I'm gone." Anyda said, pointing to a dozen cartons piled up in the corner of the sunroom. Looking at me, she added "it will be your problem to get them there."

I figured. They also made preparations relative to living wills, internment and all of the other details associated with a future they refuse to discuss. The thought of one of them living without the other is too terribly painful to imagine.

So in the meantime, they make regular visits to their trusted doctor and do everything they can to take expert care of each other and extend their lengthy love affair as long as humanly possible.

Will we still be living in our home, taking care of a Schnauzer or two in our later years? Or at an all-lesbian assisted living facility? We don't have such a luxury here yet, but there has been plenty of hypotheses. Knowing this community, it will happen.

I can picture it now. I'll be scribbling on yellow legal pads and Bonnie will be flirting with the baby dykes on staff. And beating the heck out of everyone at gin rummy. We should be so very, very lucky. ▼

June 2005

As my sister and I celebrated at a family party last week, we got to talking—and she was shocked at some of the things she learned. So I'm going to share them with you to put a human face on this ridiculous special rights business.

My sister Gwen has been married to her husband Rick for 19 years.

I have been partnered with Bonnie for 23 years as well as married for two years in the eyes of the Canadian government.

These two sisters and their spouses have all paid into social security since bell bottoms were hot the first time and Lyndon Johnson was president.

If, heaven forbid, something happens to my sister or her hubby, the surviving baby boomer can collect a social security death benefit, then cash the 401K and keep the house (and all 18 cats in it) without inheritance taxes. If there was a pension involved, the surviving spouse could claim it, which would be important, because 18 cats eat a lot of Friskies. The merry widow or widower might not be so merry but at least they could keep themselves in cat litter.

If something happens to me or Bonnie, one of us could be stuck paying a crippling tax bill on the spouse's IRA. We'd be coughing up a staggering estate tax on half the damn house, and not receive a penny in Social Security death benefit or any survivor benefit from all the years our spouse paid into the system. In fact, if one of us had a pension (sadly, we aren't that lucky), it would just...zzzpppft, disappear as if no one remained behind needing to put dog kibble on the table.

But that's not the worst of it.

If one of our quartet doesn't die, but is merely very sick, the difference is even more appalling. Say my sister or her mate get cat scratch fever and need expensive nursing home care.

The healthy spouse will still have a place to live since my sister's ailing husband could qualify for Medicaid without having to sell his home. That's because the government recognizes that his legally wed wife and all her cats would still need a roof over their fuzzy heads.

If Bonnie or I had to go to a nursing home, the healthy spouse would have to sell the house in order for Medicaid to kick in. Great. One of us and a pair of Schnauzers will be living in a camper in a Wal-Mart parking lot. The government would probably make better provisions for a surviving Schnauzer than a remaining gay partner.

Even as we worry about future tragedies, we see daily inequities. My sister's husband and I each have a job with health insurance benefits. And my sister is covered under hubby's health plan.

My employer wanted to offer domestic partner coverage—and I was willing to pay for my mate's policy, but the insurance company nixed the idea. And even if they had agreed, I would have had to pay federal income tax on Bonnie's premium amount as if it were salary. If my sister's husband had been treated this way he'd have developed distemper.

So since we can't get insurance for Bonnie, even IF we are willing to pay the extra tax, she has to rely on the Veteran's Administration for her health care. Frankly, it's a darn good thing this particular gay was in the military.

And speaking of the armed services, my sister's husband got a student deferment during the Vietnam era and never served, so he didn't have access to the VA home loan benefit. If he had, he could have financed their home through a lower cost VA loan.

Well, Bonnie did serve during that conflict (albeit stateside) and applied for a VA loan for our first house. The real estate agent snidely told her she could only borrow money on half the cost of the mortgage because technically she was only buying half the house. Useless benefit. BaDaBoom.

It's enough to make you sick, but it had better not. When

my sister was hospitalized with an intestinal ailment (hair-balls?), there was no question that her husband could have round the clock access to her hospital room.

When Bonnie was laid up for seven weeks several years ago, I had to come out of the closet to roughly a platoon of people before I was granted family status, and though I sat at Bonnie's bedside every day for what seemed like a millennium, I still got the fish eye at every shift change.

The really frightening fact remained that while I pitched in day and night as an unpaid member of her health care team, any one of the hospital staff could have tossed me out on my butt, legally unable to visit, much less help. Just thinking about it gives me kennel cough.

So you have four people here. Two couples. And a lotta house pets. Both couples have sworn to the for-better-for-worse thing, and in the ensuing years have actually seen better and worse and better again.

Gwen and Rick were able to have a wedding in their own country, with all of their friends and family in attendance. Bonnie and I had to sneak across the border to Canada and leave our friends and family to join us only through digital photos.

To his credit and my enduring thanks, my Dad paid for both weddings.

So there is it. Two long term relationships. Two couples tossing the occasional flea bomb. Two happy households. Except for our choice in companion animals, we're pretty much the same. And each couple forks over the requisite taxes. But according to the Human Rights Campaign, Gwen and Rick have over a thousand important, life-altering, financially and emotionally important rights that we do not have.

Special rights my ass.

America may be the land of the free, but you have to pay Uncle Sam through the nose for your benefits. If you are straight, you get what you pay for. If you're gay, you don't.

I'm so mad I'm foaming at the mouth and may need Rabies shots....▼

June 2005

With murderer Scott Peterson safely behind bars and Michael Jackson's infamous acquittal on child molestation charges (don't get me started on that) the country is abuzz with legal groupies. Story after story fixates on those who stray from the righteous, flaunt the rules, and laugh in the face of authority.

Of course, the airwaves (or cables) are filled with this crime stuff (Runaway Bride! Aruba Tourist missing!) so nobody has to cover any real news and find out how many people are being killed in Iraq or how low the dollar has sunk in foreign lands.

The line between news and entertainment (infotainment?) is blurring so badly that real juries are letting people go free because they aren't getting the kind of proof they see every night on *CSI*. I hope the acquitted Robert Blake is appropriately appreciative of what prosecutors are calling this *CSI* effect.

And now that the Watergate scandal's Deep Throat has been revealed, the only mystery left is whether or not I have aged as badly as Woodward and Bernstein. Gee, did you look at those guys? Do we look as old as they do?

Since crime is such big news these days, with criminals all over the evening news, I was shocked that nobody got wind of one of the biggest criminal cases ever to hit Sussex County. We are obsessed with criminals and they are us.

It's true. My mate and I did something so heinous, so egregious, so totally against the law that our auto insurance rates skyrocketed, people smirked as they viewed our driving records and we were sentenced to spend an entire afternoon wrangling with the geniuses who work, and I use that term loosely, at the Motor Vehicle Department.

What was this wicked attack against convention, our crime of the new century? You'll be aghast.

The whole sordid affair began when my spouse called me

at my office to say we were looking for cheaper car insurance. Okay, whatever.

After getting her new quote she called back, shrieking that she was about to be charged a whopping $75 extra each month because of some serious black mark the insurance company discovered on her driving record.

Okay, she's been caught speeding a time or two but this sounded worse than going 37 in a 25 mph zone in Ellendale.

"The clerk said it was something very, very bad, like resisting arrest, or stealing a car," Bonnie told me.

"What do you mean LIKE resisting arrest? Either you did or didn't." I pictured my mate being handcuffed, thrown to the hood of the Volkswagen and frisked by some surly female trooper.

"Don't you think this is something you might remember?" I suggested.

And if she had stolen a car, why wasn't there a Cadillac CTS in my garage? Stealing a car? I think not.

"The report didn't say exactly what you did?" I inquired.

"No," Bonnie whined, "the insurance company just said that the code for the infraction indicated something really, really bad and I'd have to pay a lot if I still wanted insurance."

Certain this was some bureaucratic boondoggle I drove home, picked up my criminal element and set off for the county seat.

Ah, Bonnie and Clyde arrived at the DMV. At least when you take a number at the bakery, your wait is rewarded by a bagel. At the DMV, you wait and all you get is attitude. A snippy clerk searched Bonnie's driving record.

"Yes, it's right here," she said. "You were stopped in Bridgeville, got a $45 ticket, which you paid several days later."

Ah, lovely Bridgeville-if-you–lived-here-you'd-be-home-now-Delaware.

"It was for unauthorized use," continued the clerk.

"Unauthorized use of what?" I asked. Hell, it was Bridgeville, maybe it was unauthorized use of scrapple.

The woman slowly, painfully slowly, reached for the code book and looked up the offense. With the urgency of a sloth she found a page and slowly, slowly, walked over to the copier and started printing the information.

"Wait a minute," Bonnie said, with a glimmer of recall.

She proceeded to remind me of our being stopped by an officer under Bridgeville's towering Rapa Scrapple sign and being written up for having a license plate holder that covered up a little bit of the '04 sticker on her car's tag.

"That's it? Unauthorized use of a plastic license plate holder?"

The clerk slowly, very slowly picked the copy up from the copier and painstakingly handed it to us.

There it was: Unauthorized use of an automotive accessory that obscures the license plate date sticker.... Or something to that effect.

I got louder. "Unauthorized use of a little plastic thingy with rainbow colored *DOGGY PAWS* on it?"

By this time, dozens of sleepy people who had been waiting since Christmas for their ever-lovely drivers license portraits began staring at us, because I was still standing there shouting to the clerk "Our insurance rates are skyrocketing because we bought a decorative license plate holder with red, green and yellow *PAW PRINTS* on it?"

"That's it," said the clerk, hoping this crazy woman would take her photocopy of the law and go away. "That's it."

But I assure you, that wasn't IT.

Butch and Sundance had to wrangle with several different insurance companies before we found one that would give Bonnie a reasonable rate despite this scandalous driving record. And now we have to go and try to get this absurd conviction off the books, because every time somebody checks her driving record it's going to come up with those terrible words "unauthorized use" and she's going to seem like a smarmy little felon.

So let this be a warning to you—and you know who you

are—who have the audacity to surround your Delaware plates with little personalized license plate holders—those little rainbow frames, those audacious "Go Eagles" accessories, those patently illegal plate holders advertising your brand of car, your auto dealer, or heaven forbid, your love of animals.

Go ahead and buy those goodies if you must—some of my favorite stores have them displayed all over the walls—but please, please put them on the front bumper and not over your damn license plate. We don't want to see you on *America's Most Wanted.*

Frankly, I'm surprised Woodward and Bernstein missed this one. Hey, maybe there's a book deal here, or a TV show...*Paw and Order, Criminal Intent.* ▼

June 2005

It was 93 degrees out by noon, as we stood right up at the police barricade at Fifth Avenue and 22nd Street waiting for the front of the New York City Pride Parade to reach us.

In my sweaty hand was the 2005 Pride Guide, a glossy magazine listing events, the parade route, Pride organizers, judges and grand marshals, and a page headed Accolade. It described the awards ceremony, to be held in the fall, to honor those individuals and organizations which embody the diversity of pride throughout the year.

I stared at the page. Above the story, in italic typeface, was the quote *"Pride parades were born of brave individuals having the courage to come out as gay in often hostile, unsafe environments,"* and it was attributed to Fay Jacobs, *As I Lay Frying.*

I had no idea who chose to put the quote there, when the decision was made, where they bought my book, or what prompted Pride organizers to use those particular words— although I'm happy they did.

I knew ahead of time about this honor. A friend e-mailed us the previous week, saying there was a quote of mine in the New York Pride Guide and I was pleased and curious. I couldn't imagine what kind of quote (Schnauzers, boating or lawnmowers didn't seem appropriate) but I figured it was probably going to be a quote among many, having something to do with diversity.

But there were my words, all by themselves, heading the page, in a publication in the hands of thousands and thousands of people and on the window sills or stacked up, free for the taking, in hundreds of New York City bars and restaurants.

I was by parts astounded, honored, flattered, and incredulous. And proud, for I meant what I said and this was Pride

2005. It made me think about how far I had come over the decades, from confusion to panic, to a toe out of the closet, to building a life with Bonnie, wonderful friends and family, to Rehoboth and life as a writer, to a Canadian same-sex wedding and now to a sweltering New York street surrounded by thousands of people with their own complex coming out histories.

When I showed the quote to Bonnie, her face lit up. "Cool!" she said.

But it was far from cool as sweat trickled down our necks, and the sun beat down, as we strained our eyes uptown to see if the parade was near.

And then we heard it. The thundering sound of motorcycle engines revving their way toward us. Ah, dykes on bikes leading the parade! They were followed by the New York Police Department marching band, followed by a three hour parade of floats, dancers, music, placards, whistles, shouts and cheers. Along with the marchers, floats from bars, churches, health organizations, gay sports teams, liquor companies, banks and more, there were lots of laughs and some somber moments. This year's parade theme: "Equal Rights, no more, no less" was never far from peoples' consciousness. And the true diversity of the New York community shone bright. Latino contingents (Ah, the costumes and good looking people from Brazil!), Harlem Pride floats, Asian groups ("OUT, not take-out!") black, brown, white all together, it was a refreshing and joyous mix. Gay firefighters, police contingents, flight attendants (duh!), rugby teams, you name it. We loved D-Flag (women and their dogs), gay dads with a sign "We love our straight son," the naughty signs, and so much more.

One of the most touching groups (a few marching, a few riding) were some Stonewall riot veterans, one with a sign "Class of '69." They got sustained cheers and thanks from the crowd.

And of course politics had its day. New York Mayor Bloomberg led the way, with prospective mayoral candidates battling for applause behind him. Al Sharpton shook hands, led by TV crews moonwalking backwards in front of him for film at 11. There was Senator Chuck Schumer, Congressman Jerry Nadler, and so many more. A huge whoop of joy and cheers went up for political superstar Hillary Clinton, clad in her ubiquitous black pants suit and waving to crowd shouts of "Sister Hillary!"

A contingent of VW bugs chugged by with the waving Fab 5 of Queer Eye, and walkers skipped along with "Honk if You're Queer" bumper stickers. The new gay cable network Logo had a float, as did the Gay and Lesbian Task Force, and P-Flag with a float advertising their "Stay Close" campaign—with a huge photo of Chrissy Gephardt and her parents.

As bystanders right against the rail, we were handed dozens and dozens of stickers, hand-outs and postcards advertising events plus a lifetime supply of condoms, which we passed back to some boys behind us.

Sharing elbow room with us at the front were two lesbians from Brooklyn, and it turned out that one of them had, until recently, worked at InsightOut Bookclub, and knew of my book. Disney had it right. It's a small world after all.

By 3 p.m. we were parched, sweaty and risking third degree sunburn as the parade showed no signs of abating. We had a friend volunteering at a party in the building behind us, at the *In the Life* offices. If you are not familiar with the show, it's a terrific PBS gay news magazine and I'm a big fan. We took refuge at the air conditioned party, toasted Pride with a Mimosa and still had an awesome view of the parade from the *In the Life* office windows.

From there, as the parade chugged along, Bonnie and I fought our way through the throngs lining Fifth Avenue, down to 10th Street and across to Christopher Street to the food and souvenir vendors. The streets were packed as far as our queer eyes could see.

We met friends at Julius', and in small world Part II, my cousin Kenn was there, with a group of his friends and we all had a reunion, burgers, and beer.

Then, after buying the requisite Pride T-shirt with the Keith Haring design on it and swigging our third large bottle of water we realized how far we had walked and how much further still we had to go to get back to our car on 25th Street. It seemed physically impossible.

"We'll never get a taxi down here," Bonnie whined as I spied a yellow cab with its vacancy light on. But a group of young guys signaled the cab just as we saw it and it stopped to pick them up. The guys looked at us, we looked at the guys, and they must have taken pity on the two old sunburned lesbians clutching pride guides, staggering unsteadily and looking like Stonewall survivors ourselves. They insisted we take the cab. To those anonymous guys, we will forever be indebted.

And as we slowly pulled away from Christopher Street, I could see the streets still teeming with people, the gutters littered a foot deep in plastic water bottles and other garbage, and the corner trash can bursting with, among pizza boxes and coke cans, hundreds of discarded Pride Guides.

Fame is so fleeting. Happy Pride 2005.▼

July 2005

I knew my foray into golf had gotten out of hand when somebody called me a jock. Quick, phone *The New York Times*.

It had nothing to do with my actual golf skill, but that my golfing buddies didn't know enough to come in out of the rain.

We're on the course and it starts to drizzle, then rain, then pour. I expected CNN's Anderson Cooper to arrive to broadcast while being blown horizontal.

Several players gave up at drizzle and almost everybody was in the bar by rain. It was considerably into pour by the time I could drag my soggy butt off the course. That's what I get for playing with three serious golfers.

Meanwhile, this reporter cannot reveal her anonymous source despite the threat of jail, but I can divulge that the lounge conversation went like this:

Bonnie: "Oh my God, she's going to kill me."

League Member: "Why?"

Bonnie: "I told her to leave her raincoat in the car."

Another League Member: "You mean Fay Jacobs is still out there?"

Third league Member: "I know she is. Her tee shot bounced off the roof of our cart as we drove by."

For the record, I was aiming in the other direction. But it did serve them right for rushing back to the clubhouse at drizzle.

So I drip into the bar, wringing wet, and somebody says, "I can't believe you stayed out there so long. What a jock!"

I may not be getting better at golf, but I'm having my Outward Bound.

Along with precipitation, golf offers intimacy with pestilence. Last week I was attacked by a swarm of horse flies the size of Sea Biscuit. My teammates sprang into action and spritzed me with Skin-so-Soft and a shot of Deep Woods Off. Now there's a nice fragrance.

On the next hole I was informed that the previous week somebody had spied an electrical line wrapped around an adjacent tree. Wisely, they drove me past the site before revealing that the utility cable turned out to be a reptile. Oy, I was on an aversion therapy tour. Next week I'm expecting a plague of frogs.

At least I'm doing well in the accessory department. My fuzzy Schnauzer club head covers arrived. Call me if you ever need doggy hand puppets. Every once in a while their beards get top heavy on the clubs and a faux Schnauzer topples onto the fairway. I'm going to have to start offering a reward for their return.

And I have to say, the costumes are cool. Imagine my surprise on my maiden golf outing when I was given a glove monogrammed with a giant FJ. "You shouldn't have..." They didn't. Turns out that FootJoy manufactures golf stuff and everything I wear can have my initials on it. Cool. I now have FJ shoes, sox, and a ball marker. I'm looking for an FJ fly swatter.

Today, I came home and found a visor with a big FJ on the front hanging on my doorknob with a little note: "Got this for you. Has your name written all over it."

Okay, eventually I have to tell you how I'm doing at the actual game of golf. Here's a clue. One week my quartet included a woman actively undergoing chemotherapy, a woman with arthritis who has had at least 18 joints replaced, and a woman with a prosthetic leg. They all played better than me.

Okay, to be fair, all three gals are experienced, superior players despite their challenges, but it does make one consider the point of continuing in the sport.

Although, golf is great exercise—especially for me. If four of us tee off, three golfers then jump in the carts to ride a hundred yards or more to their golf balls. Me, I trudge the fifty feet to my ball and whack at it again. I rarely hit it far enough to even use the cart (my first off-road vehicle) and generally wind up walking most of the course. Yes, the exercise is going well indeed.

So I forge on. One day my companion sank a putt and I congratulated her on her birdie.

"Hey, you're getting the terms down!" she said.

"Language I get, it's sports where I suck."

At my next lesson, my mentor made me change my stance, my grip, my swing, everything but my underpants. This was necessary because, how shall I delicately put this? My tits were in the way. We gals with large bingo bongos need to stand further from the ball so we don't interrupt our swing by whacking ourselves in the hooters.

I made the adjustment, stood further from the ball, took a good swing, missed my boobs, and sent the ball far enough to lose it in the wheat field next to the course. I'd need a hay baler and combine to find it.

But they tell me the shot was good, despite it costing me a stroke. Better to cost one than have one, I say.

In fact, this whole sports thing may have the desired effect of relieving my stress and giving me a hobby. I could turn into a jock yet. Stop snickering. Do you know any lipstick lezzies who would spurn White Diamonds or Chanel in favor of Deep Woods Off? Me, neither. ▼

August 2005

"Have you got a column ready for me?" my editor had the audacity to ask, one hour before the CAMP Rehoboth Follies started. Like I've had time to write anything.

And it was an especially risky question because he knew I could retaliate by tattling that when he asked, he was wearing a pink tutu.

Honestly, living in Rehoboth is like being at adult sleep-away camp. And I use the word adult loosely. If you've ever been to camp or heard tales of counselors, bunks, color war or dining hall etiquette, you may relate.

Here at Camp Runamuck we swim, go boating, have cook-outs, do arts and crafts, play sports, have dances and do every damn camp-like thing except wake up with reveille and gather at the flagpole in the morning. Hold it. When I go to the boardwalk, I walk right past the flagpole.

Of course, back in the day, I was cranky as hell because I was sent to a co-ed camp. Worried that I wasn't boy crazy, my parents were probably the only ones hoping their daughter would climb out the bungalow window to sneak over to the boy's bunks. Little did they know I was suffering in silence with a crush on my counselor.

So just like my tortured past, here at our adult camp, we have separate boys' and girls' waterfronts (although there's a great amount of crossover), many co-ed activities (which I now love, go figure) and that mid-summer tradition, "Sing." For the uninitiated, Sing is a competition, where different age groups present songs and skits making fun of various counselors, activities and camp lore.

I can recall sitting up late at night with my pals, re-writing popular songs with silly lyrics to take good-natured jabs at our friends and shared experiences. Wait a minute, that was last week when I was re-writing popular songs with silly words for the CAMP Rehoboth Follies. And we made lanyards to hang pink triangles on our costumes.

Yup, the correlation between summer camp skit night, where we'd rehearse for two days and be willing to humiliate ourselves for a laugh has amazing resonance here. Just ask Tinky Winky, a.k.a. my spouse, who was drafted for Follies.

And speaking of the Follies, I have to report that the following morning in the dining hall...er, Crystal Restaurant, the Delmarva Divas ate their bacon and eggs with their Gold Barbie, won the night before, sitting on the table. Honest.

Actually, the old fashioned mid-twentieth century generic summer camp is probably extinct. Specialized camps are all the rage now, with computer camps, dude ranch camps, fat camps (the kind where you trim the fat as opposed to what's happened to me at adult camp) and of course, drama camp. We've got that one covered in spades.

I guess our corollary to Wilderness Camp is an overnight to Western Delaware.

I just read about a Hogwarts camp where Harry Potter maniacs can make potions by mixing Alka Seltzer and Jello. I don't know about you, but I just went to a party where Jello shots were available—that would be Jello and Vodka. We waited until morning for the Alka-Seltzer.

Ahhh, all those starry nights, with boys sitting around the campfire telling scary stories and girls sitting around the campfire gossiping. I think we reverse the roles around here, but we have horror stories and gossip to beat the band. No marshmallows, though.

Hey, remember lights out when the counselors yelled, "One more sound and I'm coming in!" Now we have a noise ordinance to deal with and our bars and restaurants get pretty much the same treatment. And just as we did as kids, we try to behave, but every once in a while....

And though I've never heard of Rehoboth bunk mates short-sheeting a friend's bed, I do not put it out of the realm of possibility. Actually, it would be a great hint to guests who over-stay their welcome. As for another tradition—camp Visiting Day—instead of once a summer, we have visiting day around here weekend after weekend after weekend. I wonder if I remember the correct technique for short sheeting?

Oh, we were so bad as teen campers. As a 16-year-old counselor-in-training I would run off with my friends to smoke Newport Lights (ptooey!) clandestinely in the bathroom stalls. Do we see any parallels here?

And while we don't have an official Color War, which splits the whole camp into two teams at the end of the summer, we do have our annual Drag Volleyball (how campy is that!) with its two rival teams inviting hundreds of campers to take sides and cheer.

We've come a long way baby from Kool-Aid and lousy camp food, but we're still happy campers. That's because along with our Rehoboth camp activities we have five star restaurants, legendary happy hours, and S'Mores.

Oh Lord, Kum-Ba-Yah.▼

July 2005

The CAMP Rehoboth Community Center is now a reality. After a lot of planning, public input, lesbian processing, successful fundraising, gay guy decorating, and plenty of hard work, we and the bank now own two buildings, with a beautiful court-yard between them in downtown Rehoboth Beach.

The first time I went to a community center was over 25 years ago. Peeking out of my very musty closet, I'd traveled to downtown Washington, D.C. from the 'burbs, heading for a place called the Women's Center. I correctly suspected that the name of the place was code for Lesbian Center.

What happened there is why I am here—in Rehoboth, in my long-term relationship, and possibly here at all.

I'd been in the D.C. area for over 15 years but had never driven downtown solo. D.C. intimidated me then and does now. There are four of every damn street. Northeast this and Southwest that. And those diagonal streets, names brimming with patriotism like Constitution and Independence Avenues, form trapezoidal mazes from which the only exit is a plunge into the reflecting pool by the Capitol.

Lore has it that D.C.'s ubiquitous traffic circles were designed by inebriated City Architect Pierre L'Enfant, who kept putting his sweaty beer mug on his map plans and oops, made a ring. "We'll call this one Dupont Circle...."

So there I was, in alien territory, seeking a place to feel comfortable. That first visit to a welcoming space set me on my way.

You have to kiss lots of Toadettes before you find your princess and go to lots of inappropriate venues before you find your niche. My Women's Center visit led me first to a lesbian square dance. Hee-Haw!

I sat pasted along a wall, watching 30 or 40 women doseydo in Dale Evans get-ups. While it wasn't my kind of thing, I got to see women enjoying being together as couples. Actually, I noticed many women in sleeveless shirts, who had obviously shunned underarm shaving (it was, after all, the late 1970s). Then and there I determined if I was coming out of the closet I was taking my razor with me.

The next event was a lecture on Women and the Outdoors—which to me, was that distance between the car and Macy's. These gals meant spelunking and backpacking.

I didn't know what was worse—hating myself for thinking I might be a lesbian, or hating myself because I hated square dances and mountain climbing and figured those were the only lesbian options. Geez, the gay community was just one more place I wouldn't fit in. So evolved was my internal homophobia, I thought it odd, or queer if you will, that a gay group held meetings at a place called The Ethical Society. Snicker, snicker.

But after a few more weird forays—a meeting on lesbians and depression (which, based on me, was redundant), a potluck where all the women but me dressed like Johnny Cash, and an unfortunate evening spent learning to play pool, things turned around nicely.

My Women's Center connections led me to a party in D.C. hosted by a friendly woman (remember this, there will be a quiz), where I met someone who invited me to an event, where I was introduced to another woman, whose friend lived near my home in the suburbs and...suddenly there were parties and dates and friendships.

To this day, some of the women I met that fledgling year are still dear friends. Incredibly, many of them now live in Rehoboth.

And the funny thing is, as I became more comfortable with myself and my new life, I became more adventurous and outdoorsy. After meeting Bonnie and getting to love both her and her passion for boating, I became one of those formerly daunting women and the outdoors. Although, I drew the line at camping.

My second community center experience happened here.

In 1995 Bonnie and I, knowing only a handful of people in Rehoboth, came to town by boat, docked just outside Rehoboth in Dewey Beach, and planned to spend summer weekends here. In our first week, Bonnie and I were subject to the rants of a homophobic chef at a Dewey burger joint. He spewed hatred with a side of fries. I was so upset I didn't know if I wanted to remain here for the summer.

I had seen the magazine *Letters from CAMP Rehoboth* and made my way to the tiny courtyard office with a letter to the editor I'd written. Though I didn't know a soul there, I received a warm welcome and immediate help. Not only did the editor run my letter, but he contacted Dewey officials who promised to look into the situation. I don't know whether it was the bad burgers or the community action, but the offending restaurant and its owner were soon gone.

Hearing we lived on our boat and had cruised here from Chesapeake Bay, editor Steve suggested I write about the trip for Letters. Before we knew it, I was a columnist, Bonnie was donating volunteer time for something called Sundance, and we were up to our armpits (shaved, of course) in both CAMP Rehoboth and Rehoboth Beach.

Within a year we were so deep in local activities, friends and the brother and sisterhood, we bought a condo here. From there, the ties CAMP helped us make, and the torture of crawling over the Bay Bridge every weekend, caused what would have been unthinkable a short time before: we ditched our corporate, dressed-for-success lives in Maryland and ran away to the beach. My father thought we were mental cases until he visited and began to see the liberating effect of our being able to live openly and proudly in our own hometown.

Fast forward. Hundreds of people gathered for CAMP's Community Center Founders' Circle fundraiser recently, producing palpable energy, genuine excitement and spectacular generosity.

Still, there are gay people in town who wonder why we

need to build a full-service community center. Based on some image conjured by the words "community center," they may feel disinterested; not needing a place to play checkers; having no use for meeting rooms, a library, art gallery, or *Letters* office.

To them I say, please reconsider. Whatever physical shape the building takes, it really will be "the heart of the community." More than a place to buy tickets, run a magazine, publicize events, hold meetings and welcome people who need help or companionship, it will be the future of gay Rehoboth.

To me, it will insure that Rehoboth Beach stays a gay friendly resort and hometown for all of us, even if we never attend a single event, meeting, or envelope stuffing party there. For everyone who loves Rehoboth, gay or straight, this community center will anchor the activities and atmosphere everyone enjoys in Rehoboth.

After all, years from now, when some homophobic goof ball makes insulting comments to some young gay man or lesbian just arriving in town, we want them to be able to head to the community center and discover what a safe and heartwarming hometown this can be.

And by the way, just last month I ran into the woman whose DC home had been the site of that lesbian potluck dinner so many, many years ago on my coming out journey. She and her partner have a place here now and I watched them joyously purchase one of the paintings auctioned at the Founder's Circle Ball. I guess that's why they call it a Founder's CIRCLE. What comes around goes around, and we want to make sure the tradition continues.▼

August 2005

They say that if you remember the 1960s you weren't there.

I was there. My memories are appropriately fuzzy.

The recollections that do still exist came trickling back last week as Bonnie and I prepared to attend a 60th birthday party with a psychedelic 60s theme.

First let me say that the downtown shop featuring 60s gear (is it still called a Head Shop?) must have had a great week. Throngs of old people (how old am I? I want a caller ID on my side of the phone to remind me who I'm calling) kept asking for tie-dyed clothes and other 60s accouterments. The clerks took to asking if we were going to "that party." Duh, yes. Why else would I buy a purple tie-dyed shirt festooned with peace symbols?

Actually, when I think about it, I could amortize the outfit by marching, once again, in front of 1600 Pennsylvania Avenue protesting a prolonged, bloody, senseless war. You'd think that the first time would have been enough.

My freshman year at American U. in Washington, D.C. was 1966. I arrived on campus with a suitcase full of preppy pink Villager clothes, Bass Weejuns penny loafers, a record player bellowing "I Want to Hold Your Ha-a-a-a-and" and a penchant for showing up in class dressed to the nines, including pre-pantyhose hosiery, false eyelashes (I swear!!!) and more lipstick on my puckers than you'll find in barrel of lipstick lesbians.

Within weeks, thanks to an intervention by my roommates, I wore holey denims with shredded bell bottoms, scraggy tie-dyed shirts, day-glo buttons, macramé headbands, and a face scrubbed clean of Maybelline. Those special Brownies were heavenly.

On Thanksgiving my parents wrung their hands over the stranger who came to dinner.

As the 60s turned increasingly psychedelic, our mop-topped Beatles morphed into Sgt. Pepper's Lonely Hearts Club Band and we pulled all-nighters in the dorm—panicked cramming fueled by No-Doze, Mateus wine and smoke from a bong.

While I studied (and I use that term loosely), I got to experience the apex of the protest era.

During the huge 1967 march against the Vietnam War I rode up and down Constitution Avenue, my head poking out of the moon roof (although that term had yet to be coined) of my boyfriend's VW bus. I photographed the protesters with my Kodak camera (with Flash Cubes). We traipsed up the steps of the Lincoln Memorial and gazed back at a sea of people, protest signs and civil disobedience. We were rebels with a cause.

My first political campaign had me licking the proverbial envelopes for Robert Kennedy's presidential bid. I was sure he could change the world and I wept as Walter Cronkite announced that my hero had been assassinated in that California hotel kitchen. It was my very first in a long line of political disillusionments and disappointments.

I was at the District Building in D.C., when the city went up in flames following the Martin Luther King assassination. Some of his disciples burned their own neighborhoods, and my friends and I manned the phones trying to find milk and diapers for families without resources.

As amazing as the political memories are, so too are my recollections of pop culture: Peter, Paul & Mary concerts (girls in peasant skirts, guys in Nehru jackets), Peter Max paintings, hootenannys in the dorm (how many deaths will it take till too many people have died? Sorry.), a win for the hapless NY Mets, and illegal substances everywhere you looked. We lived in an earthquake of cultural upheaval.

Gloria Steinem renamed us *Ms.*, we watched men take a step for mankind on the moon, wondered if Teddy knew Mary Jo was asleep in his car on the Chappaquiddick Bridge, said goodbye to Marilyn, watched *Funny Girl* and hummed Dylan's

Lay, Lady, Lay.

Abortion wasn't legal but you knew where to go. One of my friends almost died from a botched backroom job.

And we protested everything from the bombs in Cambodia (for which we got tear gassed by DC civil defense troops) to the school cafeteria menu (resulting in the first Roy Rogers Roast Beef restaurant opening on campus).

We took our Flower Power seriously.

"No more falsehoods or derisions
Golden living dreams of visions
Mystic crystal revelations
And the mind's true liberation, Aquarius!"
It was indeed the Age of Aquarius.

Now, it's 40 years later (40 years!) and the aged of Aquarius are partying in a Rehoboth Beach backyard.

Some things don't change. I never went back to eyeliner. I did lose the guitar, though. And shame on me, I had to Google the words to "Blowin' in the Wind." But most of us Boomers are still protesting in one way or another. Now we write letters to the editor instead of taking over campus buildings.

In fact, feeling uncommonly frisky in our tie-dye, my spouse and I partied hearty, followed the birthday bash by dancing at Cloud 9, then on to Louie's Pizza for food to sober us up for the ride home. It was almost an all-nighter.

The only difference is that back in the old days we didn't need to gobble an aspirin and Nexium nightcap, sleep with three pillows to stave off reflux, and have to get up to pee several times a night—no matter how much 3.2 beer we drank.

Peace and love, sisters and brothers. ▼

August 2005

I love this town.

Although, for the past two weeks I've been kicking myself for saying "yes" to participating in a fundraiser at Café Zeus.

When a brave Sussex County AIDS Council volunteer asked me to volunteer, he made it sound innocuous.

All I'd have to do is climb up to the big white lifeguard chair in the Zeus courtyard, and spend five minutes at the Sunday tea dance asking for SCAC donations. How difficult could it be?

Well, that was before I found out what usually goes on in that courtyard for Happy Hour. Then I was plain scared.

Part of the Zeus bar culture is a fabulously well-attended Sunday tea dance where the lifeguard chair is filled by mus-cled, six-pack-ab-sporting lifeguard types, with and without body jewelry, with and without shirts on, promoting the sale of beverages to guys who appreciate the abs, body jewelry and shirtlessness. Sometimes the shots are delivered using flat abdomens as serving trays. Sometimes there's CPR practice involved.

What could they possibly want with *me*? My panic was only slightly assuaged knowing that other Rehoboth fools, favorite middle-aged bartenders, local coffee baristas and a certain *Letters* editor were similarly hoodwinked into participating.

After all, SCAC desperately needs money for its transporta-tion fund—the only way many clients have of getting to their doctors. How difficult could it be to raise the cash?

How difficult? When I got to the Zeus courtyard on Sunday I found out. First off, the damn lifeguard chair looked three sto-ries high. Yeah, there were steps, but they were further apart than these thighs have been in a decade. Short of hiring a crane, I'd need a sand bag and pulley system to hike me up.

As the event began and the first life-guard victim took his seat, I sidled up to the bar for a cocktail. I know that worrying doesn't solve anything, but it gives you something to do until the trouble starts. And there was going to be trouble.

The "lifeguard" before me was a buff, bejeweled *Baywatch* clone. Twenty dollar bills for SCAC flew at the young man as he poured drinks into willing jaws—not an act to follow.

They called my name and I walked to the side of the chair, hauled my ass up the first two steps, and from what has been reported to me (I have post traumatic stress amnesia), climbed Everest only with the assistance of three dykes and a boost from a body builder in leather swim trunks.

Ah, the cheers! No, not for me. People cheered that I made it into the stupid chair so they wouldn't have to put down their drinks to make room for the ambulance gurney.

Once at cruising altitude, I loved the view: throngs of people braving the oppressive heat to drink for a good cause. A bunch of my buddies had shown up to support SCAC and their stupid friend, who was now waving a microphone and trying to figure out how to please this crowd to get donations. Singing "Let me Entertain You" and taking off a glove wasn't it.

Perhaps reverse psychology might work. I gazed across the ocean of mostly young male faces and found myself hollering "give me the money…or the clothes come off!"

You should have seen the rush. Tens, twenties, all for SCAC.

"Show me the money!"

People plunked bills into the silver wine cooler collection pail and others stood below me, mouths agape like baby birds, with mama here pouring pink liquor into them.

For the Miss Manners crowd we had tiny shot glasses so they wouldn't have to rely on my aim. Good thing, because I missed a lot of mouths, dousing donors and causing shrieks, applause, laughter and sticky tee-shirts. I think I gave somebody a nasal enema.

By minute three my loyal and long-suffering friends had all

coughed up their cash, my previous victims were rinsing off and I was desperate.

"Calling all Schnauzer lovers! " I yelled, and amazingly a Schnauzer owner appeared with some currency.

It was a hundred degrees in that courtyard, and I was schvitzing like no other Jewish girl had ever schvitzed. "Okay, kids," I screamed above the din, "deadline for *Letters* is tomorrow and if you don't come across with the cash I'll tell embarrassing fables about each and every one of you."

That brought forth another flurry of fives, brave shot drinkers, and more and more money.

Finally, the longest five minutes in the history of beverage service was over. Yay!!!!

Oh god, I had to get down. By this time I'd stopped asking myself how difficult it could be. Would they let me just stay up there along with the next "lifeguards?" Then I could wait for happy hour to end and summon the volunteer fire department to retrieve me with the bucket truck. I looked down. It was a really long way to Tipperary. Thelma and Louise flashed through my mind; should I take a swan dive out into the crowd?

I stood up, inched my way toward the ladder and dangled one foot, searching for base camp. The lesbian posse below gripped my swollen ankles, guiding me to the next step. Arguuuhhhh! There were so many people participating in the dismount I felt like a balloon in the Macy's Parade. Finally, I hit terra firma to another round of cheers, mostly because people were relieved to have this particular circus act over.

How difficult could it be, indeed. I understand that there were many thousands of dollars raised thanks to the incredible generosity of Café Zeus and the many, many greenback-tossing participants. And I got a column topic where none existed mere hours before.

So for those who witnessed this whole discomforting affair, as they say in the play *Tea and Sympathy*, "When you think of this, and you will, be kind."

I love this town.▼

August 2005

Well, it's the end of August and exactly one year since I wrote my last its-the-end-of-August and nothing is happening column.

These dog days of summer (although, in my house it's always dog days) are infamous for no real news to speak of, no juicy scandals and nothing much happening anywhere. August is when we get newspaper headlines like last week's, "Woman downs 35 Bratwursts in 10 Minutes to win speed-eating title."

Was she on the Rehoboth Beach Diet, evil twin to the South Beach Diet?

Friends and relatives are here, rushing to take advantage of the waning summer and one more funnel cake. And friends don't let friends pig-out alone.

So it's with a delightfully sugary aftertaste that I sit on a boardwalk bench and ponder how different this August is. I am riveted to the news, because there actually is news.

While POTUS (walkie-talkie Homeland Security shorthand for President of the United States) pedals around his Crawford, Texas ranch, piddling away the entire month of August, one woman is starting a revolution.

Cindy Sheehan, if you haven't heard of her, went down to Crawford to ask the President what her cherished son was fighting for when he lost his life in Iraq. All this grieving and angry woman wanted to do is have a few minutes of face time with the president of the United States. She gave up her son for her country and she wants to ask her country's leader to explain why.

Seems like a reasonable request to me. The Prez dissed her. He couldn't hop off his bike and have a conversation with her?

By day ten of her vigil, he hadn't.

Regardless of your political leanings or ideology, it's public relations 101 to get out in the open and explain yourself. Hiding and obfuscating is never, ever a winning strategy.

So an amazing thing is happening down there in Texas. Other mothers of fallen soldiers, or dads, or friends, or people just fearing they will lose loved ones in Iraq are showing up in Crawford to support Cindy Sheehan. And the camp has a name: Camp Casey, after the son Cindy lost to the Iraqi insurgency.

The thing is, thanks to the bizarre refusal of POTUS to act presidential, preferring instead to hide and obfuscate, there's a growing backlash igniting a fervent anti-war movement where only a fledgling one existed. Camp Caseys are cropping up all over the country, as groups in other cities hold vigils and rallies in honor or Cindy and in memory of Casey.

Of course, talking TV heads on the Fox Network are having a field day sliming the reputation of Cindy Sheehan with talk of her divorce and other family issues to make her look pathetic and unpatriotic.

And the Rovian PR machine has recruited the Swift Boat Women's Auxilliary for Truth with another mother who lost a son in the mid-east to call Cindy unpatriotic.

It reminds me of two bumper stickers I saw this week and one local story.

One bumper sticker said "Support Our Troops, Bring them Home." The other said "Dissent is patriotic."

Has it occurred to anybody else that our current political climate once again denigrates dissenters and calls anti-war activists or their sympathizers unpatriotic? Didn't we learn that lesson more than 30 years ago?

Cindy Sheehan is camped in Crawford *because* she supports our troops and wants to make certain that the cause they are fighting for really is in the best interest of our country and its people. Okay, she disagrees with the President's policies. Does that mean he should disregard her and send his minions to mount a PR campaign to trash her? Come on, people, the least our commander in chief should do is talk to her.

But refusing the recognize dissenters has become our national game plan. It's happening right here in Delaware.

According to *News Journal* columnist Al Mascitti, disagreeing with Pennsylvania Senator Rick Santorum almost landed two local teenagers in jail.

Santorum, you see, is promoting, among other nonsense, the theory that gay marriage will lead to legalized bestiality. What can I say here? How can a single comment, or a paragraph of comments adequately relay my disgust at being so marginalized that Santorum thinks I'd throw over my spouse for a romp in the hay with a goat?

But Santorum the great thinker, held a book signing at a Barnes & Noble in Wilmington last week. He also invited people to chat with him at the signing.

Apparently, two teens wanted to ask Santorum about his views and tell him that they respectfully disagreed with his positions, specifically against women working outside the home, against birth control and oh, yeah, the goat thing. When Santorum's handlers heard there might be two youngsters asking him about his views, he asked security to have them removed—with threats of jail time if they didn't leave. Hello, is this still America where we have freedom of speech? If Santorum is free to publish his cockamamie ideas, aren't readers free to say they disagree??? Santorum doesn't seem to think so.

"These are all honor students," one of the parents said. "I don't know when they passed a law in Delaware that said you can't have a cup of coffee and discuss your opposition to a book."

Al Mascitti said, "They haven't, but give them time." I share his fear. The way we are going, goats in Delaware will have protection from discrimination before gay people. Maybe we should follow Cindy Sheehan's example, pitch a tent at the state house, and ask the Democratic Senate

Leadership to come out and talk to us.

Bet they wouldn't.

Its time to get our heads up out of the sand here at the beach or simply in front of TV reality shows, and pay attention. There's a lot more going on this August than one woman swallowing 35 sausages. ▼

September 2005

We sat on the sofa, fighting to keep our eyes open. 11:02 p.m. It's one thing to doze during *Law and Order*, but for this show we needed to stay uncharacteristically conscious. When the program finally came on, we still didn't know if this was "our" episode or not.

Back in July, we had a whirlwind trip to NYC to be interviewed for the PBS show *In the Life*. If you haven't seen this monthly news show, you should try to find it. Good luck. The show has been running 13 years, but PBS affiliates get to hide it anywhere they want on the schedule, if they run it at all. I can't imagine it coming on in South Dakota. If it does make it to the schedule, it's at 11 pm, midnight or even 3 a.m. when they figure big bigots and their little bigots are sound asleep, revving up for the following day's homophobia. You got it—*In The Life* is about our lives; gay people. It's our news.

But with the emergence of Digital Video Recorders, I never miss an episode.

That's good, because when the producer asked if I wanted to be interviewed on the show, I didn't say "Hey, what?" and sound like a nincompoop from the provinces. The producer had read my book and wanted to include me and my spouse in a series of interviews about coming out. "Can the two of you come up to New York on Friday, if that's not too much trouble?"

A tax-deductible trip to the Big Apple is my kind of trouble.

We raced up the Jersey Turnpike early Friday morning, making it to New York's "trés gay" Chelsea Pines Inn on 14th Street in record time. The proprietor happens to be my high school boyfriend who's trés gay himself. We're still trying to figure out what was in the water on prom night that turned both of us queer.

So we checked in and shopped until the appointed interview hour. Despite being in the city of my culinary fantasies we spurned glorious New York pizza (a completely different food group than Delaware pizza), chocolate egg creams, and a street corner falafel, for fear of blotching our interview clothes. You just know a glob of oozy, gooey cheese would have leapt onto our continental shelves.

So it was with nervous and growling stomachs that we arrived at the Fifth Avenue offices of *In the Life*.

The producer ushered me into the studio first, wired me for sound (got those stomach gurgles?) and leapt right into it.

"How did you tell you parents you were gay? How did they react? Set the scene for us. Do you remember how that made you feel?"

Did I ever. Like it was yesterday, not almost a quarter of a century ago. I remember phoning my father to tell him that Bonnie and I were buying a house together. He begged me not to buy a place "with another girl," insisting "You'll never find a husband that way. What do you want to go and do that for?"

Sweat emerged on my forehead as Bonnie stood across the room, flailing her arms and mouthing "Tell him, dammit, just tell him."

Finally I blurted, "I'm buying the house with Bonnie because, um, we want to spend the rest of our lives together...um, as a couple, uh, if you know what I, um, mean." It wasn't my glibbest moment.

"I...think...I...do," said Dad.

"Well, how do you feel about this news?" I asked, not really wanting to know and wondering why I asked.

His answer, in total, was the phrase "Well...(deep breath) this *IS* 1982."

Then he hollered to my stepmother, "Joan, can you get me a Scotch?" and we continued the conversation.

The producer probed. "How did you and Bonnie meet? What's life like in Rehoboth? Are you proud of your life as a lesbian?"

And she didn't want just the facts, ma'am. She wanted to know how all of it *felt* and what it *meant* to me. For a person used to coughing up words, I got mush-mouthed as she said "delve, delve" like a submarine captain yells "dive, dive."

So I bared my soul for 45 minutes.

When it was Bonnie's turn she told some pretty shocking tales of her own coming out amid 1970s military witch hunts. She recounted her first softball game followed by her first visit to a gay bar and the woman with big blue eyes who made her come out to her 18-year-old self.

We'd spent a combined 90 minutes under the lights for the interview, which was more like a free therapy session.

And when it was over, we grabbed a corned beef sandwich, stopped in for a drink at the Stonewall Inn and headed off to a night of wine, women and song.

So two months later, we're sitting in front of the TV at 11 o'clock at night, fighting to stay conscious for our 15 minutes of fame. And then we saw it. My face. My very round face, taking up most of the 27 inch TV screen and looking, well, puffy. The old tale that TV adds ten pounds is true. It added it all in my jowls. I looked like Gloria Swanson getting ready for her close-up but with slightly less eyeliner.

But wait. I was talking. There it was, the recounting of the phone call with Dad, all magnificent 45 seconds of it. Blip, the camera blacked out and came up on Bonnie, bigger than life and talking about the woman with the blue, blue eyes. She looked less jowly than I did, but I think the ten pounds were in her eyebrows. By the time I blinked we were onto a PBS fundraising pitch.

That was it? An hour and a half of true confessions in 90 seconds? Fifteen minutes of fame readjusted for inflation?

We glimpsed ourselves again when the program came back on, little head shots in a film strip type graphic on the screen. I was right next to a picture of Kate Clinton, the episode's host. She must be very thin, because she did not look at all puffy.

Well, the trip to NY had been herds of fun we agreed. Then we crashed for the night.

The next day the phone rang.

"We saw you on TV," said my stepmother Joan, "you looked wonderful. And I remember that phone call you talked about."

"I didn't really ask for a Scotch, did I?" asked my father.

"Yes, actually you did."

"And we told all our friends to watch," said Joan, "And they did. I've gotten several calls saying 'We saw Fay on television last night.' Everyone has been so complimentary."

Well, one thing is certain. Fame may be fleeting but a heck of a lot of attitudes have changed for the better since 1982. Bonnie and I know we have been very lucky to be able to experience so much more unqualified acceptance and so much less dispiriting discrimination than our friends Anyda and Muriel, those grand Rehoboth icons, did when they were in their heyday. We can only imagine what valuable contributions, besides the Sarah Aldridge novels, Anyda and Muriel could have made in the struggle for gay equality if they had been able to be open about their incredible journey and their glorious same sex marriage.

Mr. DeMille, we're *all* ready for our close-ups now.▼

September 2005

With the destruction of New Orleans by Hurricane Katrina playing on TV or in my head 24 hours a day, it's impossible to think of a light-hearted thing to say.

I've been picturing our gulf coast sister resorts, families in crisis, folks who lost everything and pets left behind.

I hope my favorite gay bar on Bourbon Street in New Orleans, Café Lafitte in Exile, is still there. Just as I hope its regulars, who loved to sip that now eerily-named New Orleans drink, The Hurricane, got out safely, with places to stay and means to recover their lives.

Disasters make me think about connections and people. About counting my blessings.

And one of those blessings was a friend who rescued me. She didn't swoop down in a helicopter and pluck me off a rooftop amid swiftly rising water, but she might as well have.

I showed up at age 30, on the doorstep of this liberal, socially conscious, recently widowed, heterosexual friend in her mid-fifties. I stood there with two cat-carriers (inhabited), the clothes on my back and the need for a place to reinvent myself.

She invited me to make a nest in a downstairs apartment in her Maryland home, and for four years Mary Jane and I had a grand time as she tried to teach me to cook, taught me to drink booze without mixers, proved absolutely non-judgmental in a hostile and homophobic world, and gave me the courage and good-natured push to come out of the closet.

In addition, she had Schnauzers. She gets alternating credit and blame for my Schnauzer fixation. My first dog, Max, was a birthday gift from her. Bonnie called him the gift that kept on giving. Sometimes she meant love, sometimes other things.

Actually, Mary Jane was pretty much responsible for

Bonnie, too.

It was a windy March night in 1982 when Mary Jane would rather have had me stay home to share linguini, clam sauce and *Cagney & Lacey*, but she urged me to go out to a dance "and meet somebody for heaven's sake."

I did. But the rest may not have been history, because, as months went by, as much as I adored Bonnie, I was plagued with guilt just thinking about telling Mary Jane I was moving out. I was certain I couldn't do it.

A short time later Mary Jane picked a terribly uncharacteristic fight with me over Margarita glasses left sticky, which quickly escalated to, "I think you better consider getting a place of your own." I never asked and she never confessed, but we both knew she picked that fight so I'd be able to leave.

Bonnie and I stayed close to Mary Jane all these years, until she was frail, battered by disease (although still enjoying booze without mixers) and ready to go. She passed away at age 81 two weeks before Hurricane Katrina and took with her a large chunk of my heart.

But just as the subsequent New Orleans disaster sharpened my grief for her passing, it also urged attention to the important stuff.

Despite droning Katrina coverage, my rage at the inept and insensitive bureaucratic emergency response, and my sadness at losing my friend Mary Jane, I noticed the sun did shine in Rehoboth and we did have a Pride Festival on Sept.10 at our state park.

There, as I sat in my beach chair, hawking books, Bonnie shilling for me, our friend Marge arrived.

Marge is memorable. She had been Bonnie's friend since 1968 military days (and you thought there were no gays in the military!). She is a back-to-the-land militant feminist, lesbian separatist; cowboy-hat and Southwestern jewelry-wearing, outspoken gem of a dyke. When we met we had nothing in common except Bonnie.

One day in the early 80s she showed up in our redneck

Maryland town wearing a t-shirt with a drawing of, forgive me, hairy labia on it. Showing up in it at my house was shocking enough, but she wanted to go to the local diner wearing it. She reluctantly agreed to change when she saw me starting to hyperventilate.

But I remember her loudly proclaiming herself a "militant lesbian feminist" several times during dinner, to the total disgust of nuclear families at neighboring tables. Barely uncloseted, with still-smoldering internal homophobia, I was appalled. Damn, I'd like to go back to that silly community now and shout, "We're queer! I'm here, Get a life."

It's a funny thing about Marge. Bonnie and I sometimes went years without seeing her and then we'd run into her, by chance, at a D.C. March on Washington, amid 250,000 people. It happened in 1987 and then again in 1993 in the midst of a million people. And this was before cell phones made meeting up a breeze.

Sometimes Marge would pass through town, call and we'd have a meal together—and then we wouldn't see her again for years. But there was always a special connection.

This time Marge found the surprise link. Several weeks before our Pride event she was deep in the woods at a lesbian retreat, dancing nekked and listening to women's music, when she went back to her cabin to read for a while. She sat on her cabin steps. A friend sat nearby, book in hand as well.

She heard her friend chuckle.

"Whatcha reading?" Marge asked.

Her friend passed her the book.

Marge stared at the cover and whooped, "Oh my gawddess I know this gal!" She flipped through the pages, shaking her head and exclaiming, "I'm stunned, it's about Fay and Bonnie-girl. Oh my gaaawwwwddess."

So we got an e-mail asking about the book, telling us she was heading our way to attend the Nanticoke Indian Pow-Wow held every year near here, and arranging to meet at Pride.

At the festival we pow-wowed too, catching up and re-connecting. Marge was off to Arizona, to (can you guess?) an all-lesbian retirement community.

We sat and laughed. The sun shone. Couples, troupes, singles, dual mommies with strollers, people we knew and people we didn't listened to music, shopped the vendors, made new connections and celebrated existing ones.

I am more determined than ever to celebrate those connections, cherish our friendships, and, as Suede sang here a few weeks ago, see the rose petals in life, not the thorns.

I had finished this column, having talked about connections until I was blue in the face, and was preparing to hit the "send" button to submit it to *Letters*, when an e-mail popped up.

"Hello you two wonderful womyn. It was so great visiting with you all at your pride event. It was the highlight of my trip. I absolutely love the connections we all make, and it's especially great to have them for many, many years...may the fun continue. You're always welcome to bask in the beauty of my new home in Arizona. Sleep well and love to you both. Marge."

Her echo of the connection theme proved a teeny bit spooky. But divine.

So I'm retooling the end of this column and as soon as I send it, I'm going to lift a Martini in memory of my rescuer Mary Jane, consider having some tofu in honor of Marge (it's the thought that counts, right?) and look up the recipe for an official New Orleans Hurricane.

Here's to recovery down South, precious friends, Gay Pride and Vodka without tonic. ▼

October 2005

I intended to write a fluffy column this time. Following weeks of flood coverage, with Anderson Cooper interviewing anybody wearing waders, I felt we needed a break.

But that was before I read about the Vatican's new edict on gay priests. While I know little about the Catholic hierarchy I do know something about gay people. And the former has just pissed off one of the latter.

To be specific, if the Church does this dreadful discriminatory thing, seminaries nationwide will soon post "For Rent" signs. Ban gay guys from giving compassionate assistance to congregations and who'll be left in the profession, Nascar Dads?

It would be like banning lesbians from the military for goodness sake. Oh, right, our government thinks it does that.

But this new Salem-style witch hunt is so wrong-headed, so totally bass ackwards, it's delusional. You mean the Vatican just found out that a portion of the flock is queer? Give me a break.

Barring gay seminarians will make gay priests who have been serving admirably feel appallingly betrayed. Why stick with a fraternity that would blackball you from pledging? It's the reverse of Groucho's famous line that he'd never belong to a club that would have somebody like him for a member.

Let's face it. Young people questioning their sexuality haven't had it easy. Rather than crumble under pressure to conform, lots of gay people escaped to the priesthood, the nunnery, the military (mostly for the girls) or, God love it, musical theatre (mostly for the boys).

By the time gay people figured out why they felt "different" they were already enmeshed in the clergy, the infantry or dinner theatre.

Presumably, the troops and troupes had a little more freedom to express their newly uncloseted orientation. Not so with the priesthood. A vow is a vow.

Or is it? I'll never forget Father Frank putting the moves on a friend of mine after officiating at her sister's wedding. The affair lasted several years. There are gay priests who lead double lives, too. The bottom line is that a vow of celibacy is tough for anybody. I'll bet the strays are equally straight and gay.

But what, pray tell, about pedophiles? Everybody but bigots knows that gay people and pedophiles are not synonymous; both hets and homos can suffer from the illness of pedophilia.

But in a shameful, scandalous history, the church has refused to recognize the rampant pedophilia in its ranks. In fact they colluded with the abusers by playing Sick Priest Hopscotch—spiriting pedophiles out of towns before they could be tarred and feathered and then unleashing the beasts on other unsuspecting communities.

In this whole sorry mess, the priestly pedophiles have been shuttled around like astronauts, sheltered from criminal and civil prosecution. Want to travel? Be a pedophile priest.

But has the Vatican announced a rooting out of this problem? Nooo. They're protecting the damn pedophiles by scapegoating gay folks.

I'm mad and concerned. Exactly how will the authorities screen for homosexuals? A questionnaire?

"Did Stephen Sondheim write *Company* or *Mama Mia*?

"Would you rather wear Prada or Keds?"

"Who played Vickie Lester opposite James Mason in *A Star is Born*?"

And if they do ban homosexuals from the priesthood, when the dust settles the Church will be made up of a few compassionate and truly religious heterosexual men, a bunch of offended gay priests, and a trove of pedophiles taking refuge in the church because it's a great place to meet kids—or more likely, men whose Church-ordered repressed sexuality, homo or hetero, has caused them to behave very, very badly indeed.

Meanwhile, gays are barred from serving. The poster

priest for this debate should be The Rev. Mychal F. Judge, the New York City Fire Department chaplain who died in the 9/11 rubble.

Judge was out to his friends as a celibate gay man, admitting his orientation but keeping his vows. This man gave his life to assist the New York firefighters trapped in the towers. According to *The New York Times*, this man had a 40-year career, ministering to firefighters, their grieving widows, AIDS patients, homeless people, Flight 800 victims' families, and countless others. He was, and still is, one of the most beloved Roman Catholic priests in New York—in fact, there is a movement to canonize him.

Under the Vatican's new rules, this man would not have been allowed to be ordained.

In this shocking burst of wrong-headed bigotry, the Church is blaming homosexuals for its own inability to call a pedophile a pedophile.

Someday, and I hope sooner than later, our country will wake up, follow the lead of more progressive nations and see that homosexual Americans, in the religious or secular life, want a "Gay Agenda" that looks suspiciously like the aspirations of The Constitution of the United States.

And, like previously racist politicians or vocal anti-Semites, the Catholic Church is going to be very embarrassed. Very.

Let my people come...to any calling they choose. ▼

October 2005

Sitting in the movie theatre with a newspaper on my head, uncooked rice-a-roni dripping from my hair and people pumping water from super-soakers into the back of my neck, I doubted whether my parents ever behaved this way on a Saturday night in their fifties. Or The 50s for that matter.

Somehow I cannot picture them heaving minute rice, tossing toilet paper (Great Scott!) and screaming "Asshole!" and "Slut!" at a movie screen. No, the *Rocky Horror Picture Show* is my generation's schtik, and we've been having our way with it for more than a quarter of a century.

In celebration of another anniversary of what is inarguably the worst movie musical of all time (okay, musical comedy queens, except perhaps for Lucille Ball defaming *Mame*), when Halloween comes around, so does *Rocky Horror*.

For readers who are *Rocky Horror* virgins, having wondered what the fuss has been at midnight shows since the 70s, here's the scoop. This horror movie spoof starred a young, handsome Barry Bostwick and an even younger, gorgeous Susan Sarandon, as hopelessly boring newlyweds who stumble into the castle of a Transylvanian transvestite (Tim Curry), a man with an equal-opportunity libido.

Suffice it to say that the film was so awful moviegoers started talking back and throwing things at the screen. Pretty soon it became a cult thing, with a script of sorts and specific props for audience participation. It's a stunning example of mankind's ingenuity in the face of artistic failure.

And the damn thing is still playing nightly all over the country. Theaters full of purported adults everywhere are doing Time Warp choreography and screaming "Slut!" as scantily clad Sarandon gets turned to into plaster a statute. Dead Woman Walking.

And if you think Tim Curry in fishnet stockings and a black leather corset is outrageous, you should see how some of the audience members show up.

On this particular night I passed on the chance to run around in a Sarandon-like slip or dripping in ghoulish make-up and blood-red lips. Others were not so timid. Some of the most genteel people in town showed up in scandalous garb, mimicking their favorite characters.

While I didn't dress, I prepared.

Yesterday, I checked out the more than 40 *Rocky Horror* sites on the internet—official and unofficial audience participation scripts, on-line memorabilia shops, fan club pages and some really disgusting suggestions for activities to engage in while the movie is showing. I will spare you.

While *Rocky Horror* is a Halloween staple, Rehoboth has also been the scene of a well-attended *Sound of Music* sing-a-long, costumes encouraged. Nuns, novices and bitchy baronesses came out of the woodwork. I'll never think of solving a problem like Maria the same way again.

While Halloween may be the ultimate gay holiday, Labor Day's no slouch. We have a Drag volleyball match every year with thousands of people swarming to Rehoboth's Poodle Beach to watch the delicious spectacle. Oddly, it's damn good volleyball, too.

Two teams of burley guys (and one brave drag king this year) take to the court in meticulously planned drag get-up, complete with team musical numbers and choreography. The cool thing is that these queens can really play the game. They may be amateur drags (and therein lies the fun) but they certainly can spike and serve.

Over the years we've had many team themes to admire. From a troop consisting entirely of Dorothys from Oz to one sporting the many incarnations of Madonna; a crew of Trashy Barbies to Famous Royalty, and most memorably Broadway divas vs. the Bridal Party from Hell with a rainbow of bridesmaid gowns. Close your eyes and picture Evita spiking the ball to the Mother of the Bride who, in turn, pounds the ball back to Liza Minelli. It's a volley hard to forget.

Even our community center fundraising occasionally requires local adults to behave like our inner children. Every year, for our huge silent and live auction, hundreds of volunteers devote hours and hours and then more hours turning the staid Rehoboth Convention Center into a hot circuit party dance club. It's amazing what some fabric and $30,000 worth of lighting can do.

The non-artistic among us spend weeks picking up auction donations and logging, labeling, displaying, counting, accounting, gluing, framing and more.

The few hours I spend assisting is nothing compared to the sacrifice made by so many. But I often help out when the varsity squad labeling their four hundredth item suffers temporary writer's block.

Last year, faced with a donated bust of the poet Milton, the chief writer said, "I can't use stunning, exquisite, lovely or fabulous one more time. Quick, get me a superlative."

Called in from the bullsh*t pen, I too, got a brain cramp after two dozen promotional come-ons. I got to a fruit and nut gift basket and described it as "perfect for the fruits and nuts at your next party." They replaced me.

By the way, the auction and dance cleared over $160,000 for the community, thanks to all those volunteers and generous attendees.

But far and away, my favorite childish event is the annual Follies. It began many years ago, during the worst of the plague, with backyard drag. Various share houses fielded an act for a once-a-summer bash. What followed was a themed night of drinking, dancing and amateur drag, with big bucks raised for our local AIDS charity. If the police eventually arrived, the party was deemed a success.

These days, the party has come out of the neighborhoods and into the Rehoboth Beach Convention Center. The police still come, but only to watch and cheer. The diversity of the audience astounds us.

The really wonderful part is that lesbians have crashed the party—not, as you might suspect, as typical drag kings. No, some of us set out to decry the age-old myth that lesbians have no sense of humor. ("How many lesbians does it take to change a light bulb? That's not funny.")

In 2002 we put together a troupe making wicked fun of ourselves. Wearing overalls and painter's pants, lugging hefty power tools, our all-girl entry was sandwiched among a dozen boy groups doing campy lip synch drag and lewd skits. We actually sang original lyrics to "Nothing Like a Dame." The crowd thought we were a hoot and the judges awarded us the coveted Bronze Barbie for Third Place. But the best part is that the guys thought we were funny.

The next year we raised the bar by adding clumsy chore-ography and exceedingly sturdy scenery. Where the boys had flowing art deco backdrops, our stuff was built like a brick out-house. In fact, it *was* an outhouse.

The male contestants pranced around in gorgeous, gaudy gowns while we womenfolk donned cowboy boots and chaps for a skit about a lesbian old-age home on the range. We called it *Oklahomo*.

That year we snagged Miss Silver Barbie.

By the third year, we figured there was only one way to win the thing. We knew it was risky, but a girl's gotta do what a girl's gotta do. To compete we had to do boy drag. We conspired to do the *Victor/Victoria* thing and be girls dressing like boys dressing like girls.

Our drag alter-egos were charmers like Miss Rhoda Kill (dead pelts hanging from her gown), Miss Lotta Chutzpah (an enormous Menorah for a tiara) and Miss Anita Shave (hideous hairy harpie). God knows this was not lesbian chic. These par-ticular lipstick lesbians were more Sonny than Cher, more Charles Brolin than Babs.

With oversize netting tutus, we all looked like giant kitchen scrubbies.

For the first part of our skit our sturdy scenery formed a nightclub called *La Cage Aux Faux* as we scampered around in high drag, singing (what else) *I Enjoy Being a Girl*. During the blackout after the last note of the song, we stripped to jeans, tees and cordless drills, changed the set to say La Cage Aux Lowes, and sang (what else) *I Am What I Am*.

We took the Gold Barbie, and, like any sensible group, Rolling Stones not withstanding, we retired at the top of our game.

Which brings me back to *Rocky Horror* and tossing toasted croutons at the cue "Let's have a toast", twirling noisemakers and shouting "Slut!" at that perky, jail bait, Susan Sarandon. With so much rice in my brassiere, a hot flash could cook dinner for two.

We dykes may be getting older, but, thank god, we'll never mature.▼

November 2005

LETTERS FROM CAMP REHOBOTH
AIN'T NO SUN UP IN THE SKY

The weather graphic showed seven little clouds, spewing rain. "Chance of rain 80% for the next week." "An historic convergence of storms." Grab your galoshes and welcome to P-Town's Women's Week 2005.

Bonnie and I packed ourselves, rain gear and dogs for a road trip. A&M Books had sent me on a press junket! Bonnie and I would have gladly paid our way for the privilege, but the ever-generous Muriel insisted on slipping Bonnie a check for expenses.

I was due in Provincetown, Massachusetts for a book signing and reading on Friday, Oct. 14, but we headed up on Tuesday to experience the wonders of this legendary P-town extravaganza.

It was raining cats and dogs, which if you think about it, is appropriate for a week with lesbians traveling with their pets. With howling winds and roiling surf (not even the butchest dykes dared to whale watch), the week still rocked.

No less than nine comediennes performed all over town, most with a couple of shows a day and one funnier than the next. We laughed so hard we ran out of panties.

Three shows ran simultaneously at the Crown & Anchor, and four other venues offered comics along with blues, jazz, folk and any other kind of music you could want.

In between deluges, it was raining (wo)men behind Town Hall. Two teams of scary-looking gals played touch football, refereed by Kate Clinton. The game involved lots of fumbling and falling into weather-induced mud, plus requisite tackling, grunting and cheering.

But that was nothing compared to the Good Old Fashioned Lesbian Revival inside Town Hall. Kate, Cris Williamson, comics Vicki Shaw, Suzanne Westenhoefer and Judy Gold stood

178

together on stage, testifyin' about coming out, kickin' butt and fightin' for equal rights. Naturally the revival included a signer and Indian drum corps. I felt the power. I was healed.

Rubbing elbows with thousands of lesbians in bars and restaurants is a dream come true anytime, but when you're eating lobster, and clam rolls, it's to die for—but not without guilt.

Our luck, my book tour took us to P-Town on the holiest Jewish holiday of the year, the Day of Atonement, when my tribe is supposed to fast all day. Strike me dead. I broke the fast right out of the sack with freshly made Portuguese rolls for breakfast. By lunchtime I disgracefully chowed down on a lobster roll, a big religious gaff, requiring extra atonement in some circles. I'll be atoning until Joan Rivers looks her age.

Forgive me though—it was all worth it. So was the evening's wet t-shirt contest. I know, I'm supposed to be past trivial pursuits like ogling. But how could we turn away from firm young things jiggling in the bar's inflatable swimming pool? Help me out here, is this kind of thing degrading to women when womyn run the contests? Just asking.

We did get some real culture and laughs at a play at the Provincetown Playhouse about a lesbian adopting a baby and a younger sister transitioning into a younger brother.

The audience was as entertaining as the play. It included a cornucopia of women who might have been men, or the other way around, oldsters, youngsters, boomers, pierced eyebrows, mullets, shaved heads, lipstick lezzies, gals with goatees—a profusion of dykedom and the people who love them.

The next day we saw a one-woman show about journalist Lorena Hickock, who lived in the White House with her "special friend" Eleanor Roosevelt. In this meticulously researched show, we shared the charming and sometimes sad tale of a clandestine love story that smoldered despite politics, war and impossible circumstances. Now *that's* dyke drama.

As for the book business, I had a blast. The reading took place on stage at the Crown & Anchor, and lots of women showed up at 9 a.m. on a bleak, rainy morning to hear well-

known authors like Karin Kallmaker, Radclyffe and Ellen Hart—
and unknown author, me.

I have to admit, it was exhilarating to read one of my
columns out loud and hear people laughing about life in
Rehoboth. And I was pleased by the number of women who
showed up later at the friendly Now Voyager Book Shop, to
chat with me and buy my book.

Any illusions of grandeur were easily quashed when later
in the day I found myself walking, in a squall, dogs in front, me
in back carrying their poop in a plastic bag. Reality check.

Meanwhile when the rain held up for an afternoon, we
walked the wet beach, explored the pier, visited that enormous
P-Town monument and joined a zillion other lesbians walking
their canine companions up and down Commercial Street. Oh
how I'd love to see the same kind of women's week parade in
Rehoboth. And there's no reason we can't make it happen.

In fact, Rehoboth mirrors P-Town in a lot of great ways—
gay friendly small town beach resort, fabulous restaurants,
adorable B&B's, an artist's haven, etc.

Unfortunately, we share some not-so-good things as well:
quaint properties being bulldozed while condos and town-
houses multiply like rabbits; skyrocketing housing prices, and
both locals and young visitors being priced out. Oh, and P-
Town's biggest dance club, the historic Boatslip has been sold
for, what else, condos. With our Renegade club gone we are
twin cities, separated at birth.

Here in Rehoboth we should be able to ramp up our fes-
tivities and roll out an even bigger welcome mat than we do
now. I'm envisioning our Spring Women's Weekend growing
into a nationally known party, bringing women, their pets, and
their cash to Rehoboth each Spring.

We'd love to see you visit! You'll probably find me walking
the boardwalk, Moxie & Paddy in front, me at the rear, holding
a little plastic bag. To them I'm one of the pack, not an author
with a book at #341,853 on Amazon.com. ▼

December 2005

It was Christmas morning and Bonnie and I headed over to Laurel Street for breakfast. Bonnie promised to make pancakes and Muriel would insist, once again, that I try her cheesy grits (no really, they were actually cheddar grits).

But the minute we arrived we knew something was wrong. Anyda, who is usually up giving orders to the roosters, was still in the bedroom. She started to make her way down the hall but had to lean on the doorway to the dining room on her way. Bonnie helped her to a chair.

"What's the matter?"

Muriel piped up. "She had a terrible night. I don't know what's wrong."

"Are you sick?" I asked. "What can we do for you?"

Anyda just stared blankly ahead, not answering.

"Do you want us to take you to the hospital," Bonnie quietly asked. There was a too long pause.

"Maybe you'd better," Anyda whispered in Bonnie's ear. "But let's have breakfast first. I don't want to ruin Muriel's holiday." Oh so typical.

We hurriedly prepared pancakes, three of us ate a little, Anyda had only a mouthful or two. Then we told Muriel we were taking Anyda to the hospital.

We called a friend to stay with Muriel, helped Anyda into the car, sped to the emergency room and called ahead for a wheelchair to get Anyda into building.

There were tests, scans, questions, x-rays, moments of quiet, a lot of hand-holding. We knew that Anyda had been having stomach trouble for a while, easily attributable to age. She had also been hospitalized for a bleeding ulcer two months before, but that had cleared up nicely. Anyda continued to complain of weakness though, and was aggravated she wasn't getting her strength back. She was furious about it. But we figured that a bleeding ulcer can take a lot out of anybody, much less someone of 94.

By afternoon, the emergency room doctor came into Anyda's cubicle and pulled the curtain around the three of us.

To his credit, he spoke directly to Anyda instead of to us. It was probably Anyda's commanding personality that prevented her from being treated as an invisible old lady. All the same, I knew at that moment how terribly frail and tired she was. And a little pissed off, although she would never put it that way.

"We have found a mass in your abdomen. We need to see if it's cancer and then decide on a treatment plan."

Startled, Anyda addressed the doctor very slowly and very clearly. "There will be no treatment. I am almost 95 years old. Why would I have treatment?"

The doctor had no answer. Anyda nodded. Case closed. Eventually she was admitted to the hospital and transferred to a room upstairs. Other friends arrived to hold the fort and we returned to Laurel Street to get Muriel and bring her to be with Anyda.

Ever concerned for others, Anyda insisted, vehemently, that we leave the hospital and carry on with our regular holiday plans—Christmas dinner in our neighborhood with a large group of friends. Anyda announced she'd be fine with Muriel by her side.

By this time, other family-like friends had arrived and promised to take Muriel back home when she was ready. From what I understand, the pair spent about an hour together, mostly just holding hands before Muriel tired and needed to return to Laurel Street.

The situation reminded everyone of a time several years before when Muriel was hospitalized with heart trouble. Most people, including the doctors, thought she wouldn't be coming home. The entire time she was hospitalized, and for weeks following, while Muriel was miraculously improving in a convalescent home, Anyda stayed by her side day and night, sleeping in a chair in her room, or in a stray empty bed.

When Bonnie was hospitalized several years ago, I tried to stay day and night and couldn't do it. No matter how much I wanted to do so, it was too exhausting.

It wasn't too exhausting for elderly, iron-willed Anyda.

And even now, in her mid-nineties she was no shrinking violet. After tests confirmed the diagnosis, she demanded she be checked out of the hospital, called Betsy to come get her and headed home. Arrangements were made.

Hospice staff set up a bed in the living room. Friends came and went. Cocktail hour went on as always. For many hours during each day, Muriel would sit in her wheel chair, by the hospital bed. Anyda kept insisting that the doctors were wrong. She was furious about being confined and took to telling visitors that they should help her get up and dressed—and if they couldn't do that, they might as well just go home.

Although she was absolutely furious at her deteriorating condition, she continued to rule the roost, giving orders to hospice staff, requesting not just tea, but Prince of Wales tea, discussing headlines in the *Washington Post* (Oooh, that horrible Rumsfeld creature!) and demanding her nightly 5 p.m. cocktail.

The parade of visitors spoke to Anyda and Muriel's vast circle of friends. And at cocktail hour Anyda would remind me not to make Muriel's drink too strong. And Muriel would hold the glass up to the light and complain that the drink looked awfully pale.

Charlie bartended; Betsy did errands. They both spent a great deal of time by Anyda's bedside and with Muriel, who sat in her recliner, mostly lost in thought, in the sunroom. Charlie cooked some of the ladies' favorite things; Bonnie continued to make Muriel smile a little, and then went about changing the cat litter, feeding the critters and doing other familiar chores. We circled the wagons. Charlie and Betsy held the fort like heroes. Bonnie was at the house as much as she could be. I spent time in the living room, reading letters, old and new to Anyda, talking about book projects and keeping that brilliant mind engaged. One afternoon she said to me, "You know, you are the future of A&M Books."

I knew. I was honored. I didn't want it just yet.

"You know the vision, you must remember the vision."

I knew, I would.

New Years' Eve came and went. We put up a good front, toasting to 2006, but knew Anyda probably wouldn't see much of it.

One day, as Anyda napped, Muriel, Bonnie, and I argued the merits of Dewars versus Johnny Walker. Although Anyda had been spending most of her time asleep and had not been engaged in our conversations for the past day or two, as we continued the comparison, she raised her head, looked at us with authority and announced "the virtue of Johnny Walker is that it can be found all over the globe." We drank to that.

Muriel retreated into silence, reading a little, eating very little, taking her pills, and reluctantly scooting, in her wheelchair, off to the bedroom at night.

Charlie, Betsy and Bonnie took turns staying overnight so there was a family face by the bed in addition to the hired caregiver. The trio helped bathe Anyda, give her pain medication, and get her anything she requested. After a few days, it wasn't much more than tea. Then, not even that. ▼

January 2006

After Anyda passed away, I sat down to write her obituary, attempting to convey an incredible 94 years in less than 500 words.

ANYDA MARCHANT
ATTORNEY, NOVELIST, PUBLISHER
1911-2006

Anyda Marchant, 94, retired attorney, novelist, and publisher died January 11 at her home in Rehoboth Beach, DE.

Ms. Marchant was born in Rio de Janeiro, Brazil, moving with her family to Washington, DC at age six. After earning her undergraduate degree, followed in 1933, by her law degree from the National University of Washington, DC (now George Washington University), she was admitted to practice in Virginia and DC, and before the U.S. Court of Claims and the U. S. Supreme Court. As a law student, she served for a year as assistant to women's rights pioneer Alice Paul, who was then doing research for an Equal Rights Amendment.

In 1940, she was appointed assistant in the Law Library of Congress in the Latin American Law section. She returned to Rio to work and then did a brief stint as a translator at the 1948 Pan American Union conference in Bogotá, Columbia. From there she went to work at a New York law firm, and then back in Washington as one of the first female attorneys for the law firm now known as Covington and Burling. After this, she was briefly with the Bureau of Domestic and Foreign Commerce of the U.S. Department of Commerce, and with a private practice representing claimants before the U. S. Court of Claims for compensation arising from military service in the Philippines during the Japanese invasion. She then moved to the legal department of the World Bank. She served the World Bank for

18 years until retiring in 1972.

That same year, Marchant and her life partner Muriel Crawford founded the Naiad Press as a vehicle for publishing Marchant's first novel, *The Latecomer*, written under the pen name Sarah Aldridge. From there, Naiad became an avenue for the publication of other feminist and lesbian literature. In 1974 Naiad Press was formally incorporated in Delaware when Marchant and Crawford added Barbara Greer and Donna McBride as shareholders. Marchant served as Naiad president from its inception until the mid-1990's. Naiad published eleven Sarah Aldridge novels and grew to be a powerhouse in feminist publishing. In 1995 Marchant and Crawford withdrew from Naiad and began their own publishing company, A&M Books in their hometown of Rehoboth Beach. A&M published the last three Sarah Aldridge novels along with the book *As I Lay Frying, a Rehoboth Beach Memoir* by author Fay Jacobs. Passionate about supporting feminist writers, Marchant continued her publishing and mentoring activities until very recently, highlighted by A&M's October 2005 release of the novel *Celebrating Hotchclaw* by feminist literary icon Ann Allen Shockley.

Marchant is survived by Crawford, her partner of 57 years, as well as a large circle of loving friends.

An obituary or other comments about Anyda's passing appeared in The Washington Post, The Advocate, *Chicago's* Windy City Times, The Washington Blade, *and many more mainstream and gay and lesbian papers, magazines and online newsletters, plus many publishing industry publications. And of course, our local Rehoboth area newspapers, noting the loss of a local legend.*

Losing Anyda broke my heart.

But it was an honor to speak at her memorial service.

I met Anyda when she was 84 years young. For a decade she's been my friend, mentor, publisher and the most demanding boss I've ever had. I wish I had had more time.

Anyda was born in 1911 and I can only begin to imagine the events, the innovations and the history she experienced in 94 brilliant years.

To put it in perspective, one day Anyda and I sat debating the relative power of First Lady Hillary Clinton vs. first lady Nancy Reagan. "Well," said Anyda, "neither could hold a candle to Florence Harding." I had to look it up—Florence was First Lady in 1921.

Anyda was the feminist's feminist. She worked for Women's rights pioneer Alice Paul, researching the very possibility of an Equal Rights Amendment—in 1932.

During World War II, Anyda's supervisor at the Library of Congress was drafted and she was promoted to his job. At war's end, she dutifully stepped aside so he could return to his position—but then, on principle, left the Library rather than take a lesser job—in 1945.

When Anyda was hired as one of the first female attorneys at a prestigious law firm, she met Muriel Crawford—beginning 57 years of devotion to each other. And this was 1948—before any public respect for, or even acknowledgement of same sex relationships. Theirs was a courageous, willful and against many odds, joyous path.

Through the years the couple shared adventures around the globe for Anyda's job with the World Bank. They began spending time in Rehoboth Beach, buying their first home here almost a half century ago. Anyda and Muriel hosted Delaware's first-ever National Organization of Women meeting. Anyda loved describing the women arriving at the house, as neighbors lurked, one actually hiding behind a tree, to see which Rehoboth females had the courage to show up. Rehoboth had its consciousness raised.

In 1972, Anyda retired, wrote novels and, with Muriel, founded Naiad Press—which became the most successful independent feminist publisher in the United States and the world.

Anyda wrote; Muriel transcribed. They opened their home and big front porch for cocktails and conversation with a diverse crowd of neighbors, writers, musicians, clergy, young, old, gay, straight, locals, visitors, democrats, and even Republicans.

In 1995, Anyda and Muriel started A&M Books of Rehoboth. Anyda's 14th novel was published in 2003 when the novelist was 92. For her next project, in 2004, she published the works of a little known Rehoboth columnist. I was honored. But perhaps one of Anyda's proudest professional moments, came with the publication of a new novel by legendary feminist author Ann Allen Shockley—just this past October. In my later years, I hope I can be half as giddy with glee as Anyda was the day the new books arrived from the printer.

The remnants of 2005 and the first 11 days of 2006 were tough. She was home in a hospital bed in the living room, but she insisted it be tilted at the perfect angle so she could see Muriel in her chair in the back sunroom and call "Yoohoo, Sweetie" and wave.

Two days before the end, I got the opportunity to read a letter to Anyda from a woman named Carol Seajay—former editor of the *Feminist Bookstore News* and a superstar in the publishing industry. In part, the letter read *"Anyda, it was your vision of a possible world in your first lesbian novel and your vision that we could have such books, and your vision and skills that launched our first, grand lesbian publishing house—and published books that have gone out all over the world, changed countless women's lives, giving hope and opening doors. Yours was an awesome body of work and I hope you are fiercely proud of it all."*

She was. And everyone was proud of her. And just this week—January 2006 I received an e-mail from two young women from Utah, telling me of their isolation there and asking if the Sarah Aldridge books were still available. Thanks Anyda, from them and from me. ▼

January 2006

Please don't think badly of me for the following story. It's one of those blasphemous yarns, skirting, okay, plunging face forward into the mush of questionable taste. But it happened. And when polled, even my rabbi thought it was okay to share it. So here goes.

Over the past two weeks I attended two memorial services, a week apart. One for an acquaintance and the other for Anyda.

Prior to the services, following two weeks of terrible sadness and loss, I was sitting at this very computer, writing a eulogy for the service a week hence. I turned to the Internet to check a historical fact and was stunned by AOL's headline: "Oscar Winner Shelley Winters Dead at 85."

I stared at the screen, not knowing whether, as they say, to poop or go blind. "Alrighty!" I yelped, followed by a crushing sense of doom.

It's like this. A while ago, some immortal-feeling twenty-somethings started a unique combination of gambling and drinking called The Dead Pool. Clusters of young people get together and select names of elderly celebrities. Each player antes up a set amount for the jackpot and when a celeb falls off their perch the person holding the winning name, if you can call this winning, collects.

I know, it's a ghoul pool. Perfectly horrid.

On the other hand, in a world filled with terrorists winning elections, our own government spying on us, hateful discrimination and Bird Flu panic there's never enough reason to celebrate, so why not take advantage of every opportunity?

Borrowing from this 20-something fad, our group of old-somethings launched the Rainbow Dead Pool Society. Some energetic New Jersey gals put it together and soon invited a slew of us to participate. In our version, we pick names, ante up, then when there's a loss, host a party to send off the dearly departed. Costumes are encouraged. We try to make it a great celebration, respectful in every way. Unless of course, too many Bloody Marys are involved and then you never know to what sacrilegious depths we will sink.

The gang has held a royal send off for Prince Rainier, went ape at a party for Fay Wray, and held a simply delicious soiree for Julia Child, among others.

Yep, you're getting it. After paying my dues for a while now I finally, oh, forgive me, hit the jackpot with Shelley Winters.

And that meant, in addition to receiving the funds, I'd have to use said money to throw an immediate "memorial service" for Shelley—because we had to rush to pay, along with our respects, our damn dues in case another AARP headliner suddenly kicked the bucket. The phrase "unfortunate timing" doesn't even begin to cover it. I was hearing strains of "There's Got to Be a Morning After," from *The Poseidon Adventure* ringing in my ears. Pun intended, I was sunk.

Gingerly, I shared the absurd news of our "good fortune" with my spouse. She was appalled—both by the untimely circumstances and the realization that we'd have to hostess Shelley's "memorial" the following Sunday, immediately after the real memorial service for Anyda on Saturday. It was so horrible it was hilarious, may I not burn in hell for saying so.

After we got through a spectacular spell of guilty laughter, I sent out e-mail invitations to Society Members about our upcoming Shelley Winters brunch. Then, I tried to put the whole sordid mess out of my mind. After all there were two truly sad occasions to attend within the next seven days, the first of which was the following morning.

That's when things got dicey. I was eating a canapé, following a very touching and incredibly sad service for a member of our community, when a Society pal whispers, "Congratulations on Shelley," in my ear. "Not here..." I murmured, expecting lightning to strike.

Then another very close friend of the wonderful person we were memorializing also referred to my win and I had to put my hand over his mouth—but not before persons in the vicinity heard the word "congratulations."

"Congratulations for what?" somebody asked as I broke out in a sweat knowing that over MY dead body would the words "Dead Pool" come out of my mouth at this particular time and place.

Avoiding the question, and sending the evil eye to a quartet of people who seemed poised to spill the beans, I fled, to mill about the room, paying my real respects to the family.

Although there were at least ten society members at the service, I dared not look at any of them. In fact, every time I saw somebody approaching with a twinkle in their eye, I'd hide behind the potted palms. It was all I could do to keep my decorum until I got out to the car, where, sad to say, I disgusted myself by exploding into howls of laughter.

Returning home, I went about my business, deciding what to prepare, purchase, or plan for Saturday's real memorial service and Sunday's incongruously fake one. Frankly, it wasn't hard. In both instances we'd celebrate lives well lived, and use ample booze and good food to get us through.

As for the authentic memorial service, we capped a crushingly sad week, with a true celebration of a literary life very well lived.

We sent Shelley Winters off gloriously, too. I hung her *Washington Post* obituary over the fireplace, decorated the house with photos from Shelley's Oscar nods for *Diary of Anne Frank*, and *A Patch of Blue*, played *Poseidon* on the DVD and enjoyed the time with our friends. One person arrived with a patch of blue material on her sweater and three yokels showed up dressed as if they'd been in the drink from the Poseidon. We all had a good laugh. A lot of good laughs. Especially me, being quite glad that the sad, bad week was history.

So we all anted up our dues for the next round of the celebrity Dead Pool and I collected my winnings—some of which I'd already spent on the brunch. To assuage some guilt, the rest went to pay bills. But however much I won in the pool, the money was, of course, totally inconsequential compared to the way the friends we lost that week had enriched our lives. And it probably goes without saying (but I'll say it anyway) that both of our dearly departed would have been tickled by the abject absurdity of this whole irreverent dead pool business.

Timing is everything. Live, love, laugh.▼

March 2006

Ok, I'm scared.

Some days it's hard to get out of bed I'm so terrified. I'd have a fight or flight response but I don't know who to slap or where to run. It starts when the clock radio goes off in the morning and doesn't stop until I fall asleep watching CFN: the cable fear network.

Come on, don't pretend you haven't noticed. We are all in terrible, terrible danger from thousands of hideous, well... things. These amorphous THINGS are all on the way, all about to happen, imminent, pending, coming soon to kitchen, powder room, neighborhood, city, or sneeze near you. Be afraid, be very afraid.

These kinds of warnings used to herald horror movies, but now they announce our daily life. From tsunamis to color coded security alerts, bird flu to bacteria, we're just sitting ducks. And those ducks are looking for flu shots.

For a while I took all the warnings, if not seriously, at least like bona fide news. But now it's clear that, with only a few exceptions, (like the polar cap melting, which NO ONE is taking seriously) these scare tactics are designed only to boost network market share. We're being scared silly for ratings.

So I started a tally. The following are real headlines, TV graphics or things somber anchor people warned us about this week alone:

Killer Bird Flu: Just a breath away!

Tsunami: It could happen here!

Radon: A killer in your basement!

Is Delmarva prepared for a Category 5? (Ya think?)

Startling new report! Killer infections for people already on antibiotics!

Honey bees turn killer! (Somebody should check a

Thesaurus for a synonym for "killer.").

Antibacterial soaps: Are we being scammed?

Are YOU ready for a chemical attack? (Okay. How the hell do I get ready for a chemical attack? I'd look stupid eating a bagel in a hazmat suit).

Is nuclear waste driving by your neighborhood? (By itself?)

Panic at sea! Dozens missing from cruise ships! (Not gay cruises. Nobody jumps those ships for fear people will dish about them.)

Mobile phones and radiation: Are you talking yourself to death? (No, but Rush Limbaugh might be. Although it has nothing to do with his phone).

And, of course, daily we get the ubiquitous *Health Scare Over* (pick one) *pesticides, Mad Cow Disease, Ebola Fever, Flesh-Eating Bacteria, Anthrax*, and this year's winner and new champion, *Avian Flu.*

Remember SARS? China had a run on doctor's masks and people walked around with brassiere cups covering their noses and mouths? That was scary. But what the hell happened to that doomsday plague?

It's enough to give me a headache but thanks to the recent Headache drug health scare I can't remember which pills won't kill me. As far as I'm concerned, the only true health scare is whether we can afford, or even get health insurance anymore. Our elected officials should be fixing that scary mess rather than rearranging the deckchairs on the titanic snafu that is our current congressional agenda.

Now that I've got that off my chest (*Mammograms: Is the machine at your hospital safe?*), I'm trying to figure out how to relax while everyone's yelling duck and cover, the sky is falling. All the media covers is stuff that COULD happen, rather than what actually IS happening.

Washington Post superstars Woodward and Bernstein have a theory about the death of investigative journalism. They say it takes too long. It's boring. It took months of picking through garbage, badgering secretaries and meeting with furtive moles in parking garages to bring down Nixon. With the current ratings race, nobody has that kind of time. I think they're on to something.

Why should talking heads investigate anything at all when they can just shout specious warnings. *Identity theft! Computer Viruses! Brokeback Mountain!*

But the granddaddy boondoggle of the warning wars is the daily debunking of food, vitamin, and diet claims.

This week we were warned that oatmeal, estrogen and calcium, CANNOT protect your arteries, heart and bones after all. This was good for my health because I'd been guilty about not chowing down on Tums, fiber, and hormones. I feel better now.

But not much. I keep embracing diet advice only to have it change faster than you can say low carb lasagna. One week we're warned fat is bad, next it's good; pasta is good, then it's bad; You say tomato, I say tomahto. Alcohol causes cancer but helps the heart. The heart causes angst that's bad for the immune system. And nobody doesn't like Sara Lee.

For all the dire predictions, when the media had a legitimate reason to warn us they failed. There was no orange alert warning us Dick Cheney had a gun.

Amid all the shrieking admonitions I'm still sure of only two things—semi-sweet chocolate and red wine have been declared good for your health. I'm not listening to another medical warning past that.

And if I'm forced to be terrified by the media day and night I should do something to calm my blood pressure.

Pour me a Pinot Noir with a snickers chaser. ▼

April 2006

Indulge me please, as I need to have a rather serious conversation here. I've stewed about this topic since last fall in Provincetown and it's been increasingly on my mind since I began watching the Logo network. If you don't now have the incredible luxury of watching Gay-TV 24/7 on Logo, I wish you all access to this cable channel in the near future. It's a blast.

Among Logo's pleasures, guilty and otherwise, is the show *TransGeneration*. It's a documentary about several college students who, leaving the physical and emotional confines of home, become ensconced on campus, find others like them, and begin transitioning from their natal gender to the one which they feel they rightly claim.

I get their struggle. Really understand it. And no, it's not because I think I was born in the wrong body. Although one with a faster metabolism would have been nice.

For my part, I was a total tomboy kid, a barely passable excuse for a straight woman through my twenties, and a liberated lesbian as I crept out of the closet wearing my current identity. I like women, I like being a woman, and I like being married to a woman.

And despite wishing I could have been blessed with smaller pores, I feel right in *MY* skin. I cannot speak for others.

Those others include the leading lady in the movie *TransAmerica* starring Felicity Huffman, who should have won the Oscar for her dead-on portrayal of a pre-op transsexual. There was not one single moment during the movie when I didn't believe that this warm, funny, needy, determined person was becoming the woman she felt she was born to be.

I get it. If a person is absolutely sure they were born the wrong gender I applaud the courageous decision to make things right. I am thankful modern medicine can assist them.

These brave people choose to leave the "otherness" of gay life (although not all transsexuals identify as gay before their journey) for a life as the gender they believe they truly are—although, even with a more comfortable gender, the chance of facing "otherness" is still pretty high—but at least it's "otherness" that feels more truthful to them.

Which brings me to thoughts of a night at the Provincetown theatre last fall. Before the curtain went up, I noticed dozens of young people, looking very much like young boys, in ultra-masculine outfits, crew cut hair, with various stages of hairy upper lips and chins. They had been very obviously taking male hormones. I mean no woman can grow a beard like that until she's at least 60. Seriously, though, who is prescribing hormones to these youngsters?

Many of these kids held hands with very feminine dates. Several of these youngsters paired off together. It was quite clear that these were teenagers or early twenty-somethings living as, or transitioning to become, the opposite gender.

So here's my problem. Neither the gang at the theatre nor the kids on Logo's *TransGeneration* were women transitioning to men or men transitioning to women. They were girls journeying toward boyhood and vice versa.

Have they really lived enough life to know they are making the right decision? Okay, before you start excoriating me for being insensitive and/or clueless, let me say that I know that for many people there is no "decision" about it. There are cases of children as young as three years old clearly demonstrating that they have been born the wrong gender. So, too are there teens and adults for whom the path to transition seems like the right answer from the very first.

But what if the recently uncloseted discussions, television shows, movies, magazine articles and books about transgenderism shine an overly bright spotlight on this subject? What if the 18-year old effeminate guy can't imagine a future as a handsome gay man who can comfortably camp it up socially? What if the dearth of role models for butch lesbians has left some of them thinking that changing gender is the only answer? Would you want to live with the consequences of some decisions you made as a teen or twenty-year-old? Not I.

When I was 18, I was determined to follow a high school boyfriend to college in a tiny, wintery, conservative town. What a bad idea that would have been. Thankfully, the school rejected me. When I was 23, I smugly said to my boss, "Give me the duties you hired me for or fire me!" Guess what happened.

Hell, at age 24 I married an accordion player. What if I had to live with *that* the rest of my life?

Take the skinny white kid with the goofy clothes and dreadlocks standing in front of me at Staples yesterday. He probably sees himself that way permanently. In ten years he might be in a three-piece suit hawking mutual funds. Or not. But his choice probably shouldn't be etched in stone right now.

I just think that for almost every path we take in life there's an opportunity to veer off or turn around onto another road. I'm worried about these youngsters who are jumping on the Transgender Express, full speed ahead, toward a pretty irrevocable destination—without stopping at a lot of stations to experience options along the way.

Am I alone here? Is my worry politically incorrect?

I know that much counseling is required before hormones are prescribed and a great deal of time is spent evaluating and educating pre-op transsexuals before many of the required surgeries take place.

But these transgender kids are getting their hormones from somewhere. In many cases, I bet counseling and safeguards don't come with the drugs. All I'm saying is that I wish our strong young butch girls and our adorable nelly boys wouldn't shoot themselves up, cut anything off or make any permanent changes until they have explored the richness of life's choices.

I don't go to work these days wearing a Roy Rogers holster and I don't come home to a man playing "Lady of Spain" on his instrument. ▼

May 2006

It's Spring at Food Lion Estates. If I'd known just how much of my disposable income would go for mulch, I'd be writing from my condo instead.

I didn't know it was possible to go to Lowe's three times in a day. I socialize more over shredded hardwood than cocktails. And it's the same couples there every weekend. We've conducted entire friendships in the Garden Supplies check-out line.

Have you seen the platoon of Subaru Outbacks in the parking lot? It's becoming the standard vehicle for team lesbian (I love their ads: *"Subaru: It's not a choice, it's the way we're built."*). These cars are piled so high with mulch they hardly need the identifying rainbow stickers.

So we've been landscaping. With a zeal formerly reserved for shoe shopping, I careened around the garden section acquiring all manner of variegated, compacted, dwarfed, pygmy holly things. I don't know much about plants, but all their names sound like medical conditions.

Of course, Bonnie always has to stop by the tool department. Now I'm not intentionally stoking the fires of stereotyping, but what is it about girls and their power tools? No matter how many battery-operated screwdrivers they have, they want new ones. I don't think my mate will be truly happy until every electric socket in the house has some kind of re-chargeable, chuckless, 14 volt appliance hanging out of it.

Meanwhile, back at the south forty, while I was in the house stretching the making of a couple of sandwiches into a full-time job, Bonnie got the new plants in the ground. Then she proceeded to connect a bunch of intentionally leaky soaker hoses (named, no doubt for their cost) around the planting beds. Oops, we were a couple of clasps short.

So I was re-deployed to Lowes, where I realized I didn't understand the project. Did I need male-female connectors, male-male connectors, female-female, female-to-male, male-to-female? It was like choosing from the list of local support groups. Finally, I grabbed a pansexual assortment so the gender identity specialist at home could decide.

Once those super soakers started splurting, we moved on. Lesbians, rev your engines. Step One: level the playing field. In order to install stones leading from the deck to the garage, Bonnie explained that we had to dig the Panama Canal along the house and transfer the resulting rubble twelve feet away.

I found this somewhat ironic since once, back in Maryland, we did a project requiring adding a yard of dirt to our lawn. Being math-challenged, I pictured a yard of dirt as the height and width of a yard-stick. Fooly, fooly. A dump truck deposited Mt. St. Victoire on the driveway. I still remember frantically being called into service to help spread the soil before a monsoon came and washed $300 worth of dirt down the storm sewers and into Chesapeake Bay.

So now, in a stunning example of what goes around comes around, Bonnie's telling me we must dig up a yard of dirt from one place and shovel it over to another.

"I'll dig and toss," she says. "You just tamp."

You know, when we used to have a boat, and needed to redistribute weight aboard, I was always sent to the bow as ballast. If you ask me, tamping is the same unskilled labor as ballast, only for landlubbers. I was instructed to march around on the newly dumped dirt, packing it down evenly.

Dutifully I pounded the fresh dirt pile, knees high, arms swinging, getting into quite a rhythm. Bonnie decided this backyard Bolero looked like fun and soon the two of us were tamping and stomping in circles. The tired, thirsty Saturday morning herds diving past our house to the beach must have thought they were hallucinating. Was that Lucy and Ethel stomping grapes?

Naturally, before we could set anything in stone over the

mud pile, the rains came and continued for an entire week. Add two Schnauzers and God save the carpets.

Three times a day we'd lure the dogs back in from the mosh pit, grab them up before their paws or snouts touched any carpet or wall and toss them into the tub. One memorable moment at Schnauzerhaven Day Spa came when we lathered and rinsed the filthy pooches, then focused on cleaning the tub. Sadly, since we'd used all our limbs just to get the boys into the house without touching anything, we'd neglected the teeny little task of closing the sliding glass door.

While I was scrubbing the damn tub, the beasts were right back outside rolling in the mud patch.

So we went to the pet store and invested in puppy galoshes. Those were incredulous little dogs when we made them put boots on before going out to pee. At first they just stared at the foreign objects hanging on their feet. When they finally tried to walk, they shook their booty and high stepped like Clydesdales.

Of course, if we didn't get the Velcro fasteners closed tightly, they'd go do their business, come back for a booty check, fail to produce 8 for 8 and I'd be sent to the tar pits with a flashlight. There is no rap tune about searching for this kind of booty.

But after a week, the rains stopped, the yard dried and we were able to host a season opener for the blender. Friends arrived, Margaritas got mixed, it was great in the great outdoors. Lovely dusk in our beautiful yard.

Maybe it was all that rain, or our proximity to wetlands, but suddenly our garden party was beset by mosquitoes so big they had serial numbers on their sides. Quick! Get the Off! Light the Citronella buckets. Battle Stations!!!

I'll have another Deep Woods Margarita, please…and if you need me, I'll be in the house.▼

May 2006

No coffee beans were injured in the making of this story.

Let's face it. There are jobs people can and cannot do. My career is talking and writing. I seem to be able to direct plays. But I flunked algebra and probably still hold the New York State SAT record for the widest split ever recorded between Math and English. And I'm a complete bust at anything requiring eye-hand coordination.

I learned this once at a dinner theatre where folks drank Kahlua and Cream and Brandy Alexanders with their comedies. One night we were short a cocktail waitress and some genius suggested the director pitch in.

Now I know I got good tips. I used my talking skills to let my customers in on scurrilous backstage gossip and despite my spilling a Sloe Gin Fizz down my pants (eye-hand thing), people had fun. Good tips.

But by evening's end, my tip pocket was empty thanks to my fuzzy math in making change. I was the first person in dinner theatre history ever to make more money in show biz than waiting tables. So food service was not a career path for me.

Fast forward thirty years. A friend, who shall remain blameless, is part owner of a coffee shop. One morning her co-owners went to a coffee convention while she stayed here to hold the fort. At 8 a.m. I got an S.O.S. call asking me to make an emergency run for capers and cream cheese.

By the time capers-r-us delivered, it was clear that the lone barista was in deep Cappuccino. A line of customers stretched out the door into the alleyway and toward the street. These folks didn't seem unruly but it was just a matter of time, as they hadn't been caffeinated yet.

To thwart potential civil disobedience I figured an unskilled barista was better than nothing. In hindsight, perhaps a tactical error.

I fought my way around the counter and into the coffee business. "I can help for a few minutes," I said to no one in particular as you couldn't hear squat over people shouting for double skinny raspberry chocolate Macchiatos.

"Here, can you rinse the spout of this bottle?"

How hard can that be? I unscrewed the cap, withdrew the spout and shot Ghiradelli chocolate syrup straight down the inside of my shirt. I fought the urge to bow my head and lick.

From there I followed orders to wipe crumbs off the sandwich and bagel station, identify empty coffee urns, joke with the customers and keep out of the chocolate brownies.

"Fill this container with San Francisco Blend beans and pour them into the grinder."

Okay Frisco Blend, Frisco Blend. I located it on the top row. I held the cup under the wide-mouthed spout, reached up and pulled the handle, releasing a torrent of beans into the cup. Did I mention the eye-hand coordination thing? By the time my cup runneth over and I lunged to close the floodgate, coffee beans flew at my face like buckshot. And Dick Cheney wasn't even there.

I got to San Francisco alright, but instead of flowers in my hair I had coffee beans.

It was only 10:30 a.m. and I longed for a breakfast blend: vodka and ice. A friend walked into the shop, spied me juggling a pair of drooling coffee filters in one hand and a pot of hot java in the other and burst out laughing. "Now what????" he sputtered.

"I'm helping," I said. At least I hoped I was helping.

"I have a feeling we'll read about this," he said, and I had a feeling he was right. After all, column deadlines come up fast around here.

Besides, I feel an renewed obligation to uphold the ancient art of memoir—unlike author James Frey who, after a spat with Oprah, has been charged with inventing much of the outrageous material in his best selling memoir *A Million Little*

Pieces—or, A Million Little Lies, which apparently would have been more accurate.

I know people sometimes don't believe me when I swear that all my column stories are true. Which is why, with a deadline coming up, I figured I could get a thousand words out of a day in the life of a coffee peon.

So, truth is, I continued my tour of duty trying not to slip on the splattered coffee beans and trying equally hard to reserve the luscious pastries for the general public.

"I'll have lox, on a sesame bagel with cream cheese," said a customer.

Hey, here was something I actually knew how to do—although cutting and shmearing a bagel with my paws in surgical gloves felt more like *M*A*S*H* than haute cuisine. Then I discovered that capers have a propensity to roll off the lox and bounce all over the floor. In food service, the 5-second rule does not apply, so capers bounced were capers lost. While an open-faced bagel with capers symmetrically dotting the smoked salmon may look professional, these customers got their capers embedded in cream cheese sockets secured by a lox blanket so the little suckers stayed put. Function over form.

Who were these customers? It was a cold day in March (as opposed to a cold day in hell, which is when I pictured myself doing this kind of work) but town was packed. While honcho barista was pleased, she wished the crowds hadn't come on a day when she was stuck dealing with the sorcerer's apprentice.

Hour by hour, Lucy Ricardo and Ethel Mertz (why does my life continue to mirror those broads?) raced to keep espresso orders from backing up. My premier attempt at actually brewing coffee was a tragic pot of brown sludge (flavor of the week: Nuclear Waste), but I improved as the day went on. Sumatran, Nicaraguan, Guatemalan, Costa Rican, customer orders sounded like the blue questions from Trivial Pursuit.

When business slacked off mid-day, Ms. Barista took a moment to duck next door for refills for the soda case. The second she left, thirteen people appeared (this is true; it's a memoir), requesting things like Mocha Macchiato and double shot vanilla chai espresso grande. My face surely said I didn't know Chai Tea from Tai Chi.

I explained that the real barista had left me holding the tea bag and would be back momentarily. I offered to get cups of plain coffee or tea for anyone wanting something so pedestrian.

Hours passed. Gee, the last time I'd spent this much time in a coffee house we were singing "Puff the Magic Dragon." Eventually, my mate came to help vacuum the floor. "You've spilled the beans before, but never like this," she said.

While I am now retired from my fledgling career in food service, it was really a major buzz. I'm proud that I sliced bagels all day without slitting my wrists (accidentally or on purpose) and I now know the difference between an espresso shot and buckshot (does the Vice-President? Sorry, I cannot help myself.)

And I did not, during my tenure, violate any health or food handling rules (happy, Pam?). When I got home, I found capers in my shoe laces and my tits covered in Ghiradelli chocolate. Same s**t different day? Not in Rehoboth.▼

May 2006

I hope New Orleans is coming back. While there is still misery everywhere you look (I saw shiny blue tarps on every third rooftop from my airplane window), and tales of insurance and FEMA horrors, there are great signs of life, too. Especially in the French Quarter, which was spared the water, but not Hurricane Katrina's winds and the eventual evacuation of almost all restaurant, hotel and shop employees—many of which are still not back because they have nothing to come back to.

But New Orleans is making lemonade, spiked with bourbon of course, out of their Category 5 lemon.

I was in NOLA for the Saints and Sinners GLBT Literary Conference, where I was invited to read, along with many others, from our recently published works. Two days earlier, I'd packed a carton of books and dropped it off at my friendly UPS store. The books flew first class, non-stop, but I had to take an economy class puddle jumper from Philly to Charlotte to New Orleans. The City might be the Big Easy but getting there isn't.

I'm sitting in the airport, ready to board when I get a frantic call from my UPS man. He tracked my books and they were refused at the hotel and sent back north.

"What the…???"

"I will try to intercept them on the way back and get this straightened out," he said.

I had the reading copy of my book in my carry-on luggage, but no others. Naturally, the point of showing up and reading is to sell books. No books to sell and I'd be up the Mississippi without a paddle-wheeler.

When I got to my French Quarter hotel—a wonderfully shabby-chic B&B half a block off Bourbon Street, complete with a steamy, tropical-plant filled interior garden—I checked in and inquired about the book snafu. I got a stricken look from the clerk.

"Oh, I hope it wasn't my mix-up," she said, with an expression that told me it was. "You see, the FEMA people stayed here until last week, and they were forever getting packages. I might have thought your box was for them and declined to accept it."

"But here," she continued, "I'll upgrade your room."

Whoopee.

I slipped the key into the aged lock on the 12-foot high, many paint-layered door and entered the stage set for *A Streetcar Named Desire*—two ancient Victorian sofas, an imposing bed with ornate wooden headboard, a dramatic chandelier and, I bet, Tennessee Williams in the closet—so to speak.

Like Blanche Dubois, I careened around the room soaking up the Southern charm and steamy atmosphere, until I was jarred by my cell phone. It was my UPS man. "Can I get more books to pack and send overnight?" he asked.

What can Brown do for you, indeed. Taking only a small leap of faith, since Mr. UPS seemed like a good guy, I revealed my hidden house key location and where to find the books in the garage. That would be everywhere. Overnighting them might make it in time.

After the call, I marched myself down the street to the conference hotel to meet the other Saints and Sinners. First, I finally met Carol Seajay, the San Francisco legend who has worked for over three decades promoting lesbian literature, most notably with her publication *Feminist Bookstore News*. In the 70s and 80s, when independent women's bookstores thrived and served as community lifelines for lesbians all over the country, it was Carol who pulled the network together.

As giant bookstore chains and the internet squelched and shuttered many of our independent bookstores, Carol's publication closed shop, too. But now, seeing a need to reconnect readers, Carol has a new publication, called *Books to Watch Out For*. (You can check it out at bookstowatchoutfor.com).

Talking with Carol was so fascinating I didn't dwell on the

UPS man sprinting through my house, rooting through my garage. I wasn't worried about anything sinister, mind you, but I hated to have him see the mess I left.

A cocktail party followed, where publishers, authors, publicists and New Orleans literati chatted it up. Mid-cocktail my cell phone vibrated. "Good news!" says UPS guy. "I intercepted your package and it will be back at your hotel by 8 a.m. tomorrow. I didn't even have to go to your house!" Saved.

Finally able to relax, I schmoozed with the Sinners, since by that time the Saints were all back at their hotels, brushing their teeth. We trolled Bourbon Street, watching balconies full of drunken straight boys calling for the women below to show their bosoms—and tossing beads to them if they did. We sampled Po Boys—the sandwiches, but that's not to say that some of the literary sinners didn't sample other kinds as well—and sipped Hurricanes in souvenir glasses, to the tune of live jazz from almost every storefront on the block.

I suspected New Orleans' sense of humor was returning with shops selling tee-shirts announcing "Show me your tits and in 8-10 weeks FEMA will send you your beads," or "Katrina Gave me a Blow Job I'll Never Forget." And then there was the all-purpose shirt "I Got Bourbon Faced on Sh*t Street."

I stopped short of that.

The next day at 8 a.m., as I walked to the actual conference, a few people were still in the bars, and the sound of trash trucks scooping street debris replaced the previous evening's sound of music.

I attended a panel discussion about on-line publishing and a talk by *The Hours* author Michael Cunningham. I listened to a lesbian read the male erotica she wrote, thinking what's up with that? And when it came time, I read a couple of my columns to an assembled crowd, followed by some actual book sales. I also learned from the pros, that GLBT publishing is a tough game.

That night, post gumbo, I chose sinner again, for in lieu of early to bed I attended my very first drag king show. It was adorable, which is probably not a review the kings would appreciate. But they were puppies. Skinny little gender queers, with spirit gum whiskers on their faces, butching it up, lip synching to macho songs. The cast was energetic, with stage names like, forgive them, Lick Draw McGraw. I guess the kings' aim was titillation and/or humor, but adorable was what they were. Drag queens are intrinsically funny. Not so the kings, but they sure tried.

On Sunday morning, after a breakfast of beignets and chicory coffee at Café du Monde, I noticed more signs of New Orleans rebirth. Store windows displayed shirts saying "Make Levees, Not War," and "Re-Cover, Re-Build, Re-New Orleans."

I really hope they can.

As for this author, her weekend was saved by that dogged UPS man, who spent the better part of three days plastered to his computer, tracking my miserable carton of books.

As Blanche Dubois surely said one day in my hotel room, "I have always relied on the kindness of strangers." ▼

June 2006

I have good news and bad news. The good news is that a study from the Stockholm Brain Institute ("Come have your head examined with us!") says that lesbian brains react differently to certain sex hormones than heterosexual women's brains, thereby adding to the evidence that homosexuality has a physical basis rather than being "caused" by learned behavior. That's good.

But the bad news is that our brains react similarly to straight men. Ouch!!!!

Well, not quite the same, and that's a good thing because these days many straight men are reverting to cavemen when it comes to their behavior. And I for one don't want to be associated with it.

Naturally, I'm not talking about all straight men, anymore than Mary Cheney represents all gay women (Not! More about her later) but I've noticed a disturbing trend whereby straight men are once again being congratulated for being boorish, sexist and homophobic.

I'm talking about the subtle creep of creeps into commercials, TV shows and everyday life. In a single prime-time hour I saw a man proudly trick his wife into staying home with the kids while he went fishing, a restaurant showing a huddle of men grunting "Beef!" and that icky Dodge commercial with the silly little fairy. In it, a big hairy guy throws a fairy (a literal one, with wings) against a wall and the fairy's wand turns the macho guy into a lithe little fellow in strange socks, walking a tiny Chihuahua. We get the point.

In fact, after seeing a Yellow Book ad with women, no, girls prancing around in outfits previously only seen in darkened lap dance emporiums, it prompts the question "what do streetwalkers wear these days to stand out from the herd?"

Then I picked up a magazine and found t-shirts being marketed to teens with slogans like "I'm a Virgin...this is a very old t-shirt" or "Porn Star" on them. Click!

Are you seasoned enough to remember the old *Ms. Magazine* "Click" campaign? For years, the last page of *Ms. Magazine* featured advertisements, sent in by readers, that were insulting or degrading to women. The magazine used to print them with "click!" as a caption, hoping that people would hear that click in their heads when confronted with other sexist stimuli.

Watching TV last night I heard the click so often I thought the room was infested with crickets. Or was that poor Betty Friedan flipping in her final resting place?

The media is bad enough, but recently, a friend, introducing herself to colleagues in a professional class, told the group she was a feminist—and was met by the sucking of air and groans.

What's that about??? Are we so far into post-feminism that feminism becomes the F-word? Is sisterhood less about powerful women helping women and more about the tabloids following two anorexic women fighting over loutish Charlie Sheen?

Everyone knows that sixties and seventies-era feminism paved the way for more women legislators, doctors, lawyers and CEOs than ever before. But does the present generation of young professionals know how that happened?

Have they been told that their grandmothers advised their mothers to go to teachers college or nursing school "to have something to fall back on." Now God bless our fabulous teachers and nurses—I would not be up to either job, but nobody's grandmother told them to get an MBA in case they didn't get their MRS. Instead, mothers told daughters not to worry about dropping out of college to get married because heck, they wouldn't be using their expensive educations anyway.

Mortified as I am to admit this, when my own mother gave me the line about having something to fall back on I bought it. Not only did I go to college thinking that picking a husband was more important than picking a major, but if you recall, I started off wearing hose, heels, and, I swear it, false eyelashes every day to class.

To digress, one night, I parked my gluey eyelashes on the wall in my dorm room and the next morning as I staggered out of bed I saw two huge spiders on the wall and pulverized my Long and Lush Max Factors.

Fortunately, by October of freshwoman year, I'd been introduced to books by Gloria Steinem and "hippie" clothes. I failed to tell Mom that the only thing I wound up falling back on were pillows on the floor of apartments lit by lava lamps and featuring some groovy second hand smoke.

Oddly, I had no interest in this free love era (can you believe they called it that!). It took me another decade to work that problem out, but I did begin to understand the burgeoning theory that women mattered.

But now, my lesbian brain (the one that does not react like a straight man, thank you very much), is worried.

Are self-avowed feminists really being mocked? Is advertising once again celebrating women as sex objects? Is it okay for Jay Leno to make *Brokeback Mountain* jokes night after night? It would be hell to go backwards. I don't think I'd survive having to wear hosiery and heels to the Super G like my mother did.

And while we're talking about going backwards, there's Mary Cheney. Boy did she get it backwards. She couldn't come out and denounce her father's party, cronies and compatriots when they were campaigning to get elected. Noooo, she kept quiet like the good little woman, facilitating their election so they could trample gay rights, threaten the first amendment, kick privacy rights to the curb and gleefully plan to etch discrimination into the Constitution. And NOW she's cashing in by talking about being gay in America. Not to help the cause, mind you, but to help her sell her self-serving book. Too little, too late, too selfish.

Meanwhile back at that Scandinavian brain facility, ("Good

morning, Brain Institute, Press One for Lobotomies") scientists held sniffing contests, with men and women, gay and straight inhaling male and female pheromones—those pesky little love aromas.

The good doctors deduced that heterosexual women found the male and female pheromones about equally pleasant, while straight men and lesbians liked the female pheromone more than the male one. Men and lesbians also found the male hormone more irritating than the female one.

That's nice. Frankly, I'm just plain irritated.

If we don't stop those alphabet generations from undoing the gains women achieved almost 40 years ago, we aging baby boomers are liable to have to pick up protest signs, ("not too heavy, I've got rotator cuff problems") take to the streets (grab those Rockport walkers with the arch supports) and start singing protest songs. Nobody wants that.

So I'm making an appeal to our youngsters. Guys, don't be oafs. Gals, don't be objectified. Everybody, don't let feminism become a dirty word. And whatever you do, don't listen to Mary (Benedict Arnold) Cheney.

Because you really don't want to see me climbing the Capitol steps (hand me the oxygen, dear) waving a NOW poster and singing "I Am Woman Hear Me Roar."

For all our sakes, I hope Feminism isn't dead, that it's just taking a snooze. ▼

June 2006

I'm sitting in a hotel room in New Orleans, after seeing, in person, almost eight months following a hurricane, the most unimaginable destruction of neighborhoods. Meanwhile, the President of the U.S. is on TV fighting for a constitutional amendment against (omigod!) gay marriage.

What's wrong with this picture?

With 80 percent of New Orleans still up to its butt in mold and rotten sheetrock without, in large part, electricity, drinking water, grocery stores, gas stations or any open businesses, our self-described Decider has decided to abandon this historic city completely, and use his bully pulpit (and I do mean bully) to warn America that if they don't write discrimination against gays into the Constitution NOW, the apocalypse is coming. Guess what. It already happened in New Orleans. So here I am back in this devastated city, having been to a book conference here three weeks ago. Now I'm here for my day job with the Rehoboth Beach Main Street organization, affiliated with the National Trust for Historic Preservation. On my last trip I stayed in the French Quarter, sold books, ate crawfish, drank frozen Hand Grenades and bought t-shirts. We heard about the horrible affects of Katrina, but life in the Quarter seemed to be coming back.

Today, though, I got to see the unholy mess left in New Orleans neighborhoods for myself and now I'm mad as hell. In fact, as furious as I am at Decider-in-Chief for trying to rally his bigoted base with a strictly for show Constitutional Amendment banning same sex marriage—an amendment that has zero chance of approval, therefore making it a fools mission in every sense, I'm just as mad at him for abandoning New Orleans and the whole gulf coast.

Let's face it, he toured the same communities I just did; he saw muddy water lines up to second stories in ruined neighborhoods; he saw holes in rooftops where people had to be cut out of their attics (and there are street after street of them); he saw homes where people died.

And what did this compassionate conservative do? He posed for photo ops in the only neighborhood still intact, and then walked away to obsess about (gasp) same sex marriage. If he's a compassionate conservative I'm that bitch Ann Coulter.

As we toured the city, dining at restaurants that have managed to reopen, and listening to great musicians, we heard the same plea over and over. Go back and tell people how bad it is. Tell them we need help. Tell them we must rebuild New Orleans and preserve its special culture. Tell people the truth. So here I go.

What Katrina's wind did is being repaired. What the rain wrought has been sopped up.

But the havoc that the broken levees and burned out pumping stations caused is not fixed. Yes, the levees are being repaired and built to slightly better standards. But the neighborhoods flooded by this man-made part of the disaster are not back, in any way, shape or living form.

The best way to describe what I saw is this: a hurricane hits your community (okay, if you are land-locked, pretend you live on a coast). And two days later, when people think the emergency is over, a swift-moving flood from a storm surge on both a bay on one side of town and the ocean on the other inundates much of the area. Your Main Street and three or four blocks on either side—your tourist area—is dry. But your city neighborhoods and suburbs are completely flooded. Picture it. Picture the flood itself. Neighborhoods, rich and poor alike, up to their roof eaves in mucky water, ruining furniture, appliances, books, photo albums, clothing, computers and cars. Killing over a thousand people—including some people you know.

It's not just the poor neighborhoods where people had no transportation out. No, lots of people stayed to ride it out because the levees by the bay had never ever failed before. Now picture the scene eight months later, when NONE, I mean NONE of the neighborhoods have come back to life. There's nobody living in the homes on the bay or by the ocean. Everything from mobile homes and one story cottages to $500,000 houses sits rotting from the water and virulent mold. There are Mercedes, BMWs and Lexuses left to rust in washed out driveways. Shrubs and trees are brown and dead, killed by saltwater and neglect. Beautiful homes have crude writing on them, 12-feet high, noting that they have been checked by the police and animal rescue teams. Sometimes the writing spells out the terrible things rescuers found inside. Sometimes the writing warns looters to stay away; sometimes it carries the message "We'll be back!"

There are square holes in rooftops where rescuers sawed into the attics to save the occupants. Those roofs with jagged holes are where the occupants chopped and clawed their way out.

But my god, it's eight months later. The neighborhoods are still dark and deserted. Why aren't people fixing up their houses? Well, a very few are, if they managed to be on the short list for a FEMA trailer to park in their yard. First they get rid of all the debris that once was their belongings, then they gut the house down to its studs to fight the mold and water damage. Oh, they must supply their own generator and water, because no utilities are connected. There's not a food store open. No gas stations. No restaurants. Even cell phones get spotty connections. Contractors are overworked, materials impossible to come by and it's dark and scary at night because no streetlights or traffic signals light up any of the roads. Picture it. Suburban neighborhoods with hundreds of homes deserted; the blocks near the beach with not a soul living there; whole communities without a light on except for a trailer or two parked along the street.

But these are the lucky people, because they either had money in the bank to start to repair their properties, or they settled with insurance companies. I say lucky, because most of their neighbors are still in the middle of a boxing match between the people they have paid thousands of dollars to for homeowners insurance and the ones they paid thousands of dollars to for flood insurance. Each group has been insisting the other is responsible for this particular disaster.

But humans are a resilient bunch. And folks in your town fight to bring back the community they love. In fact, area musicians, chefs, artists, police and fire officials all go back to work despite their homes being uninhabitable. Most of them drive to work from rental apartments over an hour away.

And your wonderful neighbors work together to help their friends and family, tell their elected officials that the town deserves to be rebuilt and must not be forgotten. You send a special message to legislators from other areas of the country who don't want to rebuild a city between a coast and a bay. You tell them that your hometown must be rebuilt—for its people, its culture and its future.

Well, that's what New Orleans is doing. And, just like residents in your town would do, New Orleanians are trying to get the word out, telling people to come back to New Orleans, spend money in their city, visit Bourbon Street and let the good times roll so the city can come back to life.

So there, I've done what they've asked. I've told their story. And I really hope readers will consider a New Orleans vacation soon. You'll have a grand time and will be greeted and entertained by very thankful people. You can do a good deed and have a great vacation at the same time.

And meanwhile, with Americans (and Iraqis) dying overseas, polar ice caps turning into giant slushies, the national debt exploding, gas at $3 a gallon while gas execs get $30 million dollar bonuses, our president is spending capital, political or otherwise on banning same-sex marriage.

Not only am I mad as hell, but I have to tell Senator Santorum that if those naughty activist judges really do manage to legislate same-sex marriage, the next fight is NOT, I repeat,

NOT a push for marriage between lesbians and squirrels or whatever his demented fantasy is.

Hopefully it's a push to get our national priorities right. I hope the good times roll again in New Orleans. For our good times we might have to wait until the next presidential election. ▼

June 2006

Last week, immediately following my New Orleans business trip, I headed to Atlanta to attend the Golden Crown Literary Society Convention—a giant celebration of lesbian fiction.

I had just arrived at my hotel room when Bonnie called to tell me that Muriel had suffered a stroke a few hours before. I was stunned. "Don't rush home," Bonnie said. "She'd want you to keep going—for Anyda. We will keep you posted."

I was attending the convention to accept, for Sarah Aldridge/Anyda Marchant, the Trailblazer Award from the Society. This was the second such award ever given; the first, last year, was given to 1960s lesbian pulp fiction writer Ann Bannon. It was Bannon who was to present the award posthumously to Anyda. I was looking forward to bringing the engraved trophy home to Muriel.

I knew she would love it, because it celebrated Anyda— and Muriel loved nothing more than to have people praise Anyda for her writing, intellect and love for literature. Muriel considered herself a happy witness to Anyda's career. Everyone else knew it was a joyous collaboration.

Several times a day I called home to ask how Muriel was doing. Bonnie reported that Muriel's friends were converging on the hospital. She knew they were there, but couldn't talk. I couldn't quite imagine it. But I wanted to be there.

When my cell phone rang at 10 p.m. two days later, I knew. Bonnie, sobbing and difficult to understand, told me that Muriel was gone. I was overwhelmed by the news. Alone in the hotel room all I could do was cry, but I knew I had to stay in Atlanta for the next day's ceremonies.

In the hotel ballroom, when the award was announced— and when it was noted that not only was it posthumous, but that Anyda's partner of almost 57 years died only a day before, there was an audible buzz. You could feel the sadness. And then, as I accepted the award for them—for it was truly the two of them responsible for their publishing history, nearly 300 women gave the pair an emotional ovation. They would have loved it.

I can't say the moment was bittersweet, because Anyda and Muriel had lived long and magnificent lives, mostly sweet, nothing bitter. I guess it was just semi-sweet, since I wished they both could have been there to see how well-loved and admired they were.

I returned home, and again, had an obituary to write.

MURIEL INEZ CRAWFORD
PUBLISHER EMERITUS
APRIL 21, 1914-JUNE 7, 2006

Muriel Inez Crawford, 92, passed away Wednesday, June 7, 2006, at her South Rehoboth Beach home, surrounded by her loving circle of friends.

Born April 21, 1914, in Washington, D.C., Crawford served as an executive secretary at the Washington law firm of Covington and Burling, followed by a position as executive secretary to the president of the Southern Railroad, now Amtrak.

Crawford, along with her partner of 57 years, Anyda Marchant, who pre-deceased Crawford this past January, began coming to Rehoboth Beach on weekends in the early 1960s. Their house became the site of legendary Saturday evening salons, where cocktails, conversation and an amazingly diverse crowd would gather. In the winter, the cocktails and conversation would relocate to the couple's home in Pompano Beach, Fla.

In 1972, the couple founded Naiad Press, an independent feminist publishing house, and then founded A&M Books of Rehoboth Beach in 1995. At the time of her death, Crawford was publisher emeritus with A&M Books.

She is survived by a niece and nephew and a family of dear friends.

The Memorial Service took place at the same church where we celebrated Anyda's life. In fact, Anyda, in her urn, was there—because the service was not so much for Muriel alone, but for the both of them, and for the end of an era in Rehoboth Beach.

The truth was, Muriel was a tag-a-long churchgoer, attending because it was so important to Anyda. As Father Max was officiating, our son Eric, the one who penned the foreword to this book exchanged a glance with me. I knew we were both thinking of Muriel watching the service from on high and thinking "Well, this is the last time I have to do this."

Although, she really would have adored the words Father Max delivered. He spoke of Anyda and Muriel's partnership, their devotion to each other and hopes for a better world, where same sex relationships could flourish in the open.

Once again I walked to the lectern and gave a eulogy.

None of us thought we would be back here so soon, but we're not really surprised, either, are we?

In the mid 1940s when Gertrude Stein, one half of one of the world's most famous female couples passed away, her partner, Alice B. Toklas referred to her future as "soldiering on alone."

When Anyda Marchant died in January, Muriel Crawford accepted her assignment to stay on alone with grace and a certain courageous calm. But it was clear that she was unenthused and tired. She tried to keep the mischievous sparkle in her eye for her friends, but it was an effort.

Right after Anyda's passing, Bonnie and I were talking about the following Saturday night's salon at the house. "I guess we won't have it anymore," Muriel said, "Everybody was just coming to see Anyda."

"Absolutely NOT, we assured her, "they came to see you both, and now we will come for Dewars and conversation with you."

And we did. And there were many, many visitors. So many,

in fact, that when Muriel was temporarily hospitalized a month before her passing, her hospital roommate could not believe the amount of calls and visitors and circle of loved ones. "She must be somebody important," said the roommate.

And she was—with her playful nature, stubborn independence and loving generosity. She touched so many lives in such a positive way.

Both the impish Muriel and the imposing Anyda will live on as Rehoboth legends, literary icons and role models for lives exceptionally well lived and loved.

And I'll always close my eyes and see Muriel's head peeking over the steering wheel of that big Lincoln. She loved to drive and until very recently, she could still be seen at the wheel, a careful but surprisingly speedy driver.

I'll tell you a little tale out of school but I'm sure Muriel and Anyda wouldn't mind.

One day, about three years ago, Muriel and Anyda returned from a visit to the doctor with a worrisome report. The doctor was worried about their drinking. He wasn't worried about the actual quantity consumed, but the fact that the ladies enjoyed two cocktails each evening in the living room before retiring. The doctor worried about their being able to maneuver, without incident, as they toddled off to the bedroom.

He cautioned them to keep the ritual to one drink only.

Surprisingly, the ladies took the news well.

It was not until two years later, when I was sent to the bedroom to get a sweater for Muriel that I learned the truth. There, on the floor by the bed, were two cut crystal glasses and a half gallon jug of Scotch.

Yes, they only had one drink each night in the living room.

When I reported my discovery to the ladies, Anyda pretended not to hear me and Muriel's eyes got that well-known twinkle as she cackled and giggled like a teenager.

At 5 p.m. tonight, wherever you are, let's raise a toast to Miss Muriel. ▼

July 2006

I live in Animal House.

Our dog groomer left town a while ago and Bonnie began clipping our pups herself. Quicker than you can say buzz cut our dogs were exceedingly naked and shorn like sheep at a Marine induction center. For the first ten days after the shearing they had to wear newborn onesie outfits to stop the shivering.

But since then my spouse has gotten much better at this grooming thing, perfecting the Schnauzer cut—feathered legs, clipped mustache, square beard, shaved sides and long eyebrows. Our boys could model for Canine Klein.

Soon, friends with Schnauzers started to drop off their pooches at the house for haircuts. Occasionally, brave friends with other breeds asked Bonnie to prune their pets too, and it's amazing how fast Bonnie could turn almost any breed into faux Schnauzers. The AKC will soon be registering the Schnorkie, Schmaltese and Schmutt.

Last weekend was particularly busy here at Schnauzerhaven. We had human and canine houseguests, non-stop events and the usual summer craziness. On Friday morning, we saw a weird shadowy thing bouncing off the walls in the sunroom and our dogs plastered against the sliding glass door like Garfield on car window suction cups.

One of our houseguests investigated. "Oh my, it's a bird, it's stuck in here," she said, at which point she started trying to shoo the panicked creature out the door. Startled, the bird dive bombed her head and there she was, barricaded in the sunroom channeling Tippi Hedren in *The Birds*.

I knew better than to inject myself into the pursuit, so I summoned my spouse. She entered our new aviary and started to chase the creature, too, which prompted the question "how many lesbians does it take to…." It was all very Keystone Kops, with the bird and its pursuers flying all over the place.

Finally, Bonnie coaxed the interloper onto her outstretched arm and escorted the bird outside. The dogs, crestfallen, couldn't believe their bad luck.

As we left the house for an afternoon downtown and ladies happy hour Moxie and Paddy stayed home enjoying their last hours of solitude. The following day we would be taking in two more Schnauzers for doggy day care.

Yes, we sometimes provide daily or overnight lodging for non-shedding breeds. Not only are we getting a reputation for having a canine safe house, but sometimes I think somebody posted us on Doggie Hotels.com. We do offer five biscuit lodging with amenities like spa service and, if Bonnie or I put our java mugs down to get dressed or visit the library, there's in-room coffee. Fortunately they do not need high speed internet access or a complimentary *USA Today*.

Unfortunately, we'd forgotten to inform our human guests about the two additional dogs that would be checking in on Saturday morning. They awoke to a terrible thunderstorm and a pack of howling animals. Discovering that the two household Schnauzers had, in the night, multiplied, our friends considered giving up martinis.

I assured everyone that the double vision was not alcohol induced and we set about preparing breakfast. We'd just popped the champagne cork for the Mimosas when the phone rang. "Is Bonnie there?"

It seems that a dog visiting friends down the street had gone under their deck and was refusing to come out. Driving rain continued unabated and it was worrisome. "They need a dog whisperer," I said.

So Bonnie threw on her raincoat and headed for this new animal emergency. Sure enough, a friend's Beagle (If Bonnie clipped it, would it be a Schneagle?) was entrenched in mud under the deck. I bet Bonnie wished she'd kept that bird as bait. Unable to succeed through her powers of persuasion, she resorted to crawling, on her belly, under the deck for the rescue. Three gay men stood watching, squirming at the thought of the muddy and perhaps varmint filled mess Bonnie was willing to crawl in.

With her mission accomplished, our drenched and mud-caked animal rescue expert arrived home to learn that our two visiting Schnauzers would not be picked up until late that night, having requested, yes, a late checkout. So it was back to cooking breakfast.

And in our house, cooking is a problem for many reasons, one of which is the obvious fact that we rarely do it. But perhaps the real reason is that our dogs are terrified when we cook. How's that for a culinary reference?

Once, back in their puppyhood, I was broiling chicken wings and the tips started to blacken and sizzle, as they will do, setting off the smoke alarm. Well, you'd think Zambelli had detonated firecrackers up those Schnauzers' butts. The dogs fled to the back of the bedroom closet, holed up there, shaking, for two hours. Now I'm sure the sound of the smoke detector hurt their sensitive ears, but I also think they were being little canine drama queens. Regardless, I tried never to let that happen again.

But from that moment on, every time we'd turn on the oven, stove or microwave, my dogs trembled, drooled and hyperventilated from post-traumatic stress syndrome. They carry on like that if we prepare anything from a turkey dinner to a pop tart.

We tried behavior modification techniques, luring the dogs toward the stove by offering them a taste of whatever was in or on the offending kitchen appliance. This worked pretty well, as they no longer ran from the room. They'd just hang around drooling and panting until we gave them a taste of our chicken or fish.

I actually think we were beginning to make progress putting their childhood smoke detector abuse behind them when it happened again. Negligently tended pork chops. The damn smoke detector went off, our dogs had flashbacks and have not trusted us in the kitchen since.

So we were cooking scrambled eggs and my houseguests asked, "What's the matter with the dogs? They're shaking."

"We're cooking," I said.

Face it, it's not encouraging for guests invited for a meal to see your dogs hiding under the coffee table in terror because you are cooking.

I was explaining the genesis of their mental illness to our wary guests when the phone rang. It was friends asking if we'd mind watching their little darling the next day. Later, we got yet another booking.

So here it is Monday night, I'm finishing up this column, and the door bell rings. It's the parents of the Schnorkie, coming to fetch their best friend. That left one Schmaltese with a late checkout, a Schnauzer with a salon appointment for Tuesday and us, eating carry-in food so we don't upset the pack by cooking. Now we're wondering if we should re-carpet or just surrender and tile the living room. Later this week we have another overnight boarder, setting up a three-dog night.

We live in a kennel. We love it. Bring on the Schnocker Spaniels.▼

August 2006

Sit down. I won a golf tournament. Well, not individually. And it was actually a team game of "best ball" and our team won third place in spite of me.

This golf thing is getting out of hand. Now that I'm an athlete, I gave up a winter trip to Naples, Florida, the shopper's paradise, for a week in Hilton Head—an island with six golf courses and twenty alligators to every permanent resident.

Of course, when the tourists descend on the island it's like Rehoboth's boardwalk in July—thousands upon thousands of straight people. To borrow a phrase from Jerry Seinfeld, "Not that there's anything wrong with that." But given Hilton Head is a golf resort, there just had to be lesbians around but I never saw any evidence of them. Except us, of course.

When we found out that they'd give us $100 if we sat through a time share lecture we saw visions of greens fees dancing in our heads. In hindsight I'd rather have made a buck as a professional alligator wrestler.

The wait in the lobby before being shuttled off to a sales person was so long they had a magician entertaining. It was like being stuck in an elevator with David Blaine, except this guy had no magic skills. Wait a minute, does David Blaine have magic skills other than a highly practiced death wish?

Anyway, this Blaine-like person kept telling hideously insulting "wife" jokes while he insisted on executing a trick where he set a twenty dollar bill on fire. After we'd been stranded with him for over 45 minutes he did manage to entertain us by setting his pants pocket on fire. We got our $100, so at least the guy wasn't a liar liar with his pants on fire, but it was painful—for everyone concerned.

For golf, though, the resort was perfect. Every day we'd be up and out early, playing the game with the gators watching our every move. One time I whacked the ball directly at a gator's jaw. Is it the alligator you run away from in a zig zag or a crocodile? Since retrieving that hook shot could have turned me into Captain Hook, I just took a stroke, tried not to have a stroke and fled zigzagedly.

The courses were long and tough, with deep ravine-like sand traps. The hardest thing for me was getting out of the sand traps—and I don't mean the ball.

I'd say that I got to practice my short game on the greens, but actually my long game is my short game and I didn't know what the heck I was doing. But I had fun. One time I teed off and my ball hit the water, skipped across it like a stone and bounced up into a sand trap. That's multitasking.

At any rate, my winter golf prepped me for our CAMP Rehoboth Women's league this spring and summer and ultimately gave me the illusion of grandeur needed to participate in the July 10th tournament. It was 96 degrees by 8:30 a.m.

From the minute we registered I realized our folly. First, it was a "links" course, explained to me as a very long, narrow "targeted" Scottish style course with hilly moguls, deep sand traps and a ridiculously narrow fairway. It looked we'd be walking the highlands calling for Heathcliff.

Our foursome completed the first hole in fifteen minutes. At this rate we'd be back to the Clubhouse by next Tuesday. Luckily, since it was the "best ball" format, if one of the other three hit a respectable shot, all I had to do was sit in the golf cart and perspire. It would have been 110 degrees in the shade had there been any shade.

However, one good thing about this fancy course was the service. A refreshment cart showed up every few holes asking us if we wanted anything to drink—and drink we did—water, Gatorade, more water, anything to keep us cool. We drank so much, that by the last time the cart came around and the gal asked, "Want anything?" I requested a catheter.

One of my teammates laughed so hard she made the catheter request moot.

As our carts sped from one hole to another, trying to keep marginally ahead of the team breathing down our golf shirts, I felt like I was in a car loaded with Borscht Belt comics running the road in the film *It's a Mad, Mad, Mad, Mad World*.

Arriving at a hole, we'd whack at the balls and then run to find whatever shots landed in the skinny fairway. "I'm not stopping to find my ball," Bonnie yelled. "I've got plenty of balls."

Well, that's true.

By the time we finished what seemed like 128 holes and the battle of bunker hell we were drenched, exhausted and a thoroughly sorry lot. So imagine our surprise at winning third place among the women's teams.

In hindsight, what helped us most was not spectacular golfing, but shopping. Since this was a charity event, you could purchase Mulligans (do-overs) and Sandies (get-out-of-the-sand trap-free cards). I may be a lousy golfer, but I'm a shopping professional—so I purchased quite a few of these goodies before we got started and, as most shopping sprees do, it made all the difference in the world.

So, tourney win behind me, and league play continuing, I seem to be sticking with this golf thing. Truth be told, the only reason I took up golf in the first place was to write a damn column about it. Who knew I'd actually like it.

But the bad thing is that I'm improving. When I started, I was a team joke. It was incongruous and hilarious. I was the league mascot. Everybody wanted to play in my foursome because the whole idea of me taking up a sport was a big yuk.

But after little more than a year, the sad truth is that I've improved just enough to ruin my game. I am now just a garden variety awful golfer, no longer a novelty, no longer so amusing. In fact, occasionally I make less than double par. It's so sad.

So for your protection and mine, this is the last you will hear about golf from me. Unless of course, I wind up in the LPGA or playing in the Dinah Shore Classic.

And I imagine you'll see me gator wrestling on Animal Planet long before that happens. ▼

August 2006

I heard it on *All Things Considered* on NPR. Age quashes our spirit of adventure.

Really? Do they know any gay people? A neuroscientist, probably funded by a stupendous government grant to study such things, states that there is a certain age when the typical American passes from the novelty stage to that of utter predictability. Old Fartism as it were. Okay, for some things, like staying up until last call at any of our local watering holes, my behavior is utterly predictable. No way, José.

However, I chuckled when the NPR correspondent explained that if a person in Nebraska hasn't tasted sushi by age 26, the likelihood of that person eating sushi in their lifetime was about the same as me getting into a size 6.

I know they didn't consider gay people in the Bell curve, because for us, it's pretty much out of the closet and into a Japanese Restaurant.

A late bloomer in every sense, I was 38 when I first tasted sushi, and in fact, I first tasted eel last week and liked it. Toto, I realize we're not in Nebraska anymore, but living in Sussex County should be relatively equivalent.

I howled when I heard that youngsters who have not had their tongues pierced by age 22 probably will never have it done. I believe this one, straight or gay. Therth no way I would conthider having my tongue pierthed, no matter what the purported benefiths.

I did, however, get a tattoo at age 56. I wasn't the only grownup client in the shop but that was just because Bonnie accompanied me. The rest of the tattooees, clearly heterosexual boys and girls, wore dental retainers and got there on learner's permits.

I just think that gay people have a wonderful spirit of

adventure well into old age. Heck, old Sarah Aldridge penned her last novel at 92. Bonnie celebrated her 40th birthday on a roller coaster. I know somebody who got her first kayak for her 75th birthday.

It probably has to do with the coming out process.

Face it, once we struggle to come out to ourselves, then to our friends, then to family, colleagues and the rest of the world—and keep having to come out, and gauge just how far to come out, every single time we meet somebody new, our spirits of adventure are pretty well practiced. Along with the thickening of our skin, but that's another whole topic.

Now far be it from me to stereotype, and I'm sure that there are pockets of adventurous adult heterosexuals all over the globe, but even according to my straight friends, gay people are often envied for their adventurous natures. "You and your friends have such a wonderful time!" I've been told, time and time again, by slightly green-eyed straight people.

Of course, they might just be envying our relatively carefree lives, unencumbered by offspring and the ensuing orthodonture, driving lessons and tuition. It's a possible explanation but I don't buy it.

After all, lots of gay people have children from previous straight relationships and even more are starting their own families these days. These nuclear family gays, male or female, still seem to have more adventure in their souls than most straight people at the same stage in life.

I think this late onset of adventure is caused by our delayed development. Which, in this case turns out to be a great thing. Unlike our straight peers, most of us gay folk (at least those as old as I am) got a very late start in the dating department. I don't know about you, but I never made out in the moonlight, took skinny dips, or went to a dance club with someone I actually wanted to share those activities with until I came out of the closet—at age 30.

I wasn't 14 the first time I kissed someone and melted, I was 31. I wasn't 18 the first time I danced til dawn at a crowded, throbbing disco, I was 33. And I wasn't a teenager when every song on the radio made me sigh or cry. I was 34.

Getting such a late start makes you want to make up for lost time. My thirties and forties were spent at Gay Roller Skating nights, all manner of bizarre theme parties and marching for gay rights with the same youthful exuberance I had when I marched against the Viet Nam war in my twenties. And that's the spirit that leads gay people to break the fuddy-duddy barrier. That's my story and I'm sticking to it.

Take last night for instance. I was driving around the neighborhood when I spied a friend of mine out riding her newly purchased Segway—that two wheeled vehicle where you stand up and buzz along, balancing yourself like a dreidel.

"Here, give it a try," she said. "Now that you're a golfer and an athlete this should be a piece of cake."

"Hah!" I answered. But for some reason, coward and klutz that I am, and pushing my sixth decade to boot, I had this inexplicable urge to try the thing. I gingerly stepped onto the Segway, had a helping hand to steady me up, and then took off, yelling "wheeee" as I went rolling down the street, jowls and chins flapping in the breeze.

And while I love our gay spirit of adventure and promise not to let the old rocking chair get me at any age, I altho promith that I will never get my tongue pierthed no matter how adventuruth it may be. ▼

August 2006

I love my iPod, even though I'm not what the electronics industry calls an "early adopter." Early adopters are those eager beavers who fiddle with new inventions before anybody else. Early adopters (EAs) bought CD players when the rest of us were still rewinding cassette tape spools with our pinky fingers.

I'm a tardy adopter. If I'd lived in the 19th century, I would have been reading Jane Austen by candlelight long after everyone else had gas, if you'll excuse the expression. I'm still wary of Halogen lights, wireless, and digital thermometers (you want to put that where???).

Which is why I'm astounded that I purchased, programmed, and actually use an iPod. And which is also why, as I drove to New York last weekend, trying to get my iPod to play through my car radio, I recognized irony when it assaulted me in the ears.

Back when Edison invented the stylus to play music on tin foil cylinders, early adopters tried out these tin foil phonographs. When Edison's cylinder gave way to shellac discs, the record player was born. Between Edison's records and Marconi's radio, a beautiful relationship grew.

Of course, the sound was awful. Jelly Roll Morton and Enrico Caruso came through with radio static and screechy needle skips on the 78 revolutions-per-minute records. Eventually, those sneaky early adopters got wind of 33 and a third rpm records and the first major format war ignited.

Did you know that in 1940 audio pioneer David Sarnoff installed the first secret recording device in the White House? It took another 34 years to see the error in that plan. Meanwhile, 33s begat 45s and the classic long-playing record, or LP, triumphed.

I came along in 1948 and by the late 50s wanted my very

own record player. I can still see that green vinyl-covered box with a flip-up lid. Inside was a turntable, an arm with a diamond needle and a clip for that little round plug to stick into 45s to keep them from becoming Sputniks. Over the next decade I listened to my first Broadway shows, The Kingston Trio, and the ubiquitous TV stars cutting records, like Richard Chamberlain Sings! He really didn't, but 12 year olds didn't care.

I practically wore out my LP of *My Fair Lady* starring Julie Andrews. That should have been a parental early warning. I really, really, really wanted Julie to be my best friend, talked about her incessantly and coveted her butch haircut.

Early adopters forged on: Hi Fidelity, FM Radio (no static!) and the new technology called stereo. Nuclear families sat in the middle of living rooms marveling at bongo drum sounds flipping from right speaker to left. Dean Martin crooned That's Amore, on speakers the size of restaurant dumpsters.

By 1966 EAs brought us new 8-Track tapes. The sound quality stank and the tapes hiccupped every time they changed tracks, usually mid-song. But heck, you could take your music with you in the car!

I finally capitulated and got an 8-Track player to listen to Sgt. Pepper while sipping cheap wine and enjoying the aroma of wafting...um, incense in the dorm.

Dammit, my 8-Track was still virginal when those vile early adopters diddled with cassette tapes. You could fast forward or reverse them and the sound was better. So everybody had to dump their 8 track players (or shove adapters into them) and switch formats again. By this time I had 300 albums but they were the same 100 releases purchased in three different formats. I still have all three versions of Carol King's *Tapestry* someplace.

Actually, cassettes held the public's attention for a long time. They hissed less than 8 Tracks but the sound on the radio, in the car or on the home stereo was merely good enough.

Then, Land Ho! In the early 80s, technology and early

adopters collided in their quest for perfection, touting the Compact Disc—a digital technology virtually eliminating tape hiss, squeaks, needle skips, and all the other humm, buzz and static we've enjoyed through the ages.

Perfect sound. Of course, I didn't buy a CD player until years later when I spilled a Pina Colada into my cassette carrying case and ruined all my 80s music—which, in hindsight, was not the tragedy I thought it was at the time.

So I purchased my music for the fourth time, but got smart, joining six record, I mean music clubs. I'd get five free CDs with each membership, plus pay for the required two more CDs at regular price simultaneously, thereafter quitting lickety-split. For the record, no pun intended, I did not replace ABBA or CATS.

Which brings me to the hell that those doggone early adopters have unleashed this time. Peer pressure finally convinced me I needed an iPod to carry with me the entire contents of my CD cabinet—which, by the way, was pretty empty, since I threw away all my bulky VHS tapes in favor of slim DVDs, requiring me to buy back my favorites yet again.

As for the iPod, I love it. Following three bleary days at the Dell, every CD I own is digitally stockpiled in the thing. If I trusted technology, which I do not, I could just throw away all those CDs and reclaim shelf space for the photo albums I refuse to convert to digital slide shows.

So as I headed up the Jersey Turnpike last weekend, I tried to enjoy selections from my entire iPodded music library played through my car radio. I had a gizmo supposed to play my iPod via wireless magic by tuning in a local radio station. What I got was barely audible Dixie Chicks along with some hideous 1960s AM radio static. Worse, the radio errantly drifted to some God Squad station railing about "ho-mo-sex-iality." Please, I'd rather listen to CATS.

When we spied a Bed, Bath & Beyond, we stopped to buy a tiny speaker system for Mr. iPod so we could turn off the squawking car radio.

Down the highway we went, unwrapped the little woofers and tweeters and discovered that the whole damn thing was made of flimsy plastic, and get this, Mr. Thomas Alva Edison—the speakers were, ta da, TIN FOIL. And it sounded like it, too.

What comes around goes around. What will those zany early adopters think of next! Wouldn't it be ridiculous if they tried to get us to give up our 54-inch TVs for 2.5 inch Podcasts? Naw, that's just way too absurd....▼

August 2006

Marketing has gone too far. Don't get me wrong, I'm a marketer. My whole career has been spent trying to get people to visit places, see things and buy things. I'm a professional.

But my skills pale in the face of some 21st century marketing practices.

I'm now being told I need an outdoor kitchen.

From Restoration Hardware to the Pottery Barn, outdoor spaces (we used to call them patios) can be more than mere decks. Not only have creaky picnic tables been supplanted by teak ensembles with Mission Style armchairs, but now you can have a whole kitchen outside. With your stainless steel three-burner barbecue grill—you know, the one that could double as the space shuttle booster, an attached Corian countertop, and even an outdoor wine cooler, so you can bring your wine outside in the heat to cool it—outdoor kitchens are really taking off. Or so the catalogues say.

"Everything you would expect from a conventional kitchen can be found with our outdoor kitchens." Really? Do they have fridges filled with last week's doggy bags and zip-loc bags of fuzzy things resembling science projects?

I was lusting after the Garden Gate catalogue, with its gorgeous outdoor tables, chairs and, get this, sideboards, when I came to my senses. I rarely use my indoor kitchen, why the hell would I need an outdoor one? To be just like my indoor kitchen, my outdoor kitchen would need a phone on direct dial to 1-800-Pizza.

Here's a good one—"a gazebo with woven panels, sturdy steel framing and mosquito netting creates an exquisite outdoor room, as beige fabric allows this structure to coordinate beautifully in any outdoor setting."

I thought green goes best with the outdoors, besides, wasn't the point of eating outside to enjoy the natural environment? You want coordinated fabric? Go in the house.

I turned the page in the catalogue and saw swagged draperies, yes, draperies, "perfect to set the mood in any screened porch." Window treatments for the porch? And see, even I'm calling what used to be curtains, window treatments. And I'm not even a gay man.

How about those outdoor heaters. "Take the chill out of the evening air with the 30" Copper Fire Pit. Elegant design and durable construction create a stylishly functional backyard centerpiece." My backyard centerpiece is an oscillating sprinkler. And a can of bug repellent.

And what's with the Media Room thing? Every new house has to have a Meeedia Room with theatre seating and a TV big enough to watch life-size football. I don't need to see sweaty men slapping each others' butts that big.

Besides, my whole house is a media room. The TV is in the Great Room—and by the way, that's the place we used to call the living room, but now builders save money by not putting up an extra wall and it's a Great Room. My computer is in the den, my music is in my ears, and I read in the bathroom. I don't need a Meeedia Room.

And I'm not even going to discuss marketing successes like caffeinated water (drink plenty of water, then hit yourself over the head with a frying pan in order to sleep). And speaking of frying pans, now we need George Foreman indoor grills (now there's something that *DOES* belong on the porch…). Then there was the salad spinner. It's lettuce for pity's sake, wash it off.

On the beach I see people using a moving van to come in for the day. They have to have their L.L. Bean pop up shelter, Crate & Barrel collapsible table, and Coleman industrial sized cooler. And wireless laptop. It's the beach, people, bring a towel, a hat, and a book (preferably, mine).

But here's the marketing plan that caught me by surprise. I opened the mail last week to find a letter to my dog Moxie from his veterinarian. It reminded him that now that he's turned eight years old its time for him to ask his Mom or Dad to make an appointment for his Senior Wellness Examination.

I looked at the dog. Was he reeling in stunned disbelief like I was, the day I opened my mail to find my AARP card? I'm surprised Moxie didn't look at me and ask for Metamucil.

The vet, by the way, is excellent, very caring and competent. But me thinks marketing has gotten the best of the practice. Senior Wellness Exam? Whatever happened to an annual Rabies shot, flea dip, and a dog biscuit? Neither Moxie nor I consider him a senior citizen, and while I'll do anything within reason to keep him healthy, two hundred bucks for "wellness" tests makes me want to be de-wormed.

Really, this marketing thing is out of hand. All of a sudden we can't survive without naturally holistic pet foods, bathroom faucets that look like exhibits in the Museum of Modern Art and my favorite must-have: GPS in the car.

First off, it's dangerous. Look at the thing while driving and you'll be the first to know exactly where you are when the garbage truck hits you. It reminds me of a depth finder in a boat, which tells you exactly how few inches of water you are in after you've already run aground.

Meanwhile, back in the car, GPS is a gimmick. Do you know anybody who actually uses it after the first week? The one time somebody demonstrated it for me, the car let us know that my own street didn't exist. "Okay, my friend says, "let's pop in the name of this restaurant we're sitting in front of. The navigation system did a good job, telling us that the pavement that we were parked upon was actually two blocks away.

Now I'm not a complete throwback. Some marketing has won me over. Like the DVR—the digital video recorder you can order from your cable company. It's fantastic. It should be marketed more. Unlike the Video Tape Recorder, its simple to operate, the time never blinks 12 o'clock, and I can watch *The L Word* any time I want.

Ditto with the cell phone and Broadband Internet Access.

But give me a break from those aggressive marketing gurus who push products or services we really don't need. Enough, already.

Though I must sheepishly admit, I've made the appointment for Moxie's wellness exam. You can never be too careful. But he's damn sure not coming home to dine on holistic kibble in our outdoor kitchen. Frankly, I'm just glad he uses the outdoor bathroom. ▼

September 2006

Ever since Georgia State Representative Billy McKinney lost a primary battle in 2002, I've been feeling uneasy. According to *The Washington Post*, he blamed his loss on the "J-E-W-S."

Nice. While it's some comfort that McKinney lost, it still made me queasy. I've spent more than half my life working to prevent discrimination against gays and lesbians. It's been my issue both personally, for small instances of discrimination, and, in a wider sense, for our community as whole.

But until some recent news articles, I never really took anti-semitism as a personal threat or a contemporary issue. Who's head's in the sand now?

I flinched when reading about the resurgence of European anti-semitism and the massive hateful propaganda, nurtured in Arab nations, that the Jews were behind 9-11.

Hearing vicious anti-Semitic rants from Iranian officials and reading of nations which refuse to recognize Israel's right to exist is very discomforting to say the least.

And we cannot forget Mel Gibson's wild eyed rant about the Jews causing all the wars in the world. Frankly, I thought that was the Republicans' job.

It's enough to make me want to "come out" as Jewish and start paying more than lip service (like eating lox and bagels), to my religious heritage.

My parents were secular Jews. They didn't attend services but they identified greatly with ethnic Judaism—and they were of the generation that refused to buy Volkswagens and Mercedes because of the manufacturer's World War II connection to the Third Reich.

Struck with a little Jewish guilt when my sister and I were young, my folks sent us to "Sunday" school on Saturday at our local temple. One day, while I was in religious class, with my mother and sister on their way to pick me up, my mom skidded the car on an icy street and wrecked her 1957 Thunderbird. Mom and Sis had only minor injuries, but that was the absolute end of my religious training. My mother took the accident as a sign from God that we should be doing other things on Saturdays. Kaput. Finito. Done.

Decades later, when a number of people here in town got together to form the first Jewish congregation in the entire county, it interested me a little.

So after a few visits on the High Holy Days, with Bonnie coming along, I began to feel a kinship with Seaside Jewish Community. With the exception of weddings, funerals, and a stray visit to DC's gay synagogue, this was my first religious experience in over 40 years (unless you count créme brulée).

Not surprisingly, I was a little lost amid the Hebrew prayers and songs, but not among the crowd. At least 10 congregants were friends from CAMP, I recognized several people from the Art League, and a few more from downtown businesses. The nice thing is that it didn't feel like a straight synagogue or a gay synagogue. There was a great mix.

So now, in addition to hosting our annual Chanukah party where we serve Bonnie's fabulous Matzo Ball soup and Latkes (potato pancakes), I am part of the budding Jewish community here.

And one the things that drew me to this congregation is the person who most often leads the services. Beth is our lay rabbi.

She does a terrific job and is a wonderfully wise and spiritual person. Also lots of fun, because long before I showed up in schul, we'd been socializing with Beth and her partner Fran. So actually she is our lay lesbian rabbi. She's a lay rabbi because she knows her stuff but hasn't been through the official rabbinical training. I do believe however, that she is an ordained lesbian.

It's been nice going to the occasional Saturday morning service and adding a bit of organized religion to my life. Somehow it feels different than all my previous forays into a synagogue. It feels integrated, with my family of choice, my gay life and my spiritual life (or at least heritage and culture) all coming together and recognized by this welcoming congregation. Adding that touch of spirituality seems appropriate to me for the very first time in my life. A touch.

And then it happened. My mate, who always enjoyed the study of religion and was herself a committed Christian until she was lobbed from her church for being gay, began to take an interest.

To be sure, Bonnie has always loved Jewish food, Jewish jokes and Jewish women. But I was a little surprised when she told me she wanted to explore converting to the Jewish faith. "Making matzo ball soup isn't enough?" I asked. No, she really wanted to study.

"A couple of pounds of pastrami won't satisfy your craving?"

Nope. She decided she liked the philosophy behind the religion and felt very comfortable with our little Jewish congregation.

So my mate started taking Hebrew lessons from Beth and practicing her alphabet and prayers by playing recorded lessons on her iPod.

I am very, very proud of her for making this choice and taking on all the hard work and introspection required to see it through.

However, I think the ability to make the requisite sounds for Hebrew and Yiddish words is genetic. Telling somebody they have a lot of Chutzpah (Yiddish for gumption) and pronouncing the CH with the properly liquid "CHuh" sound is easy for Jewish people. Non-Jews have to really work at it. It's the difference between calling a complainer a kvetch or a k-vetch.

So, I'm sitting reading and Bonnie is in the next room going over her last lesson and reading aloud. It's hard to tell if she's clearing her throat or reciting a prayer. When she gets to a particularly juicy "Chuh" in the text I wonder if she might need the Heimlich maneuver.

And so it goes. We've gotten to the point where Bonnie is explaining the meaning of the Jewish holidays to me and I'm becoming a more observant Jew by marriage. A member of the religious left as it were.

And there's no sense kvetching about it. I'm answering to a higher power: Bonnie, when she's on a mission.

And even if I did kvetch and complain, I'd just be preaching to the converted.

Shalom. ▼

September 2006

We planned a trip to China.

Insane as it sounds, on two occasions, people asked if we were going there to adopt a baby. Hah! That ship sailed a long time ago. We can hardly manage dogs.

But we went on a thoroughly enlightening and extraordinary tour. In fact, it was life-changing because it altered my thinking. Now, hearing about China on the news, I have different pictures in my mind, different feelings. I'm more hopeful about the future, actually. And I think the future is Asia.

Some quick impressions:

History. Seeing 2000 year old structures, sculptures and artifacts is humbling. Gee, Paul Revere did not invent silver. From the Forbidden City (and its stunning buildings to house Emperors, Administrators, Concubines, Eunuchs and all) to the Terra-Cotta Warriors (8,000 life-size statues of men and horses, which archeologists found guarding an emperor's tomb) we gaped and gasped.

As for The Great Wall, from afar it's majestic, powerful, and dramatic. I must admit, when we got to where it was accessible for climbing (ergo a tourist hotspot) I felt I could have been at an Epcot's Great Wall replica. Amid masses of camera-carrying tourists, vendor's hawked "I Climbed the Wall" T-shirts. But the climb turned out to be really strenuous and the Wall, a fortification stretching over 4,000 miles, is something I never thought I'd see. The first of the walls (every dynasty had their own or added to one) was built in 20 years, using human labor alone. Why should adding a lane on the highway take two years?

I always thought Chinese artists were bad at drawing mountains, making them too pointy. But no, along the Li River, the scenery really looks like that, with weirdly peaked limestone hills.

Chinese food. Okay, with the exception of one or two great meals, Chinese food is better here. We really weren't offered anything too scary, but lunches and dinners at the tourist-approved restaurants and hotels were mostly bland and boring. I perfected my chopstick technique but have lost my taste for any food requiring their use. Perhaps this weekend I'll get to Rehoboth's gourmet Chinese restaurant, Confucius, which has exquisite, non-bland Chinese food.

But I did eat Peking Duck in Beijing (which used to be called Peking) and not many people can say that. One of our best meals was on a tour where we took a bicycle rickshaw (pity the poor peddler) into the Hutong, or old town Beijing, and a local family cooked us lunch. That was terrific and we got to see their home and courtyard, which combined history (tiny rooms, coal heat, concrete walls) and modernity (TV, computer and fridge). We loved their dog—a Pekinese, of course.

Daily life. As our guide said, it's no longer Red China, but Pink China, with rampant Capitalism. A Beijing or Shanghai street has everything from Gucci and Burberry to government owned Friendship stores selling jade, T-shirts and reasonably priced clothing. There are big grocery chains, department stores and open merchandise markets where vendors, holding scarves, hats and fans, run after foreigners and yell "One dolla, One dolla!" If you are just getting back on a bus, they start yelling, "Two for one dolla!"

Stores in most cities are the width of double car garages with the entire front open by way of a garage door—and a dizzying cacophony of signs. Young people are fashion conscious, wear chic, hot eyewear and ride bikes and scooters in all weather. Tiny taxis and delivery vehicles are often trikes. But cars are becoming more prevalent (Buick is king, go figure) and the roads are impossibly jammed. One of our tour companions noted that traffic signals seem to be merely a suggestion. Fortunately, in the big cities (19 million people) there are walking tunnels under the big thoroughfares. In the small towns (*only 5 million*) crossing the street is like being on *Survivor-China*. Restaurants and cafes abound, but you can still see women on the street selling steaming sweet potatoes from a grill on the back of a bicycle.

And the construction projects! Skyscrapers, stadiums, shopping centers, and apartments are going up everywhere. As Beijing readies for the 2008 Olympics, the government is rebuilding, repaving and replanting almost the whole city— giving rise to horrendous smog.

With all the building, people joke that their national bird is the crane. They also laugh that their national flag is laundry, because on almost every hi-rise balcony, laundry hangs from bamboo poles. Many people have dryers but they hate using them.

The people. Friendly, warm, polite, short and thin. I felt like a blimp. Our guides provided a fascinating travelogue and stories galore. Henry (his American name) had a great sense of humor and delighted in telling us tales of other tour groups. At one point he was laughing about an incident where two teens misbehaved and, quoting Henry, "they stuck asses out window!" Our crew taught Henry the American word 'mooning." I'm sure that will be helpful for him to know when, following this stint in tourism, he goes for his MBA.

The tour bus usually picked us up by 9 a.m. so Bonnie and I sometimes took early morning walks to see what surrounded each hotel. Often, we were the only Caucasians on the crowded streets and we attracted attention. Once, a bike whipped around a corner and splashed muddy water all over Bonnie's shorts. People gasped, but when they saw Bonnie laugh, they laughed and came running with hankies.

On our morning jaunts and early tours, we saw large groups of people gathered in parks doing Tai Chi or other group exercises. In fact, all day long, everywhere we looked, seniors played mah jong or other board games, or practiced musical instruments and with small choirs. Workers retire fairly early to make room for younger employees. And many grandparents watch THE grandchild—per the population reduction policy mandating only one child per family. There is the potential for one very spoiled child, as four grandparents and two parents constantly hover.

The politics. The only time I felt we were in a police state was our first day, at Tiananmen Square. We saw the big square, surrounded by government buildings, but we could not go onto the square as they had visiting dignitaries. Armed soldiers stood guard and it was a little creepy. Henry, and our Beijing guide Mai, told us we could ask them anything we wanted, but ON the bus.

Pulling away from the area, we asked Mai how many people died in the 1989 uprising. She said we probably knew more than she did—but let us know she was a student at the time and sided with the protestors. Henry told us that people from small cities who want to work in Beijing or Shanghai, need a special I.D. card. He had to join the Communist Party to get one—but we could sense he was not happy about that.

But the people seem proud and patriotic, and believe they are moving toward a more open society.

Following this serious discussion, Henry lightened the mood by asking how many people we thought could fit in Tiananmen Square. "Do not be offended," he said, "but answer is 1 Million Chinese, half million Americans…just kidding," he assured us."

"When's lunch?" chimed somebody. We were a happy group.

We also talked about all the building. If the government wants to put up a new building, like Nike, they just do. Face it, they don't waste time with environmental impact statements or public hearings. And displacing people? They move people to a new place far out of town, or pay them to move. Hmmm. With the new eminent domain laws pushed by our current administration, this is sounding very familiar.

At one point, Henry mentioned that by the end of Mao's revolution, the word comrade was not used anymore. "Now, you call somebody comrade it means gay," he said. "That is okay now." He inferred that things were more open for gays in the cities now, but we saw no evidence of comrades. Except, of course, in the Beijing Minority Song and Dance Troupe we saw one night.

Our vacation itself was a good example of the political climate. All tour companies visiting China cover pretty much the same ground—and must include stops at government owned or sponsored factories. We toured rug, pearl, silk, cloisonné and jade factories, at which, adopting a pack mentality, our group frenetically and gleefully bought souvenirs and gifts. But, it did seem like compulsory shopping, although far be it for me to complain about such a thing.

Bathroom facilities. Peeing was as strenuous as climbing the Great Wall. It's that most of the bathroom stalls contain squatters—not holes in the ground like Girl Scout camp, but porcelain troughs with a button you step on to flush. These require you to plant your feet firmly on either side, pull your pant cuffs up and trousers down and balance like a Chinese acrobat to relieve yourself—all the while doing a tap dance to keep your clothing dry. I limited liquids to near dehydration. As a dyke who's last day in a dress was my sister's wedding in 1987, if I go to Asia again it will be (God help me) in miniskirts.

But it did change my thinking. I never thought I'd give a Boeing 757 bathroom a five-star rating. Relief!

Shanghai. The best for last. This beautiful, ultra modern city is the jewel of China. Lucky, lucky us, our Rehoboth friend Lyena was in Shanghai (her hometown) on a business trip when our tour was there. She took us out for an evening we will never forget. From an exquisite dinner to the lights of Nanjing Road (more neon than Vegas!) to the Bund (a section of European style buildings from the 1930s) where you could see across the river to the lights of Shanghai's tallest buildings, our private tour rocked!

Gorgeous sights, gorgeous architecture. Yes, said Lyena,

lots of Chinese people have the money for these fabulous new apartments and the prices rival Manhattan or Rehoboth's beach block. I had to laugh. For all the tea in China (and there's a lot!) I couldn't understand how people could pay 3 million dollars for an apartment, but wave their drying underpants from the balconies.

Well, It's a different culture; a different world, although we have much in common. Asia is on the ascent. Trust me, our youngsters should learn Mandarin.▼

October 2006

I am a gay American and I'm disgusted.

Naturally I'm talking about the Mark Foley scandal. What was he thinking???

I *know* what the conservative commentators are thinking, because they're shouting it. No matter what words they use to discuss the scandal, they are really just shouting "See, we told you gay people are perverts!!!!!"

WE ARE NOT. There is exactly the same percentage of perverts in the straight community as on our side—too many to take any comfort in that, by the way.

If you've been floating in a hyperbaric chamber for two weeks, Mr. Foley, a Florida Republican, resigned his House of Representatives seat last Friday after journalists discovered he'd been sending sexually explicit e-mails to teenage boys in the Congressional Page program. Yeccchhh,.

Thank you, former Congressman Foley, for giving the religious right another gay boogeyman. Thanks, too, for staying in the closet during your whole freakin' legislative career. All your buddies in the Party knew you were gay, all my friends in Florida knew you were gay, but when you got caught doing something really, really disgusting you hold your coming out party. Go ahead, pile "gay" on top of "alcoholic" and "I was abused" as part of your "I'm a victim" defense. How dare you. Same goes for Jim "I'm a Gay American" McGreevy, the ex-governor of New Jersey. While I'm happy that he now has a steady boyfriend and peace of mind, I'm furious at him for waiting until he was caught in a sleazy nepotism scandal to announce his membership in our club. The usual suspects had a field day with that one despite the fact that McGreevy didn't resign because he was gay, but because he was corrupt. Although I have to hand it to him—flinging himself from the closet on the national news probably took some of the spotlight away from his specious hiring practices.

But being gay had nothing to do with it.

Unless, of course, you factor in repression. The closet. The stress of leading a double life. When people, especially very public people, spend their whole lives hiding in the closet it takes a toll on their mental health. Voila! Some of these people finally crack up and do "inappropriate things." Let's not forget the very repressed members of the clergy, shall we, both homo and hetero.

As for "inappropriate things," Mr. Foley, farting in public is inappropriate. Pedophilia, even with someone close to the age of consent, is reprehensible.

And then there is the Nixonian question of WHAT DID THEY KNOW AND WHEN DID THEY KNOW IT.

Let me pose a question here. Picture somebody telling the Speaker of the House "I think one of your Congressmen is typing inappropriate e-mail messages to boys in the Page program." Picture the reaction.

Would the Speaker say:

1. "Gee. Go tell him to knock it off. How 'bout those Redskins" and promptly forget the conversation, or

2. "I knew that little fag would embarrass us some day. I want his head on a platter. Get him to resign immediately for personal reasons and then pray the truth doesn't come out. You have 24 hours to take care of this or you are toast."

Now there's a forgettable conversation.

One of the Speaker's spin masters even had the nerve to suggest the delay in addressing this issue (we call that a cover up, by the way) was because they didn't want to seem homophobic.

I can't stop laughing. The party that's trying to write discrimination against gay people into the Constitution says they were afraid they'd be called homophobic if they ratted on Foley? Puleeeeeze. That ship has sailed. They *dream* of being called homophobic so their voter "base" will stay with them.

Being seen as homophobic is their reason for getting out of bed in the morning.

So what's to be done, besides cringing at every mention of the scandal on TV?

Attention Family Values crowd: I have a plan. You can start by opening your hearts and minds to the idea that all people ARE created equal. What a concept. I know it won't be overnight, but sooner or later, society might become a more welcoming place for closeted gay people. Ergo, by eliminating bigotry and hatred, more people might have the freedom to live honest and open lives.

And some in that small but insidious contingent of homosexual perverts might not be tortured into the kind of mental tizzy causing at best, poor choices and at worst predatory behavior.

Flash! Helping to root out homophobia and making the world safe for gay people is one way to actually PROTECT YOUR CHILDREN! It's a lot better than your current protection plan, which relies on demonizing homos and abortion providers while teaching youngsters Hate101.

So there you have it. A plan for rooting out homosexual predators. But what should we do about heterosexual predators? I cannot say. That problem will have to be tackled by the straight team. And all those repressed and predatory priests? The Church better look those statistics in the eye and make some adjustments.

One slight comfort in all of this has been certain media reactions. I notice that the usual game of "blame the homosexuals," is being played only by spokespeople and talk show hosts from the right side of the aisle. Many journalists and left aisle commentators have gone out of their way to focus on the facts and the possible cover-up rather than buying into any gay bashing. In fact, one commentator, upon hearing Foley's statement announcing that not only is he an alcoholic, but that he had been abused as a child, and is, in fact, gay, said, "That statement is so insulting to gay people."

That's progress, I think.

In the meantime, I'm sick and tired of seeing unhappy, repressed lives, gay or straight, unravel on TV.

I am a gay American. And I am pissed.▼

November 2006

LETTERS FROM CAMP REHOBOTH

NOSE FOR NEWS

Let me say a word about health insurance. Auuggghhh!

One recent Friday I called several insurance agencies to get quotes. I'm in the rotten position of requiring a policy for a group of one. Any schmuck at a big company can get coverage for his whole family and Shitzu for less than I pay.

I spent most of the day filling out questionnaires asking "Have you ever been to a doctor?" Then I had to check a box if I've have ever had flatulence, hiccups, or a sty. The paperwork warned of loss of insurance or death, whichever comes first, if you forget so much as a 1978 nose bleed. For the record I do *not* have diabetes, kidney disease, high blood pressure (although I don't know why) cancer or heart disease. However, I did have a stress test last year for what turned out to be world class gas.

In this age of HIPPA—a government edict requiring medical personnel to swear on a stack of invoices they will never ever tell anybody anything about your health, I found it ironic that I was out sourcing my entire medical history by faxing it to a call center in Bangladesh.

The following Sunday morning I attended a Dead Pool Society Brunch. Remember the drill? We select names of elderly luminaries, ante up ten bucks and if "your" celebrity kicks the bucket you get the money and have to throw a party to usher out the dearly departed.

On this particular Sunday we were sending off that mother who knew least, Jane Wyatt. And she tried to take me with her.

First let me say, I did not even have a cocktail at the party. Honest. There are witnesses.

But as several of us left the house (I will not identify where, as I hold our charming hosts harmless), I had a teeny accident and fell flat on my face.

Based on Bonnie's forensic analysis (learned by watching *C.S.I.*) the trace evidence of mud on one of my shoes and not on the other, told the tale.

As I walked toward the driveway I put my left foot on the front of a flagstone slab. The square stone flipped up in the back, catching my right foot (hence mud on that shoe from *under* the slab) and sent me flying, face first onto the blacktop driveway where I landed with a gigantic thud. And I landed, with my full and considerable weight, entirely on my nose. A lot of things crossed my mind. While I didn't seem to be dead, I wished I were, because a platoon of my friends had just witnessed this nose dive.

Finally, as blood started trickling down the driveway, Bonnie crouched down at my head repeating "Are you okay," in varying states of panic. I mumbled, directly into the pavement, "broken nose."

By this time, somebody summoned a Dead Pooler who, when she was not waving farewell to deceased movie stars, was a nurse. She took charge, gently determining that the rest of me seemed unbroken and all that suffered was my nose. Unless, of course you count injured pride.

Somebody passed me a towel and some ice, as I heard someone else whisper "Let's see if she writes about *this*."

I was helped to my feet, shuffled into my buddy Larry's car and transported home, where Bonnie plopped me in a chair while she, Larry and a painter who happened to at the house edging the guest room, stared at me in horror. The painter started shaking his head and announcing "that looks real baaad." Thanks a lot for the expert opinion.

Soon, consensus held that the cut on the bridge of my nose might need a stitch or two after all.

A five hour emergency room wait was not appealing, so, with a bag of ice held firmly to my ballooning schnoze, we set off for the Route One "Doc in a Box" emergency clinic (even knowing I'd have to pay through the nose, ba-da-biing). It's the clinic with the 12 foot sign out front advertising "Open Seven Days a Week." It was closed. Is this a great town or what?

So we went home, where my ice bag and I flopped onto the sofa and, like Scarlett O'Hara, decided to worry about it tomorrow.

By morning at the battered woman's shelter, every bone in my body ached, both wrists and knees were solidly black and blue, and my face looked like I'd gone ten rounds with George Foreman. And losing by a nose. I had black eyes, swollen lids, large puffy bags under my black eyes, plus a nose that rivaled Jimmy Durante (ah, a name only us Dead Poolers may remember). I looked like a victim of spousal abuse.

By mid-afternoon I had seen the doctor and he sent me for x-rays. Now here's where we tip over into farce. At the radiology center, a nice woman carefully positioned my face on the machine and took pictures of my lumpy nose from every angle possible—and at this point my nose had a lot of angles.

Very quickly she checked the film and determined I could leave.

"So, is it broken?" I asked.

"You know I'm not allowed to tell you."

"Listen, I just faxed my medical history to Asia. The entire secretarial pool at Bangladeshy Insurance knows when I had my last colonoscopy and you can't tell me if my nose is broken?"

"Nope."

Back at my car, my cell phone rings. It's an underwriter from one of the insurance companies I had auditioned for, following up.

"Why do you take cholesterol medicine?"

"Because I don't want my arteries to congeal."

"Why did you have a stress test in 2005?"

"Gas."

As I'm answering, nose bandaged and raccoon-eyed, I recall my obligation to be forthright with the almighty insurance pooh-bahs.

"I have to tell you," I interrupted. "I've just had my nose x-rayed and it might be broken."

"Is this something that will require surgery?" the under-writer asked in a morbidly curious tone.

"I have no idea," I said, "but whatever happens it will be before January first and not on your company's watch." She seemed satisfied by my honesty.

By the time I got home, Bonnie was in the kitchen with an ice bag on her hand. She'd smashed it moving furniture. Great. Between her swollen hand and my bruised face, Rehoboth nosy buddies with their noses for news would promulgate the spousal abuse story.

As it turns out, my nose is broken and I have a deviated septum. I've been called a deviate before, so I wasn't shocked. I find out tomorrow whether surgical intervention is required. Hell, if they fix my nose maybe they can do my eyes at the same time.

For the moment, the black and blue is yellowing, my cut and scraped beak is healing and the only thing permanently bruised is my ego. I've fallen on my face many times before, but never this literally.

And *of course* I wrote about this. It's no skin off my nose.

Editor's note: Fay did need surgery. Now, her nose is back where it belongs, but she had to walk around in a hard cast nose cone. That happened to be Rehoboth Film Fest week, the one event where Fay was guaranteed to run into everyone she knew so they could admire her nose bra. Timing is everything. ▼

I've got two cars on the driveway and a garage stacked with books. I'm trying to learn about the world of publishing as fast as I can but I'm drowning in sell sheets, ISBN numbers, backorders, and other terminology from the publishing wars. Not to mention bubble wrap. I'm up to my ass in bubble wrap.

I wish my mentors were here to help. But of course, they are not and I'm in this alone, unless you count Bonnie who now has the official title of Fulfillment Manager for A&M Books. It means she drags heavy book cartons to the UPS Store.

This isn't the glamorous *Vanity Fair* book party kind of publishing, nor is it *New York Times* Best Seller kind of publishing, and it's certainly not the "Let's option this for Julia Roberts" kind of publishing.

But it's the keep-the-legacy-alive kind of publishing and, when I'm not too pooped to notice, I'm honored and delighted.

Anyda and Muriel represented more than half a century in the evolution of lesbian literature in America and their lives spanned almost the entire history of the gay rights movement in this country—thus far, of course. I was lucky enough to know them, love them, learn from them, and agree to try, to the best of my ability, to carry on for them.

Now before you start thinking I'm Random House, let me explain the realities of a tiny publishing house (or garage in my case). It's almost impossible to sell enough books to make any money. Not that the books don't sell. Anyda's are still selling, and I'm luckier than I ever imagined, with my book into a second printing. That's a lot of books sold—all over the country, and I am so flattered.

But the distributors, book stores and Amazon.com take a big cut (I'm not complaining—they get those books out there!) and shipping is so costly that this publisher earns just enough money to schlep the next cartons of books to UPS and send them on their way—okay, and maybe a little extra to help with travel to book events. It doesn't hurt that those events are in gay Meccas, either.

The ladies of Laurel Street never cared about what it cost—their mission was to publish books written by lesbians and get them into the hands of lesbian readers—who often had nothing else in print that related to their lives.

The A&M Books publishing house operated by me has no such luxury. We're operating hand to mouth. Or possibly foot in mouth. But either way, investment money we do not have. Which is why I chuckle when I get several e-mail inquiries a week from writers eager to have A&M (that would be me and Bonnie) publish their gay or lesbian novels, self-help books, poetry, short stories, and in one case, a children's book about gay ferrets (really).

We'd love to. Even the ferrets. But until we win Powerball or Hollywood options *As I Lay Frying* for a major motion picture (that sound you hear is me exhaling, breath not held) all A&M Books can do is be keeper of the flame for the Sarah Aldridge novels and use the funds the ladies left me to publish my second book. That was their request.

Although, I cannot predict the future. I'd like to think that someday circumstances would allow me to continue the mission of those early Naiad days and have A&M Books be a launching pad for female writers who otherwise would have no outlet. A&M (the women *and* the publishing company) did that incredible favor for me—and a whole lot of others—and I would love to pass it along. I'm working on it.

But in the meantime, I'm a teeny tiny publishing house. My den is my distribution center, with books piled four feet high and purchase orders, packing tape and the ubiquitous bubble wrap filling every available crevasse. I can easily lose a Schnauzer in the clutter.

Here in the 2006 holiday season, Bonnie and I have donned our gay apparel to keep the Yuletide gay. And, while it's only the week before Christmas, and the middle of

Chanukah, we've already had our Christmas miracle. No, not the usual one. But Mary Cheney's immaculate conception, with her parents Lynn and Dick Cheney happily looking forward to their next grandchild. Hypocrisy lives large (I'll stop with the Cheneys now. Although they have been a great target). As for my own same-sex household, we're getting ready for the spring celebration of Fay and Bonnie's 25th anniversary – that is, the informal anniversary of our becoming a couple. Was it the night we met? The night we 'did it'? The night we moved in together? Our gay anniversaries have quite a mystique, don't they? Well, like Anyda and Muriel, we're not divulging.

Although, face it, after a quarter of a century, our liaison is only informal under our antiquated federal laws and to the crazies who love them.

Actually, our Canadian marriage is a mere three and a half years old, but since that's not recognized here either, we're going with the 25th.

But even at 25, though a laudable achievement, it's a drop in the bucket by the standard set by Anyda and Muriel. We're looking forward to beating them at their own game.

And one other thing. Along with carrying on the publishing tradition, Bonnie and I, plus a cadre of Anyda and Muriel's friends, are carrying on the happy hour tradition as well.

I can still see Anyda walking slowly to the kitchen, pouring from a jug of scotch into two cut crystal glasses and bringing them both to Muriel for inspection. Muriel would determine which one had a micro milligram more of the golden liquid, taking it for her own—and then she'd sip a tiny bit from the other glass before handing it over. As their friend Tom said at Anyda's memorial service, it was a very intimate and charming tradition. It lives on in our house, mostly with the morning coffee.

So that's the news from the accidental publisher. I'm a very lucky writer. My second book is in the works and that bitch of a publisher is breathing down my neck. I'm trying to finish up before that big disco ball drops into Times Square to signal that it is 2007.

And none of this would have been possible without the ladies of Laurel Street.

It's my fondest wish that that the legacy of both Naiad Press and A&M Books live on—either through younger generations reading the old-fashioned, romantic and now classic Sarah Aldridge novels, or the telling and re-telling of the tale of the amazing couple who made publishing history.

It's ten minutes to five, time for crackers and cheese and a toast to those fabulous women who changed so many lives. They certainly changed and inspired mine.

Cheers! And make sure your drink isn't too pale.▼

A NOTE ABOUT THE AUTHOR

Fay Jacobs, a native New Yorker, spent 30 years in the Washington, DC area working in journalism, theater and public relations. Her first book, *As I Lay Frying—a Rehoboth Beach Memoir* was published in 2004. Fay has contributed feature stories and columns to such publications as *The Advocate*, *OutTraveler*, *The Baltimore Sun*, *Chesapeake Bay Magazine*, *The Washington Blade*, *The Wilmington News Journal*, *Delaware Beach Life* and more.

Since 1995 she has been a regular columnist for *Letters from CAMP Rehoboth*, and won the national 1997 Vice Versa Award for excellence.

She and Bonnie, her partner of 25 years, live in Rehoboth Beach, DE . They have two Miniature Schnauzers and a riding lawn mower.

A NOTE ABOUT THE PUBLISHER

A&M Books was established in 1995 by the late couple Anyda Marchant and Muriel Crawford. Prior to starting A&M Books, Marchant and Crawford founded Naiad Press and incorporated it in 1974 along with Barbara Grier and Donna J. McBride as shareholders.

A&M Books is the publisher of the fourteen classic Sarah Aldridge novels, all of which are still in print. A&M is also the publisher of *As I Lay Frying—a Rehoboth Beach Memoir* by Fay Jacobs and the 2005 release of *Celebrating Hotchclaw* by feminist literary icon Ann Allen Shockley.

A NOTE ABOUT THE COVER PHOTO

Reward! For the return of the frying pan.

As photographer Murray Archibald snapped away, a rogue Atlantic Ocean wave swept over both the frying pan and the photographer's knees. Fortunately, only the frying pan was swept away. Let us know if it turns up in a stream, river or ocean near you.

Books Available from A&M Books

The Sarah Aldridge Novels
(now available exclusively from A&M Books)

The Latecomer $12.00
Tottie $12.00
Cytherea's Breath $12.00
All True Lovers $12.00
The Nesting Place $12.00
Madame Aurora $12.00
Misfortune's Friend $12.00
Magdalena $12.00
Keep To Me Stranger $12.00
A Flight of Angels $12.00

Michaela $12.00
Amantha $12.00
Nina in the Wilderness $12.00
O, Mistress Mine $15.00

Any three titles available for $30

The Complete 14-Novel, Sarah Aldridge Collection $125

Other editions by A&M Books
Celebrating Hotchclaw by Ann Allen Shockley $17
As I Lay Frying—A Rehoboth Beach Memoir by Fay Jacobs $15, www.fayjacobs.com.

Books may be ordered from A&M Books of Rehoboth by calling 302-227-5558 or by sending a check or money order for the purchase price plus $2.00 shipping and handling per book ($5 for three book set, $15 for complete collection) to:

A&M Books
P.O. Box 283
Rehoboth Beach, DE 19971
You can contact A&M Books at AandMPublishers@aol.com